Sanctuary Cities

Sanctuary Cities

The Politics of Refuge

LOREN COLLINGWOOD AND
BENJAMIN GONZALEZ O'BRIEN

OXFORD
UNIVERSITY PRESS

Great Clarendon Street, Oxford, OX2 6DP,
United Kingdom

Oxford University Press is a department of the University of Oxford.
It furthers the University's objective of excellence in research, scholarship,
and education by publishing worldwide. Oxford is a registered trade mark of
Oxford University Press in the UK and in certain other countries

Published in the United States of America by Oxford University Press
198 Madison Avenue, New York, NY 10016, United States of America

British Library Cataloguing in Publication Data

Data available

Library of Congress Control Number: 2019948469

ISBN 978-0-19-093702-7

Printed by Sheridan Books, Inc.,
United States of America

The authors would like to dedicate this book to former Attorney General Jeff Sessions.

Dr. Gonzalez O'Brien also dedicates this book to his mother, who is and always will be his hero, as well as his beautiful wife, Erica, and wonderful daughter, Penelope.

Dr. Collingwood dedicates this book to his students at UCR, many who have shared their stories of struggle with him and have helped him become a better person.

Acknowledgement

This book started out as little more than a twinkle in a (not-so-young) graduate student's eye back in 2009. That year, Dr. Gonzalez O'Brien wrote a seminar paper about sanctuary cities inspired by a presentation in 2008 by Dr. Gregory Freeland of California Lutheran University on the New Sanctuary Movement. This paper, admittedly bad, lay dormant for a few years. Once the authors had both gotten jobs (no small blessing in the job market of the 2010s) the project was revived after the shooting of Kathryn Steinle. Dr. Gonzalez O'Brien and Dr. Collingwood, along with one of Loren's graduate students, the dapper Stephen Omar El-Khatib, began collaborating on a sanctuary city paper for the 2016 Western Political Science Association conference. This paper, after many, many revisions, was published as an article in *Urban Affairs Review* and found that sanctuary policy was not related to crime rates, despite the rhetoric of the Trump campaign, which had adopted opposition to sanctuary cities (and immigration more broadly) as one of its main talking points.

It just so happened that the article became publicly available around the time that the Trump administration had begun its battle against sanctuary cities throughout the United States (though to be fair, this began the day Trump took office). Unbeknownst to them, conservative media outlets like Fox and others were using their research to justify banning sanctuary cities based on a misinterpretation of a figure they had included in the paper. In July 2017 then–attorney general Jeff Sessions (2017–2018) gave a speech in Las Vegas citing their research as justification to end federal funding of sanctuary cities.

Many of the authors' colleagues and friends reached out to them to encourage them to set the record straight, which they did, penning a few pieces in the *Washington Post*, *The Hill*, and other outlets. The fact that their research generated so much media attention motivated them to consider writing a full book-length manuscript covering the broader political landscape surrounding sanctuary cities. Upon further inspection, the authors realized there was not a lot of data-driven political science research on the topic.

Thus, in the summer and fall of 2017, the authors (along with other coauthors for various pieces of this project) went on a rampage collecting data on various aspects of sanctuary city politics, including building a corpus of newspaper articles over time, state bill introductions, surveys asking about sanctuary policy and sanctuary cities, city-level outcomes relative to crime, voter turnout, minority representation on the police force, county-level detainer data, and eventually city-level 911-call data. In this process, the authors have worked with many other scholars and graduate students to whom they owe a great deal of gratitude and with whom they continue to work on various research projects as of this writing.

First, the authors would like to thank Stephen Omar El-Khatib, a graduate student at University of California, Riverside (UCR) who expended considerable effort and time building up some of the datasets used in this book (and all for free!). This includes data related to chapter 5, where we examine the relationship between sanctuary cities and crime, and chapter 4, which unpacks the state legislative process related to sanctuary cities.

Joe Tafoya helped the authors in gathering and recoding public opinion data for chapter 3, for which he has their eternal gratitude. Third, Elizabeth Hurst and Justin Reedy helped orchestrate the coding of sanctuary newspaper articles, which serve as the basis of our analysis in chapter 2. Hopefully, the fame and fortune this shout-out will bring to Dr. Reedy will allow him to finally put some books on his empty, empty shelves. Fourth, Marcel Roman did yeoman's work collecting and analyzing 911-call data in El Paso, Texas, and Tucson, Arizona. Lastly, a big thanks is owed to Jourdan Jones, a former student of Dr. Gonzalez O'Brien who helped with the archival research for chapter 1.

Early versions of part of this research were presented at WPSA 2016 in San Diego. Dr. Chris Towler offered sage comments regarding what was then little but a conference paper, and he has the authors' gratitude for helping to shape what would become that first *UAR* piece. Other bits of this work were also presented at WPSA, MPSA, PRIEC, and APSA. The authors thank all discussants and participants for their helpful feedback, especially, but not limited to, Matt Barreto, #Clicks4Kass (Kassra Oskooii), Jason Morín, Vanessa Tyson, and Jane Junn.

A very special thanks goes out to Karthick Ramakrishnan, who encouraged Dr. Gonzalez O'Brien to pursue this project back in 2009; Jennifer Merolla and Francisco Pedraza at UCR; Tom Wong at UCSD; and Allan Colbern at ASU. The authors would also like to thank Alexandra Filindra at UIC and Hannah Walker at Rutgers for providing great feedback on two of our chapters.

The authors would also like to thank Phil Wolgin and Tom Jawetz at the Center for American Progress for providing general public relations support and then for inviting them to participate in a convening on sanctuary cities in the summer of 2018. This provided added motivation to complete the project.

Another thanks to the folks at Perry World House at University of Pennsylvania for inviting us out to a sanctuary city summit held in the fall of 2018.

The authors also owe their gratitude to the Universidad Nacional Autónoma de México's Center for Research on North America for inviting them out to a February 2019 conference in Mexico City related to sanctuary cities and immigration.

Dr. Collingwood would like to say thanks to Sarah Dreier, who has been there for him in more ways than he deserves. He also wishes to thank his many co-authors over the years.

Dr. Gonzalez O'Brien would like to send his love out to all his nonacademic friends, who help keep him sane in the wacky world of academia. Benjamin also owes a debt of gratitude to Ken De Bevoise, who not only helped inspire him to pursue a Ph. D. but also to be a better teacher. His classes remain the gold standard than Dr. Gonzalez O'Brien hopes to one day live up to. A special thanks, as always, goes out to his amazing wife, Erica O'Brien, who has helped him pursue his dreams and stood by him since they first met way back in 1999. Dr. Gonzalez O'Brien's adorable little girl, Penelope, also reminds him daily of why work like this is so important. Hopefully through his teaching, research, and 2032 presidential run he can leave her a slightly better country. If not, he'll make sure she always know he loves her and that she can change the world. He'd also like to thank his dog, Maggie, for all the snuggles and emotional support, the staff and faculty at Highline College where he had his first "real" job, as well as the staff and faculty at San Diego State University, who welcomed him into their department in 2018. He hopes this dedication gets him one step closer to tenure.

Finally, the authors would like to thank their editor Angela Chnapko at OUP for providing excellent guidance and meeting with them in person on several occasions. She provided crucial guidance in the development of this project, and they cannot thank her enough!

Contents

List of Figures

List of Tables

Introduction

On July 1, 2015, Kathryn Steinle was shot and killed by Jose Ines Garcia Zarate, an undocumented immigrant, in San Francisco. Prior to the shooting, Garcia Zarate had been taken into custody on a marijuana possession charge, which was later dismissed, but the city had declined to honor an Immigration and Customs Enforcement (ICE) detainer request to hold him until ICE could take him into their custody based on the city's sanctuary policy. Garcia Zarate was later found not guilty of murder in the Steinle shooting, but many blamed his release, despite the request by ICE, as the reason for Steinle's death. While San Francisco had been a sanctuary city since 1989, policies that minimize city cooperation with ICE had long flown under the radar of the American public until the Steinle shooting.

Then–presidential candidate Donald Trump exploited the shooting, making opposition to sanctuary cities a central part of his 2016 campaign. During the last months of the presidential contest, Trump routinely brought up the issue of sanctuary cities as a means of burnishing his anti-immigrant and America-first credentials. In a speech in Charlotte, North Carolina, on August 18, 2016, Trump stated,

> I've embraced the crying parents who've lost their children to violence spilling across our border. Parents like Laura Wilkerson and Michelle Root and Sabine Durden and Jamiel Shaw whose children were killed by illegal immigrants. My opponent supports sanctuary cities. But where was the Sanctuary for Kate Steinle? Where was the sanctuary for the children of Laura, Michelle, Sabine, and Jamiel? Where was the sanctuary for every other parent who has suffered so horribly? These moms and dads don't get a lot of consideration from our politicians. They certainly don't get apologies. They'll never even get the time of day from Hillary Clinton. But they will always come first to me. Listen closely: we will deliver justice for all of these American families. We will create a system of immigration that makes us all proud.

In a Phoenix, August 31, 2016, campaign speech, after enumerating the deaths of other Americans killed by undocumented immigrants, Trump once again referenced Kathryn Steinle: "Another victim is Kate Steinle. Gunned down in the sanctuary city of San Francisco, by an illegal immigrant, deported five previous times. And they knew he was no good."

As the campaign reached its conclusion, Trump stated he would cancel all funding to sanctuary cities once elected. For example, in a November 7, 2016, speech in Raleigh, North Carolina, Trump noted, "Hillary supports totally open borders. There goes your country. And strongly supports sanctuary cities like San Francisco where Kate Steinle was murdered violently by an illegal immigrant deported at least five times. We will cancel all federal funding to sanctuary cities." In total, Trump covered the immigration policy area in some form or another in about 77 percent of his presidential campaign speeches, with sanctuary cities specifically mentioned in about 26 percent of these speeches. Clearly, Trump made the connection between crime and immigration generally, and sanctuary cities specifically, the central theme of his campaign.

Thus, Trump's attack on sanctuary cities can be conceptualized as an attack on progressive and welcoming immigration policy more generally. By using immigration to prime the classic dynamic of us (Americans) versus them (foreigners), Trump stamped himself as the law-and-order candidate— reminiscent of the Nixon era. And while Trump did not mention sanctuary cities a lot in his 2015–2016 tweets, Figure 1 reveals that Trump's daily immigration-related tweet count was highest on the day of Steinle's killing.[1]

In other words, beyond Trump's initial campaign speech denouncing undocumented Mexican immigrants, Trump's response to the Steinle killing helped establish him as *the* anti-immigrant candidate in the GOP presidential primary. Trump's strong and early anti-immigrant stances were critical to his success in the GOP primary. Research by Newman et al. (2018) shows that Trump's Republican primary support rose most rapidly in areas undergoing rapid Latino growth specifically in response to Trump's repeated anti-immigrant statements. As the campaign progressed, and Trump repeatedly doubled down on his anti-immigrant stances, his anti-immigrant tweets garnered increased attention in the forms of retweets and favorites (see top-right and bottom-left panels in Figure 1). Whether we look at speeches, tweets, or any other campaign communication, the evidence is clear that Trump used sanctuary city opposition as a venue for burnishing his anti-immigrant credentials and that this paid off politically.

Trump continued to attack sanctuary cities once in office, claiming they "breed crime" and issuing an executive order to strip grant funding from cities that passed these policies.[2] GOP candidates for governor in Virginia,[3] Florida,[4] and a congressional special election in Pennsylvania[5] have since

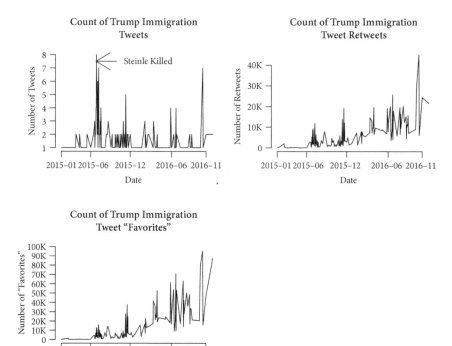

Figure 1 Daily count, retweet count, and favorite count of Trump tweets related to immigration. A tweet is considered to be about immigration if one of the following terms is included in the tweet: steinle, sanctuary, illegals, immigration, border.

campaigned on the issue. The Trump administration's aggressive enforcement operations generated a backlash, with California going so far as to declare itself a sanctuary state and to threaten fines to private employers that allow ICE to access nonpublic areas without a warrant.[6] Taken in total, sanctuary cities are now a major issue in American politics—an issue that has heretofore received relatively minimal attention in the scholarly literature.

But to understand sanctuary politics today in order to conceive of where we might be going in the future, we must ground our analysis in the history of how these policies came to pass. Sanctuary policies, which limit local cooperation in federal immigration enforcement to varying degrees, draw their name from the Sanctuary Movement, a faith-based campaign established to offer Central American refugees protection from federal immigration officers in the 1980s.

The Sanctuary Movement developed in response to the denial of asylum to individuals fleeing political violence in El Salvador and Guatemala. Between

1980 and 1985, 2.6 percent of Salvadoran and 0.8 percent of Guatemalan asylum-seekers were offered asylum, compared to 23.3 percent for all other nationalities. Some observers argued that Salvadorans and Guatemalans were denied refugee status because of U.S. support for the regimes responsible for the violence they were fleeing (Ridgley, 2008).

This denial of safe refuge led a number of faith-based groups to offer aid to refugees in the form of shelter in churches and synagogues—directly flouting antiharboring laws. The concept of sanctuary is rooted in religious tradition tracing its roots to fifth-century Roman law, but members of the Sanctuary Movement also argued that their efforts were supported by the Geneva Conventions and the United States' own Refugee Act of 1980. At its height, an estimated twenty thousand to thirty thousand church members and more than one hundred churches and synagogues across the United States participated in the program, which also enjoyed support from members of Congress (Villazor, 2007).

This support by government officials led, on June 7, 1983, to the Madison, Wisconsin, city council passing Resolution 39,105, officially commending churches in the city that were offering sanctuary to Central American refugees, many (if not most) of whom had arrived illegally. The Madison city council followed this with Resolution 41,075 on March 5, 1985, officially declaring the entire city a sanctuary for Central Americans fleeing violence in El Salvador and Guatemala. The inspiration of the Sanctuary Movement was clear in the resolutions adopted by cities like Madison in the 1980s, which frequently were ideological in character.

With a decrease in the number of Central American refugees by the end of the 1980s, sanctuary policies remained in place in many of the cities that implemented them, but media coverage of the topic faded with time. These policies also began to evolve into something different from those that had been passed in solidarity with the Sanctuary Movement. Increasingly the subject of these policies was not refugees but undocumented immigrants. They were also no longer strictly ideological, as there was a functional component: local officials wanted an increasingly large number of undocumented immigrants to feel comfortable in reporting crimes to law enforcement. Some saw the increasingly harsh rhetoric and the criminalization of the undocumented by legislation like California's Proposition 187 in 1994 and the Illegal Immigration Reform and Immigrant Responsibility Act (IIRIRA) of 1996 as driving an increasingly large wedge between immigrant communities and local officials, including law enforcement.

After the attacks of September 11, 2001, local jurisdictions increased participation with federal authorities through the 287(g) program, which allowed law enforcement to enforce immigration laws. Secure Communities, a program that shares information with ICE about deportable immigrants in custody electronically, further increased the apprehension undocumented immigrants would likely have in any interactions with local law enforcement. Many observers believed that these programs could make the job of police more difficult if Latino immigrants were afraid to call police out of fear of deportation. Sanctuary policies during the 1990s and 2000s were therefore both an ideological statement of opposition to anti-immigrant legislation and meant to foster greater trust between immigrant communities and local government.

Modern sanctuary policies forbid local officials from inquiring into individuals' immigration status and in some cases prohibit holding undocumented immigrants on ICE detainers if they have not been charged with a violent offense. Proponents of sanctuary policies claim that these policies are meant to promote cooperation between police and immigrant communities, as well as to allow undocumented immigrants to access local resources without fear that they will be asked about their status. More generally, these policies are designed to help incorporate immigrant-based communities. If individuals in these communities feel safe from deportation, they will be more likely to contribute to the improvement of their communities, and should be more likely to interact with the state to assist the latter in providing essential state services—like policing, fire protection, and so on. Because immigration enforcement is the sole jurisdiction of the federal government, sanctuary localities claim that they are not required to cooperate or assist ICE in enforcement actions. This position and reasoning constitute the precise point of the federalism conflict.

Opponents, such as Donald Trump, claim sanctuary municipalities are rewarding lawbreakers and that such policies increase crime, placing American citizens at risk. The Trump administration has repeatedly sought to link sanctuary policies to violent crime, usually through anecdotes, such as the Steinle shooting. The administration's claim is not only that these immigrants may not have had the opportunity to commit their crimes had they been held for ICE but also that the very existence of sanctuary cities attracts a criminal element. However, when we move away from anecdote to policy, and empirically weigh the potential pros and cons of such policies, the findings overwhelmingly suggest that while opposing sanctuary cities might serve to motivate anti-immigrant voters, sanctuary policies do not promote criminality but rather provide benefits for residents of these cities in terms of political incorporation.

In this book we examine sanctuary policies in detail and consider many of the questions that such policies raise: What is their history, and why did policies that initially were meant to support refugees evolve into ones meant to protect the undocumented community? How has the media, where the public gets most of its information about sanctuary policies, framed the issue, and how has this changed over time? What drives public support or opposition to these policies? Is it truly a fear of crime, or is this more related to the perceived threat from Latino immigrants? What is behind the increasing number of antisanctuary bills we've seen introduced at the state level since 2015? Do sanctuary policies increase crime, as their detractors claim, or increase trust and incorporation within the local Latino community, as proponents argue? We answer these questions in what is the first comprehensive examination of the politics of sanctuary cities in the United States.

Defining *Sanctuary*

One initial difficulty inherent in the study of sanctuary cities is that there is no concrete definition of how exactly a sanctuary city should be defined. For instance, the Ohio Jobs & Justice PAC, which maintains a list of sanctuary cities online, also includes "informal" sanctuary cities in their definition. In *informal sanctuary cities*, no resolution or policy exists on paper but instead their classification is based on observed actions, such as lack of enforcement.[7] However, this classification seems open to subjective and biased interpretations of who is illegal and what counts as lack of enforcement. In addition, some localities, such as Travis County, Texas (prior to the passage of SB-4 in 2017) may decline to honor ICE detainers for nonviolent offenders, but this is not formally part of department policy. Like informal sanctuary cities, these would be excluded from our analysis, which only includes municipalities with formal policies on the books, which can be verified and are publicly available.

Those cities with legislation or official rules in place have a gradation of sanctuary policies. Some cities or police departments only forbid law enforcement from making immigration inquiries, as with the Los Angeles Police Department's Special Order 40, which was passed in 1979. This represents one of the earliest examples of what could be called a sanctuary policy, but because the goal of Special Order 40 was not ideological—instead, it was simply meant to foster greater cooperation between the Latino immigrant community in Los Angeles and the police—it attracted little attention at the time. Some cities may also forbid local officials from collecting information related to immigration status in the dispensation of any city-level benefits. These policies are certainly contentious, but the Trump administration has most often targeted localities that take approach this a step further.

These jurisdictions, like San Francisco, in addition to forbidding local officials from inquiring into immigration status, also refuse to honor detainers by ICE for nonviolent offenders. ICE uses these detainers to have undocumented immigrants held past their release date so that they can be taken into custody and entered into deportation proceedings. Cities—and in some cases counties—that decline to honor these detainers have been the primary target of the Trump administration and other sanctuary opponents like Texas governor Greg Abbott. This represents a much more direct defiance of federal authorities than simply not collecting immigration-related information.

Some sanctuary policies do include direct ideological statements affirming the rights of immigrants or criticisms of federal immigration enforcement and policy. For example, Berkeley, California's, Resolution 63,711-N.S. states, "Whereas, the spirit and intent of Berkeley's refuge Resolutions would be violated if City funds, facilities or staff were utilized to assist the Federal government's inhumane immigration policies and practices."[8] In cities like Berkeley, sanctuary is declared not just for practical reasons but also as a way of protesting federal immigration policies. In February 2018 the mayor of Berkeley's neighbor Oakland, Libby Schaaf, made her personal commitment to the city's sanctuary policies clear in declaring that she would willingly go to jail to protect undocumented residents and later issued a news release warning of a coming ICE raid.[9]

Not all policies that could be construed as "sanctuary" policies include this explicitly ideological aspect or have as their goal protecting the rights of immigrants themselves. For the purposes of this book, we define a *sanctuary city* as a *city or police department that has passed a resolution or ordinance expressly forbidding city or law enforcement officials from inquiring into immigration status and/or cooperation with ICE*, thus incorporating both ideological and nonideological cities for the purpose of our analysis. In order to be included in our analysis, a city had to have a specific such resolution or ordinance, but we did not require that cities refuse to honor ICE detainers for undocumented immigrants taken into custody.

Proponents of sanctuary cities defend these policies by arguing that immigration is the sole responsibility of the federal government, and state and governments are not required and cannot be forced to devote resources to enforcing federal immigration policy. Therefore, sanctuary cities can be read as a subset of the broader immigration federalism framework in terms of conflict between different levels of government (Boushey and Luedtke, 2006, 2011; Gulasekaram and Ramakrishnan, 2015; Ramakrishnan and Gulasekaram, 2012). In the 1990s under IIRIRA, local officials could be deputized as immigration officers, but this was optional, as were steps

[handwritten margin note: Other goals?]

post-9/11 to encourage greater cooperation and collaboration between federal authorities and local officials such as the 287(g) program.[10] Supreme Court precedent suggests that while states, cities, or counties may opt to participate in immigration enforcement, this cannot be required. Two decisions, *New York v. U.S.*[11] in 1992 and *Printz v. U.S.*[12] in 1997, found that the federal government could not compel or coerce local officials to enforce, enact, or administer federal programs. These decisions form the legal basis for many sanctuary policies since they suggest that cities or states are in no way required to assist in federal immigration enforcement.

Additionally, while 8 U.S.C. Section 1373[13] prohibits local or state governments from enacting laws or policies that limit communication with the Department of Homeland Security (DHS) about "information regarding the immigration status or citizenship status" of individuals, sanctuary policies specifically forbid local officials from collecting this information in the first place. Since local officials do not have this information to share, proponents of sanctuary policies argue there is no violation of U.S. code.

The sanctuary debate is thus not only about policy but also about the respective roles of local, state, and federal officials in immigration enforcement. States like California and cities like Seattle argue that federalism dictates that they have a right to pass these policies. Since they do not bar ICE from conducting operations in sanctuary cities or states, there is no conflict with federal law. The Trump administration, and former Attorney General Jeff Sessions, argue that sanctuary policies are meant to obstruct federal enforcement, that they violate the free-speech rights of government employees by barring them from sharing information, and that they overstep the boundaries of state sovereignty. This tension helps to define the debate, as does the connection of these policies to an oft-demonized group in American politics: undocumented immigrants.

The Immigrant Threat and Sanctuary Cities

The politics, media coverage, and public attitudes regarding modern sanctuary cities are all influenced by the broader debate and history of undocumented immigration—specifically Latino immigration—in America. Debates around Latino immigration have always relied on threat narratives to justify restriction and increased criminalization (Gonzalez O'Brien, 2018; Masuoka and Junn, 2013; Newton, 2012; Ngai, 2004; Tichenor, 2002). These threats can be broadly characterized into three categories: economic, cultural, and criminal. All three of these threat frames are relatively common both in media coverage of

Mexican immigration, as well as Congressional debate on legislation related to undocumented immigration, though since the 1990s there has been an increasing reliance on the criminal threat frame. Jonathan Simon calls the increasing reliance on law-and-order issues to use fear as a means of attracting voters as "governing through crime" (Simon, 2006). Research has found that elites and media both tend to exaggerate the threat of victimhood individuals face from crime, which can lead to heightened anxiety (Chiricos et al., 1997, 2000; Eschholz, 1997; Simon, 2006). Furthermore, heightened anxiety attracts individuals to more negative (rather than positive) immigration news stories (Gadarian and Albertson, 2014).

We have seen a similar approach to undocumented immigration, with politicians on the right like Tom Tancredo[14], Sharron Angle[15], Pete Wilson[16], and Donald Trump relying on criminality narratives to attract votes. In particular, many Republican candidates and elected officials appear to think issues like undocumented immigration in general—and sanctuary cities in particular—play to their advantage; that is, that their party owns the issue (Petrocik, 1996). Elite messaging linking undocumented immigrants to crime has in turn influenced media coverage of the subject, which draws regularly on narratives of threat (Chavez, 2010; Santa Ana, 2002, 2013).

The passage of S.5094 in 1929, also known as the Undesirable Aliens Act—which for the first time made undocumented entry a misdemeanor and reentry a felony—effectively linked the long-standing rhetoric of immigrant criminality to the legal treatment of Latino immigrants. This criminalization of the undocumented has had significant repercussions for policymaking, with an increasing emphasis on enforcement operations to address the issue despite (or perhaps because of) the reliance of many American industries on undocumented labor. The program of Mexican repatriation between 1929 and 1936, Operation Wetback in 1954, and the Trump administration's crackdown all have their roots in S.5094 (Gonzalez O'Brien, 2018). All have sought to use mass deportation campaigns and the creation of a climate of fear to address undocumented immigration and justified this approach by citing the threat undocumented immigrants posed to American workers, culture, and safety.

Sanctuary policies are inextricably linked to the broader issue of undocumented immigration, and because of this, policy responses to them have been shaped by narratives of criminality that are now commonplace in this debate, which has a number of consequences. First, policymakers have been effectively divided into two camps on sanctuary policy, reflecting divisions on the larger topic of undocumented immigration (Wong, 2017b). GOP lawmakers profess that sanctuary policies reward criminal behavior and threaten the safety of

U.S. citizens. Democrats, who have become more reliant on the Latino vote as well as more vocal advocates of racial justice (Barreto et al., 2010; Barreto and Segura, 2014; Collingwood et al., 2014), argue that these policies are necessary to protect an already vulnerable population and allow them to access basic services like health care or law enforcement. The elevation of sanctuary policies onto the national agenda, the partisan nature of the debate, and the perceived threat from the undocumented population all affect the policy responses from conservative lawmakers. In states where immigration is a salient issue and where the GOP has control, more antisanctuary legislation is introduced. This is both to appeal to the base on a law-and-order platform as well as to address the threat posed to the electability of conservative politicians by a growing Latino population.

Politicians have long sought to attract voters based on a promise to protect them from dangerous nonwhite populations, whether this is blacks, Latinos, or other nonwhite groups (Mendelberg, 2001). The use of immigrant criminality in the sanctuary debate is thus likely to activate implicit racial threats from the Latino population, something that past research has shown that political elites sometimes seek to do for political gains (Hopkins, 2010; Newman et al., 2018; Valentino et al., 2002). The debate around sanctuary cities is not about crime generally though, and is instead focused on a particular group: undocumented immigrants. Therefore, immigrant threat is likely to play a significant role in determining public opinion, rather than fear of crime more generally, because of how the media and elites frame this issue, and its overwhelming racialization (Abrajano and Hajnal, 2015; Brader et al., 2008; Campbell et al., 2006; Key, 1949; Tolbert and Grummel, 2003).

How the media has framed sanctuary policies as they have evolved has shifted significantly as the target group of these policies has changed from refugees to undocumented immigrants. Research has shown that the media significantly influences public opinion through the tone of its coverage, as well as its quantity (Iyengar and Kinder, 1987; Scheufele, 2000; Scheufele and Tewksbury, 2007). In the 1980s, the Sanctuary Movement and city policies were most often discussed in the context of refugees and the moral imperative to protect those fleeing conflict. This changed dramatically in the 1990s and 2000s to a framing that was much more partisan and reliant on narratives of criminality, something that was quite common in stories about undocumented immigration.

Research to date has found that most media coverage of undocumented immigration, or policies related to it, tends to be negative in tone (Abrajano and Singh, 2009; Chavez, 2010; Haynes et al., 2016; Kim et al., 2011; Masuoka and Junn, 2013; Santa Ana, 2002, 2013). The media typically relies on threat narratives in discussions of undocumented immigration, which frames this negatively and can influence public opinion, particularly among those who have little knowledge about immigration (Schemer, 2012). This negative framing of undocumented immigrants is similar to the treatment of blacks in television news, where they tend to be portrayed in stories about crime or drugs, which has been found to influence perceptions of blacks (Dixon, 2007; Entman, 1990, 1992). Similarly, media framing of sanctuary policies that emphasizes crime will likely influence perceptions of these policies and public opinion. Because sanctuary policies are linked to undocumented immigrants, and Latinos are the "iconic" illegal immigrants (Ngai, 2004), public opposition will likely be driven not by broad concerns about crime but instead fear of Latino immigrants.

This book represents one of the first serious academic analyses of the politics surrounding sanctuary cities. While other scholars have analyzed the development and relevance of sanctuary cities from a historical and sociological perspective, we couch our analyses and findings squarely within the political science and immigration politics literature. Our focus is primarily on the modern-day politics of sanctuary cities; thus, we examine media coverage, public opinion, legislative activity, and policy outcomes. Our goal is to provide the public, elected officials, policy practitioners, and other academics with the latest and most relevant research on sanctuary cities to date.

In chapter 1 we examine the history of sanctuary policies in the United States and the reason they shifted from a relatively narrow focus on refugees to a far broader one on undocumented immigrants. While the Sanctuary Movement began in the 1980s with the goal of protecting Central American asylum seekers fleeing civil war and social strife, by the 1990s that movement had faded, and sanctuary policy became more about protecting undocumented immigrants. In short, immigration patterns shifted, and after 9/11, the U.S. security apparatus became more punitive. Some cities—often those with relatively high percentages of undocumented immigrants—moved to protect this population and to simultaneously send an ideological response to the federal government's increasingly punitive immigration policies.

We next look at how the media has framed sanctuary cities from the 1980s until today, with a particular eye to the changes that resulted in coverage as a result of the target group of these policies shifting. We also situate this analysis in the broader context of media coverage of undocumented immigration. First, relying on a corpus of newspaper articles about sanctuary cities and movements from 1980 to 2017, we show both through qualitative methods and quantitative dictionary-based text approaches that newspapers initially framed the issue as one about morality and religion. While crime was mentioned, it was not as salient a news frame. However, by 2016, newspapers presented the issue primarily in partisan terms, and secondarily in terms of crime. We suggest that these frames influence public opinion. Second, we corroborate these findings with a similar qualitative and quantitative text analysis of television broadcast segments featuring sanctuary cities or the Sanctuary Movement.

In chapter 3 we analyze public opinion on sanctuary cities and specifically the role played by perceptions of immigrant threat. Using a variety of data sources, but particularly four geocoded public opinion surveys from Texas and California between 2015 and 2017, we show that sanctuary policy attitudes are not determined by actual on-the-ground crime rates but by on-the-ground changes in Latino population size and current Latino population size. Local crime or murder rates are not statistically related to attitudes about sanctuary cities. Importantly, these findings hold up after controlling for alternative explanations. This finding is actually entirely unsurprising and fits squarely within the "racial-threat literature" initially proposed by Key (1949). The public—especially the white public—often conflates minority population size and growth with crime, despite contradictory evidence. This explains why politicians' arguments that sanctuary cities are full of crime or that sanctuary policies cause crime—even when they are or do not—can be so effective in swaying public opinion.

Additionally, we consider the role that partisanship has played in determining attitudes about sanctuary policy as a result of the Steinle shooting and Trump's presidential campaign. Drawing on some of the same aforementioned public opinion datasets, we now pool our data and create a time dummy for 2017 (1) versus 2015 (0). While this technique is still observational and not experimental, we can examine various hypotheses about how voters learn about sanctuary cities and sanctuary policy. While Republicans have long opposed sanctuary policies – in part because Republican elites have stressed the issue and in part because it is an easy anti-immigrant issue, Democratic voters have only recently come to support sanctuary policy. We maintain that Trump's attack on sanctuary cities helped facilitate Democrats' learning about the issue. Research shows that negative partisanship is on the rise (Abramowitz and Webster, 2016). That is, voters come to support or oppose a policy based on what party elites on the opposite side of the aisle believe and promote. We provide evidence supportive of the argument that Trump's strong antisanctuary attacks and big-city Democratic mayors' and Democratic governors' strong counter response almost certainly sent cues to Democratic voters about where they should stand on the policy. Thus, we show that Democrats—regardless of racial identification—shifted strongly in support of sanctuary cities from 2015 to 2017.

In chapter 4 we shift the focus from public opinion to policy. Taking advantage of a comprehensive dataset covering all sanctuary city and policy legislative bill introductions from 2005 to 2017 that we gathered from the National Conference of State Legislatures and the LexisNexus state bill database, we show that the Steinle killing and Trump's response almost certainly translated to an immediate rise in state legislative activity. For each state, we generate two dependent variables: a count of the number of antisanctuary bills per year, and a count of the number of prosanctuary bills per year. We then examine the correlates of both types of bill introductions for the year 2017 because 2017 saw such a rise in the number of introductions and clearly stands out from the rest of the time series.

States are a crucial interlocutor between the federal government and cities. That is, because local-level law enforcement is a product of state policy devolution, states generally have the constitutional power to dictate law enforcement policies but typically choose not to do so. However, if they so choose, states can outright ban sanctuary cities or can enforce sanctuary policy statewide. We show a massive uptick in sanctuary bill introductions—both pro and anti—in 2017. Fitting with extant literature on legislative activity, we show that conservative ideology (both legislator and mass public) is the main driver behind antisanctuary bill introductions. We show the opposite for prosanctuary legislative proposals.

We also examine the distinct role of the American Legislative Exchange Council (ALEC) in terms of promoting antisanctuary legislation around the United States. By exploiting the hack and release of over eight hundred model ALEC bills, we locate ALEC's most prominent antisanctuary city model bill. Use plagiarism software, we then textually compare ALEC's model bill to all bills in our corpus. Even in 2017, many bills have portions in them directly lifted from this model bill.

Finally, in chapter 5, we address the consequences of sanctuary policies through an analysis of crime rates in sanctuary cities, ICE-detainer requests in several large counties, 911 call behavior in response to Texas's antisanctuary SB-4's enactment, and the political incorporation of the Latino community via Latino voter turnout and Latino police-force representation.

The data compiled to examine our hypotheses in chapter 5 are extensive. First, we rely on a database of cities that passed and had on the books post-9/11 a known sanctuary city policy. To measure our dependent variable, we add on city-level crime data from the Federal Bureau of Investigation's (FBI) Universal Crime Reporting (UCR) website. We augment these data with census and political data for these cities. We gather the same data for all other cities that have at least one sanctuary city in their state. This produced a massive dataset, from which we conduct a match. Thus, our main analysis lets us compare crime rates across otherwise similarly situated cities. We find no difference in crime rate across the distinct types of cities.

Second, to examine whether county's policy responses to ICE-detainer requests systematically influence crime, we gathered monthly crime data from five counties across a roughly five-year time period. From media reports, we constructed an interrupted policy measure—locating the precise month that a county shifted to be more (or less) helpful to ICE in terms of handling ICE's detainer requests. We find no generalizable or systematic crime pattern in response to policy change involving ICE-detainer requests.

Next, via a Freedom of Information Act (FOIA) request, we gathered 911 call data across a roughly two-year period in the city of El Paso, Texas. We geocoded the data to census tract to pull in relevant demographic information. In this time series, we locate the enactment of SB-4—which banned sanctuaries in the state. Using a regression discontinuity in time design (RDiT), we show that 911 calls dropped primarily in areas of town where foreign-born noncitizens reside.

We then turn to an assessment of incorporating aspects of sanctuary policy. We gathered voter turnout data for every single registered Latino voter in the United States across a four-year time period (2006–2010). The data include geolocation information, notably city and state. We then aggregate turnout to the city level, summing up the total number of Latino voters by city for each year. We then added an indicator variable for whether the city became a sanctuary between 2006 and 2010. This indicator variable is now thought of as our treatment. We then stacked the data such that each city appears in the data twice. This technique controls for invariant city-level characteristics because we compare cities against themselves over a relatively short time span. We then estimate a difference in difference regression model where our outcome measure is voter turnout at the city level, and our treatment variable is a dummy measuring whether the city became a sanctuary city during the specified time frame.

Finally, we use a similar approach to assess whether sanctuary policy leads to greater Latino police force representation. We gathered data from the Justice Bureau's Law Enforcement Management and Administrative Statistics

(LEMAS) survey. Every few years, this survey collects data from all law enforcement agencies across the country in cities and localities with populations greater than one hundred thousand. The survey asks agencies to report a variety of statistics, including a count of total officers and their race and ethnicity. Thus, our outcome measure is the percentage of the police force in each city that is Hispanic relative to the percentage of the city that is Hispanic. We compiled the data from the 2000 and 2012 LEMAS surveys. Any city that became a sanctuary during this time is conceptualized as treated. Like our voter turnout analysis, we estimate a difference in difference regression model where we interact time and treatment to estimate the causal effect of sanctuary city status on Latino police force representation.

Our results show that sanctuary policies have no effect on crime rates, that declining to honor ICE-detainer requests does not necessarily increase or decrease crime rates, and that enacting a statewide sanctuary law almost surely reduces the likelihood that undocumented immigrants will call 911. On the other side of the coin, we show that sanctuary policies facilitate the political incorporation of the Latino community. Cities that implement sanctuary policies tend to see both a small increase in Latino voter turnout and a increase in Latino representation on the city's police force.

Over the chapters that follow we delve into all of the preceding summaries in more detail. The goal is to present a comprehensive examination of sanctuary policies, covering the evolution of sanctuary legislation (chapter 1) and how media coverage has changed between 1980 and 2017 (chapter 2). We then consider the predictors of pro- and antisanctuary attitudes among the mass public (chapter 3) before turning to what leads to the introduction of sanctuary legislation (chapter 4). We close by analyzing the costs and benefits of sanctuary policy (chapter 5). Our conclusion ties all of these threads together and includes a discussion of the role of sanctuary legislation in the broader debate around undocumented immigration.

1

The Sanctuary City in Historical Perspective

On June 7, 1983, the Madison, Wisconsin, city council passed Resolution 39,105, officially commending churches in the city that were offering sanctuary to Central American refugees, many (if not most) of whom had arrived illegally. The Madison city council followed this with Resolution 41,075 on March 5, 1985, officially declaring the entire city a sanctuary for Central Americans fleeing violence in El Salvador and Guatemala. The adoption of sanctuary resolutions by cities like Madison would mark the beginning of a clash between state and local officials and the federal government over immigration policy that continues to play out today.

Since Madison's resolution in 1985, more than two hundred localities nationwide have passed similar laws limiting the participation of local officials in the enforcement of federal immigration law.[1] In the past, these cities have received only sporadic attention from either media or politicians, but that changed drastically on July 1, 2015. On that date, Kathryn Steinle was shot and killed in San Francisco by Jose Ines Garcia Zarate, an undocumented immigrant who had been convicted of seven felonies and deported seven times. In March 2015 Garcia Zarate had been arrested for an outstanding drug warrant and briefly was in jail in San Francisco, where ICE filed a detainer asking that he be held so that he could be taken into custody for deportation. Because of its status as a sanctuary city, the detainer was declined and Garcia Zarate was released. As he was not a violent criminal and the city had declined to prosecute the marijuana-possession charge he was being held for, the request from ICE was ignored. Steinle would be killed by a bullet fired by a gun in Garcia Zarate's possession that he claimed accidentally discharged. He would later be acquitted of her murder since she was in fact killed by a bullet that had ricocheted off the ground near her.

The shooting of Steinle ignited a firestorm over San Francisco's sanctuary policy and served as a *focusing event*, defined as "sudden, relatively rare events that spark intense media and public attention" (Birkland, 1997). Republican presidential candidate Donald Trump would use the Steinle shooting to make opposition to sanctuary policies a major part of his campaign in the fall of 2015. Trump had previously argued, "When Mexico sends its people, it's not sending their best. They're sending people who have a lot of problems, and they're bringing those problems with us. They're bringing drugs. They're bringing crime. They're rapists. And some, I assume, are good people."[2] Trump seized on Steinle's shooting as proof for this statement and a further justification for the border wall his campaign had promised to build if he was elected. On the heels of Trump's statement and the Steinle shooting, nearly all the GOP presidential candidates included opposition to sanctuary cities in their platforms.

In this chapter we examine the political and historical evolution of city-level sanctuary policies from the early 1980s through 2018 as their emphasis shifted from protection of Central American refugees to the oft-demonized undocumented community. Modern sanctuary policies, like San Francisco's, draw on previous resolutions, sometimes passed earlier in response to the Central American refugee crisis in the same city. Our goal in this chapter is to examine how sanctuary resolutions passed in the 1980s differed from those passed later and to analyze the factors that led to their adoption based on the comments of public officials involved in the process.

The Curious Case of Special Order Number 40

While the root of modern sanctuary policies is often traced to the Central American refugee crisis and Sanctuary Movement of the 1980s, there was in fact a "sanctuary" policy that predated these. We define a *sanctuary city* as a city or police department that has passed a resolution or ordinance expressly forbidding city or law enforcement officials from inquiring into immigration status and/or cooperation with ICE and Los Angeles' Special Order 40 certainly fits this definition.

Special Order 40 was passed on November 27, 1979, by the Los Angeles Police Department and explicitly forbade officers from inquiring into immigration status. Procedure I of the special order specifically stated, "Officers shall not initiate police action with the objective of discovering the alien status of a person. Officers shall not arrest nor book persons for violation of Title 8, section 1325 of the United States Immigration Code (Illegal Entry)." While this law seems relatively banal, it was actually the first to explicitly forbid officers from inquiring or taking action based on immigration status and thus, based on our definition, made Los Angeles the first sanctuary city.

What is surprising is that the order passed with relatively little fanfare. As a result, it receives little attention in the scholarship on sanctuary cities. One of the main reasons is that the order was not ideological in character and was instead functional, with its goal being increased cooperation between Los Angeles' sizable Latino and undocumented community and local law enforcement.

Then–police chief Daryl Gates stated in 2008, "It was written at a different time in history, when the state attorney general said illegal entry was not our business, no one was paying attention to the influx of illegals into Southern California, and the community did not seem to be concerned" (*40 in 40*, 2008). So, despite seeming like a policy ripe for partisan conflict, Special Order 40 generated little buzz when it was passed because undocumented immigration itself was not yet seen as the hyperpartisan issue it is today. Immigration enforcement was the job of federal authorities, not local law enforcement, and the latter relied on the cooperation and trust of the undocumented community to be able to perform its duties; hence Special Order Number 40.

The legal precedent for the sanctuary city was thus set well before the beginning of the Central American refugee crisis, which would trigger the first wave of sanctuary declarations in the mid- to late 1980s. Special Order 40 did differ from many of the resolutions that would be enacted during the refugee crisis because it lacked the ideological component that would become common in later legislation. It was not passed to signal a stance on federal policy; it was just meant to make the job of police officers easier. Because of the lack of ideological commitment and fanfare it is unclear how aware residents of Los Angeles were of Special Order 40. This point is reinforced by the fact that Los Angeles, despite the existence of Special Order 40, publicly declared itself a sanctuary city on November 27, 1985. The resolution itself stated that "the climate of fear prevalent among Central American refugees . . . may potentially impair the efficiency of city government agencies, disturb the efforts of law enforcement agencies to resolve pending cases, and generally contradict the ideals of diversity and tolerance to which the City of Los Angeles subscribes" (Mathews, 1985). Special Order 40 had already been in place for six years when the above resolution was passed but the public declaration of sanctuary had ideological undertones and the effect of raising awareness of the policy itself.

While Special Order 40 had received little attention from federal authorities, this was not the case with Los Angeles' sanctuary declaration. Harold Ezell, the western regional Immigration and Naturalization Service (INS) commissioner at the time of the resolution's passage, campaigned aggressively against the resolution through a petition drive and pressed constituents to contact their city council member to express their displeasure with the resolution. Ezell's tactics were effective, and the Los Angeles City Council reversed itself less than a year later, revoking the city's sanctuary status (Mathews, 1986).[3]

Yet Special Order 40 was not challenged, despite the fact that it forbade officers from inquiring into immigration status and the resolution had only made a public declaration of sanctuary and expanded the "don't ask" provision to city employees. This case of Special Order 40 highlights the role that ideological aspects of such a declaration have in making them controversial. The sanctuary resolution did not seek to simply facilitate cooperation between police and immigrant communities but was meant as a show of solidarity with the Sanctuary Movement and as a criticism of the Reagan administration's refugee policies.

The lack of a federal response to Special Order 40 is important because it revealed the lack of costs associated with noncooperation at the time. Special Order 40 certainly had potential benefits, such as a redirection of resources and increased trust between local immigrant communities and law enforcement. If police were prohibited from inquiring or detaining individuals based on their immigration status, the resources that would normally be used to enforce federal immigration law could be directed elsewhere. With policies like Special Order 40 lacking the politicization of modern sanctuary policies, the benefits outweighed the costs. However, part of the reason that Special Order 40 did not become controversial was its nonideological foundation. It was not meant as a criticism of federal refugee or immigration policy and therefore did not attract the attention of federal authorities, as Los Angeles' later sanctuary resolution would.

Yet there was no significant spread of policies like Special Order 40 in the period following its passage. It would take a significant event to lead to their spread and the birth of the sanctuary city in name. This event was the Central American refugee crisis.

The Sanctuary Movement

While Los Angeles was the first city to pass a policy prohibiting police from inquiring into immigration status, a policy that would be mimicked in most of the sanctuary cities that would spring up in the 1980s, it was a sanctuary city in policy only. The true birth of the sanctuary city in name did not occur until the early 1980s as a result of the actions of the Central American Sanctuary Movement (Sanctuary Movement).

The Sanctuary Movement came into existence because thousands of Central Americans were fleeing political violence and seeking asylum from regimes in El Salvador and Guatemala. Most of these refugees were subsequently denied legal refugee status, so the Sanctuary Movement sprung up with the goal of providing a safe haven in the United States to those fleeing violence. In both countries, the Reagan administration was either trying to topple or prop up local regimes to prevent the Soviet Union from expanding its influence into Central America. In the case of both Guatemala and El Salvador, the administration had an active role in providing economic support or arms to groups accused of perpetrating acts of violence.

Ridgley (2008) argues that because the United States was providing substantial military and economic aid to these two countries, from which nearly all refugees were coming, it was "politically risky" to acknowledge the atrocities that this aid was enabling. Most of the Central Americans applying for refugee status were labeled instead as economic migrants and deported back to their country of origin.

Golden and MacConnell (1986) point out, "In 1981 and 1982, as the sanctuary movement was beginning, the United States, the only country in the world sending Salvadorans back to their homeland, deported an average of one thousand per month." Ridgley (2008) provides further evidence of this, citing that from 1980 to roughly 1985, only 626 of 100,000 Salvadoran applications for asylum were approved. She also points out that while the average approval rate for all nationalities was 23.3 percent between 1983 and 1986, the average approval rate was 2.6 percent for Salvadorans and 0.8 percent for Guatemalans, suggesting that these groups were being specifically targeted for nonacceptance.

A number of churches began offering sanctuary to these refugees, providing support and even transportation from the border. The official declaration of the Sanctuary Movement came on March 24, 1982, in Tucson, Arizona, by the Southside Presbyterian Church of Tucson and five East Bay, California, churches (Golden and MacConnell, 1986). While the movement did not have a leader in the traditional sense, the Reverend John M. Fife of the Southside Presbyterian Church in Tucson and Jim Corbett, a Quaker who had helped refugees cross the border before meeting Fife, are often credited with its birth.

As the movement grew and sought to bring public and media attention to the plight of the Central American refugees, and the Reagan administration continued turning away asylum seekers, the federal government eventually started cracking down on the movement. Sixteen members of the Sanctuary Movement would eventually be indicted on seventy-one counts of conspiracy and transporting and harboring undocumented immigrants. Eleven people, including Fife and Corbett, would see their cases go to trial, and six were convicted in 1986, including Fife. None would serve any time for the convictions, with all eventually released on probation. The convictions were the result of informants who were placed within the movement to gather evidence (Crittenden, 1988; Golden and MacConnell, 1986).

The convictions would do little to stop the movement, and in 1987 there were claims that the FBI was breaking into sanctuary sites to obtain documents that could be used against members. While there was never concrete evidence of FBI involvement in the break-ins, a map in the University Baptist Church archive, a sanctuary site in Seattle, Washington, shows a pattern of break-ins at sanctuary sites across the United States dating back to 1984 and continuing throughout 1987, when the map was published (see Figure 1.1). The break-ins included not just sanctuary sites but also apartments, offices, and law firms associated with the movement or its members, which a January 25, 1986, article in *The Nation* compared to the notorious COINTELPRO program that had been used to undermine the American Indian Movement and the Black Panthers, among others (Kohn, 1986).

The concept of sanctuary drew on religious traditions and traced its roots back to fifth-century Roman law. In the archives of the University Baptist Church of Seattle, there is a transcript of a radio show titled *Christian Perspectives on the News* hosted by Rev. C. Donald Cole, in which he lays out the religious foundations of sanctuary. He pointed out that churches had been refuges not only for those fleeing persecution but also criminals, based on the Old Testament, stating, "Scholars believe the custom dates to antiquity. As practiced in Christian churches, it probably has its source in the Old Testament cities of refuge. When the ancient people of Israel began to settle the land of Canaan, they designated six cities as places of asylum for fugitives.... You can read about the cities of refuge in Numbers 35 and Deuteronomy 19" (Cole, 1983).

On the subject of the churches offering sanctuary to Central American refugees, Cole argued that it would be difficult to compare modern sanctuary policies to those ancient cities of refuge, because the former were not looking to prevent illegal arrest or unjust execution, but instead a change in policy. Despite this, he continued later in the broadcast,

> This is not to say what they are doing is wrong. There is a definite analogy between their sheltering refugees from El Salvador and the underground railroad that saved refugee slaves before the Civil War.... I personally believe that most people participating in the sanctuary movement are sincere people

SANCTUARY BREAK-INS

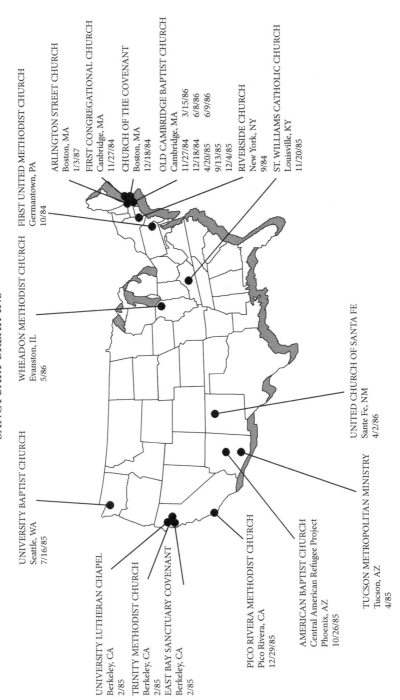

UNIVERSITY BAPTIST CHURCH
Seattle, WA
7/16/85

WHEADON METHODIST CHURCH
Evanston, IL
5/86

FIRST UNITED METHODIST CHURCH
Germantown, PA
10/84

ARLINGTON STREET CHURCH
Boston, MA
1/3/87

FIRST CONGREGATIONAL CHURCH
Cambridge, MA
11/27/84

CHURCH OF THE COVENANT
Boston, MA
12/18/84

OLD CAMBRIDGE BAPTIST CHURCH
Cambridge, MA

11/27/84	3/15/86
12/18/84	6/8/86
4/20/85	6/9/86
9/13/85	
12/4/85	

RIVERSIDE CHURCH
New York, NY
9/84

ST. WILLIAMS CATHOLIC CHURCH
Louisville, KY
11/20/85

UNITED CHURCH OF SANTA FE
Sante Fe, NM
4/2/86

UNIVERSITY LUTHERAN CHAPEL
Berkeley, CA
2/85

TRINITY METHODIST CHURCH
Berkeley, CA
2/85

EAST BAY SANCTUARY COVENANT
Berkeley, CA
2/85

PICO RIVERA METHODIST CHURCH
Pico Rivera, CA
12/29/85

AMERICAN BAPTIST CHURCH
Central American Refugee Project
Phoenix, AZ
10/26/85

TUCSON METROPOLITAN MINISTRY
Tucson, AZ
4/85

Figure 1.1 Nationwide sanctuary sites as of June 1987.

who care about refugees from Central America. They do not view them as illegal aliens; they see them as displaced people in need . . . . If the refugees are genuine refugees, not just illegals, there is Scriptural support for taking them in and not sending them back.   (Cole, 1983)

This broadcast demonstrated the difficulty in resolving a religious tradition based on preventing the abuse of criminal law by the state through unjust arrests or executions with the actions of a movement seeking a change in policy. Cole also made clear that part of the point of the Sanctuary Movement was to attract attention to the plight of Central American refugees in the hope of creating public pressure for change in the Reagan administration's treatment of Salvadoran and Guatemalans.

Similarly, modern sanctuary cities often use their open opposition to federal immigration in a way that looks to influence public opinion and media framing. By continuing to draw on a term rooted in religious tradition, cities, states, and counties evoke a powerful symbolic image of the sanctuary city as protector from injustice. During their trial, members of the movement would cite religious tradition as well as the U.S. Refugee Act of 1980 and the Geneva Conventions, which they believed the Reagan administration was violating by denying Central American applications for refuge (Crittenden, 1988).

At its height, the Sanctuary Movement encompassed hundreds of religious and faith-based groups across the country, with additional support coming from university campuses, civil rights organizations, lawyers, and a host of other concerned parties. The Sanctuary Movement grew into a nationwide phenomenon, and its members did not shy from the public eye despite the illegality of their actions. Villazor (2007) cites some astounding figures in relation to the number of individuals involved with the Sanctuary Movement. She notes that: "At the height of the sanctuary movement, an estimated 20,000 to 30,000 church members and more than 100 churches and synagogues participated in the sanctuary movement, making the conflict between the church and state inevitable."

By June 1987, toward the end of the Sanctuary Movement, there would be 393 designated sanctuary locations across the United States. Three hundred and seventy-six were religious institutions, with Roman Catholic and Unitarian denominations having the largest representation. As Figure 1.2 shows, in addition to the 376 religious institutions, 16 universities, and 1 seminary also declared themselves as sanctuaries. This has a modern equivalency in the "sanctuary campuses" that sprang up around the country following the election of Donald Trump, which sought to protect undocumented students

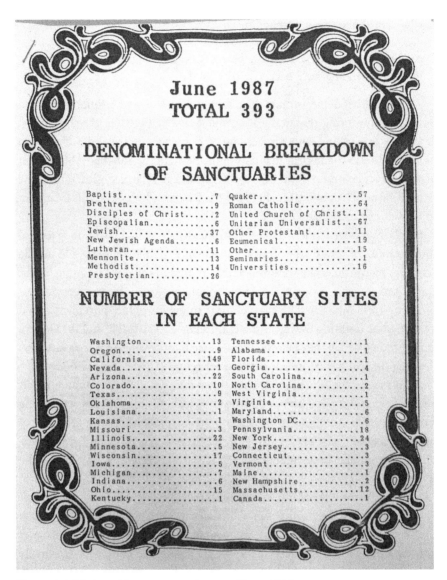

June 1987
TOTAL 393

DENOMINATIONAL BREAKDOWN
OF SANCTUARIES

Baptist	7	Quaker	57
Brethren	9	Roman Catholic	64
Disciples of Christ	2	United Church of Christ	11
Episcopalian	6	Unitarian Universalist	67
Jewish	37	Other Protestant	11
New Jewish Agenda	6	Ecumenical	19
Lutheran	11	Other	15
Mennonite	13	Seminaries	1
Methodist	14	Universities	16
Presbyterian	26		

NUMBER OF SANCTUARY SITES
IN EACH STATE

Washington	13	Tennessee	1
Oregon	9	Alabama	1
California	149	Florida	1
Nevada	1	Georgia	4
Arizona	22	South Carolina	1
Colorado	10	North Carolina	2
Texas	9	West Virginia	1
Oklahoma	2	Virginia	5
Louisiana	1	Maryland	6
Kansas	1	Washington DC	6
Missouri	3	Pennsylvania	18
Illinois	22	New York	24
Minnesota	5	New Jersey	3
Wisconsin	17	Connecticut	3
Iowa	5	Vermont	3
Michigan	7	Maine	1
Indiana	6	New Hampshire	2
Ohio	15	Massachusetts	12
Kentucky	1	Canada	1

Figure 1.2 Nationwide sanctuary sites as of June 1987.

from federal authorities and in some cases also offered free on-campus legal counsel (National Sanctuary Sites, 1987). Unsurprisingly, California led in the total number of sanctuary sites, with 149 locations by 1987.

Figure 1.3 maps locations of declared sanctuary religious organizations as of June 1987. The California Bay Area and Tucson are clearly represented on the map. Further clusters of sanctuary activism include Los Angeles and Southern California more broadly; many Lutheran and Unitarian churches

Sanctuary Church Locations Year = 1987

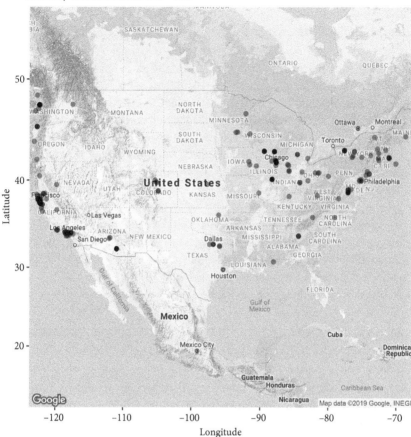

Figure 1.3 Nationwide sanctuary religious sites as of June 1987. The movement's strength, in terms of number of churches claiming sanctuary status, was deepest in California, particularly in the Bay Area and in Los Angeles. However, support existed along the West Coast, the Midwest, and throughout the Northeast and Mid-Atlantic.

in the Midwest, centered around Chicago; and the Northeast, including New York City, Philadelphia, and Washington. In general, sanctuary church and synagogue locations emerged in traditional immigration-receiving locations. It should be no surprise then, that these cities would later became epicenters of opposition to the Trump administration's anti-sanctuary policies.[4]

Churches and other faith-based groups that were members of the Sanctuary Movement also adopted resolutions formally declaring their status as a place of refuge for Central Americans. The resolution by the General Board of the

American Baptist Churches in 1985 laid out the reasons that the denomination's leadership supported the actions of churches offering sanctuary to refugees. This declaration stated,

> Painfully fresh in memory is that church and society in our own country by and large "looked away" while the Jewish victims of Nazism sought asylum in the United States. That experience has made us sensitive to the plight of persons escaping countries where the population is terrorized by bombing, death squads, and the "disappearance" of citizens.... Congregations of our denomination and other communions have risen to the occasion and publicly declared their churches to be sanctuary for endangered people. They are offering the asylum which our government routinely denies. The present situation is not attributable to the violation of immigration laws by refugees, or religiously motivated persons endeavoring to assist them, but to the unwillingness of the U.S. administration and INS to abide by international covenants and practices which our government has subscribed and which have been incorporated into U.S. law.
> (General Board of the American Baptist Churches, 1985)

In addition to arguing that it was in fact the U.S. government that was in violation of the law rather than the churches offering safe harbor to refugees, the resolution also cited that most of those churches offering sanctuary cited their religious duty to do so. Sanctuary, they argued, should be protected by the First Amendment's clause for free exercise of religion (General Board of the American Baptist Churches, 1985). The resolution ended with a call on faith groups and leaders to press Congress to grant temporary status to those fleeing violence in Central America, to investigate federal policy on refugees, and also to look into clandestine operations that were attempting to infiltrate the movement.

In May 1984 the Rabbinical Assembly similarly endorsed the idea of sanctuary, citing the experience of the Holocaust and that the U.S. government was arresting and deporting individuals who faced the "gravest danger" if they were returned to their home country. Like the later resolution by the American Baptist Assembly, the Rabbinical Assembly also noted that the United States was in violation of international law, specifically the 1951 U.N. Refugee Convention. The resolution they adopted confirmed that the assembly supported both the idea of sanctuary and those communities of faith that had sheltered Central American refugees (Rabbinical Assembly, 1984).

The Sanctuary Movement had tremendous public support according to Villazor (2007), including governmental support from forty-seven members of Congress. Mike Lowry, the representative for Washington's Seventh Con-

gressional District, which includes Seattle, wrote of his opposition to the Reagan administration's policies toward Central America to the Reverend Jamie
Robbins and Katherine Mock. Both Reverend Robbins and Ms. Mock were
associated with the University Baptist Church in Seattle, one of Washington's
sanctuary sites (Lowry, 1983a; Lowry, 1983b).

In response to letters of concern about the status of Central American
refugees and the violence in El Salvador, Guatemala, and Nicaragua, Lowry
voiced his clear opposition to the administration's policies and how these
were fueling conflict in the region. In a letter to Katherine Mock on
August 10, 1983, Lowry pointed out, "I will continue to oppose U.S. support
for the Nicaraguan 'Contra' insurgents.... U.S. support for the Contras could
create an unending cycle of violence, such as El Salvador is now experiencing"
(Lowry, 1983b).

On the subject of El Salvador, Lowry noted that the administration had
certified that the country's government was making progress on human rights,
even though there had been an increase in the number of murders in the first
six months of 1983. Lowry cosponsored House legislation that asked that the
U.S. terminate military aid and sales to the Salvadoran government, which was
embroiled in a conflict with guerrilla forces (Lowry, 1983a).

Rep. Lowry next discussed the situation in Guatemala, where "human
rights organizations indicate that 5,000 to 10,000 people have been killed by
government security forces since General Rios Montt came to power in March
of 1982" (Lowry, 1983b). While Montt had been ousted by the time of the
letter to Ms. Mock, Lowry wanted the administration to suspend military
aid to Guatemala because of the human rights abuses that had occurred and
could continue despite the change in leadership. Lastly, Lowry criticized the
administration's understanding of the unrest in Central America, which the
administration characterized as being based on outside intervention from the
Soviet Union and Cuba but was in truth based on "poverty, violence, and
oppression" (Lowry, 1983b). The clear links between the violence in Central
America, Reagan administration policies, and the refugee crisis that led to
the Sanctuary Movement helped to create a sympathetic environment for the
activists' actions.

The Sanctuary Movement would become such a popular cause among
Democrats that it was included in the 1984 Democratic Party platform, which
not only leveled criticism at the Reagan administration's handling of conflicts
in Central America, but also included support for the Sanctuary Movement.
The platform, in a section discussing the necessity of providing economic
resources to Central America, also stated, "The Democratic Administration

will work to help churches and universities which are providing sanctuary and assistance to Guatemalan, Haitian, and Salvadoran refugees, and will give all assistance to such refugees as is consistent with U.S. law" (Democratic National Committee, 1984). This support by members of Congress and the Democratic National Committee (DNC) for the Sanctuary Movement likely contributed to the declaration of city-level resolutions in the mid- to late 1980s.

The city-level statements, while they were likely influenced by growing support for the movement by political elites, were also driven at least in part by pressure from the public. For example, in King County, Washington, which includes Seattle, a public poll was conducted by Hebert Research on January 12, 1984, asking about support for the Sanctuary Movement sites in the region. The poll asked, "Do you agree or disagree with several Puget Sound churches who are illegally providing sanctuary for refugees from El Salvador who fear for their safety if they are sent back to their homeland?" (Hebert Research, 1984). As Figure 1.4 demonstrates, support for provision of sanctuary was strong, with 42.2 percent agreeing with the churches.

The poll also included some of the comments made by those on both sides. Among those who agreed, the following comments were offered: "Someone has to give them a place to stay. They're the children of God and we must all help each other;" "They really are in danger. Someone should help;" "It is morally right. Our ancestors were once in the same situation;" "It is a humanitarian gesture and God knows we need it" (Hebert Research, 1984).

Those who disagreed noted that even refugees were bound by laws, taking them in would not resolve the situation in their home countries, it would potentially take resources away from homeless Americans, and that there were already too many refugees taking advantage of the United States (Hebert Research, 1984). The support for the Sanctuary Movement by both Democratic politicians and members of the public would help lead to city-level declarations that would begin in 1983, led by Madison, Wisconsin's declaration of support on June 7, 1983.

Seattle and Berkeley

While a number of cities would become sanctuaries by the end of the 1980s, it is useful to look at the politics behind these decisions in a little more detail. Two cities represent good case studies of changes and continuity in sanctuary declarations Seattle and Berkeley. In the former, the University Baptist Church donated a large collection of documents related both to the church's decision to

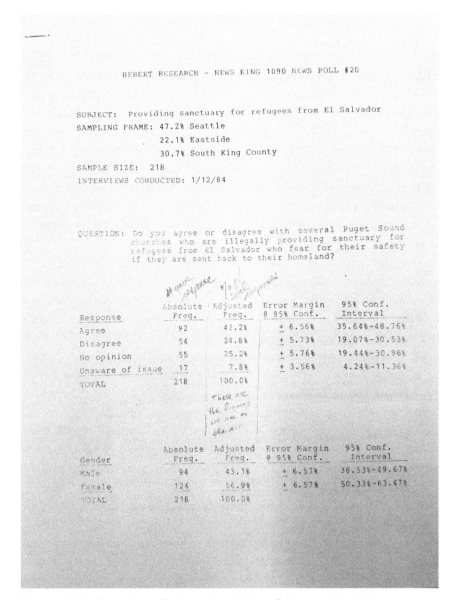

Figure 1.4 Herbert Research-News King 1090 poll, January 12, 1984.

become a sanctuary and the activism that would lead to the city's declaration in 1986. Berkeley would name itself a "city of refuge" even earlier than Seattle and it was not the first time the city had declared itself a sanctuary, which reveals the role of city-level norms in influencing sanctuary declarations.

Seattle

On Monday, January 13, 1986, the Seattle City Council passed its "city of refuge" resolution, which directed local officials to provide services to residents regardless of their immigration status, criticized the U.S. handling of the situation in Central America, and noted that refugees from El Salvador and Guatemala routinely had their applications to stay in the country declined (Maier, 1986; Seattle City Council, 1986). The resolution followed a public campaign that would lead to the passage of Initiative 28 on November 8, 1983, which expressed concern with U.S. support of Central American groups responsible for violence and also directed the city council to create a Citizens' Commission on Central America. This commission would go on to organize and facilitate meetings on sanctuary status for Seattle.

Despite what seemed like broad public support in 1986, Seattle voters would rescind the city's sanctuary status just eleven months later with Initiative 30, which stated that the citizens of Seattle supported immigration laws and criticized the politicized nature of the Citizens' Commission.[5] This reversal revealed the deep divisions on sanctuary policies, even at a time when their target was refugees, rather than undocumented immigrants.

Yet Seattle would reverse itself once again in 2003, when the City Council passed Ordinance 121063, which forbade local officials and law enforcement from inquiring into the immigration status of residents. Included in the ordinance was a rebuke of the Bush administration's post-9/11 crackdown on undocumented immigration, which was criticized as leaving immigrant communities fearful of deportation and unable to access city resources because of this fear (Seattle City Council, 2002).

In 2017 Seattle would strengthen its sanctuary policy with Resolution 31730, which members of the City Council called a "Welcoming Cities" resolution. This resolution was scathing in its criticism of both Donald Trump's rhetoric and actions on immigration, stating, "The level of anti-immigrant and anti-refugee rhetoric during the 2016 Presidential campaign, racist hate speech toward immigrant and refugee communities, and anti-immigrant and anti-refugee policies proposed by the current Presidential Administration is alarming" (Seattle City Council, 2017).

The resolution stated that Seattle would not participate in the government's 287(g) program, which allows local law enforcement to be deputized as immigration officers. It also stated that the city and city officials would not cooperate in any actions by the Department of Homeland Security that were not required by law, that they were not to deny services based on immigration status, nor was anyone to be detained based on violations of immigration law.

Berkeley

Unlike Seattle, some sanctuary cities would embrace their identity as cities of refuge from the initial adoption through the writing of this book in 2018. One such city is the liberal enclave of Berkeley, California, which passed its own sanctuary resolution on February 19, 1985. The vote on the city council had been overwhelmingly supportive, with only one council member of the nine voting against the resolution.

The sanctuary resolution encouraged the people of Berkeley to work with the sanctuaries in the city to help provide the "housing, transportation, food, medical aid, legal assistance and friendship that will be needed" (Berkeley City Council, 1985). It declared Berkeley a "city of refuge" and forbade city employees from assisting in any investigations or assisting with arrests for alleged violations of immigration laws. It also stated that city employees were not to deny public services to the sanctuary sites.

Berkeley's sanctuary policy linked itself to an earlier resolution by the city council passed on November 10, 1971, which had stated the city's support for congregations in the city offering sanctuary to those who refused to fight in the Vietnam War (Berkeley City Council, 1971). In fact, the parts of the resolution calling on the city's residents to assist those sites providing sanctuary and prohibiting city employees from assisting with or participating in investigations or arrests associated with federal law were drawn almost verbatim from the antiwar sanctuary declaration in 1971.

In the case of Berkeley, then, the city's sanctuary resolution of 1985 was part of a sanctuary tradition in the city. Berkeley's 1985 resolution, like most sanctuary city policies, was based on the Sanctuary Movement but it also drew on an older tradition in the city of resistance to federal laws that residents, and the city council, saw as morally problematic. Because states, counties, and cities are not required to assist in the enforcement of federal law, federalism offered city officials and the city itself protection from punishment by the federal government for their refusal to provide assistance in their investigations.

In 2007 the city would strengthen its existing sanctuary policy with Resolution 63711, which forbade any city employees from using city funds to assist in the enforcement of immigration law or to share the immigration status of city residents with federal authorities (Berkeley City Council, 2007). The city's long history of offering refuge led some to call Berkeley the "original" sanctuary city (O'Donoghue, 2017).

September 11 and the Rise of the Modern Sanctuary City

City-level sanctuary resolutions came in two waves. The first, covered in the preceding section, was in response to the Central American refugee crisis in the 1980s and generally ran from 1985 to 1989, by which time the number of Central Americans trying to enter the United States had declined, as had the Sanctuary Movement.[6] In 1990, Central American refugees became eligible for Temporary Protected Status (TPS), which also contributed to the decline of the movement (Mathews, 1990). The second wave of declarations came on the heels of the attacks of September 11, 2001, in response to a new federal crackdown on undocumented immigration by the newly formed Immigration and Customs Enforcement (ICE) agency.

September 11 led to a number of specific enforcement operations aimed at apprehending and deporting undocumented immigrants or moving these individuals through the system faster in hopes of increasing the ease of deportation. Operation Endgame in 2003, an initiative by ICE to arrest and deport all removable noncitizens, was the first of these linked to the 9/11 attacks, but it would be followed by Operation Stonegarden (2004), the Secure Borders Initiative (2005), Operation Streamline (2005), and Operation Return to Sender (2006) (Massey and Pren, 2012). However, this more aggressive stance of federal immigration authorities led many cities to adopt sanctuary policies in response to what they believed were the abuses inherent in these acts or operations, as well as the burden they imposed on local law enforcement by having them enforce federal immigration law.

While many cities did pass revised sanctuary resolutions in the post-9/11 period, the resolutions that had been passed in the 1980s to protect Central American immigrants also continued to protect the undocumented community since they forbade local officials from denying local services based on immigration status or inquiring into that status. However, the expansion of enforcement post-9/11 as well as the new powers the federal government was granted in the name of national security also gave ICE more tools to exploit in immigration crackdowns.

Berkeley provides an example of how policies passed in the post-9/11 environment expanded the role of city officials in sheltering undocumented

immigrants from aggressive federal enforcement. Previously, Berkeley's resolution had largely been a passive one, praising local sanctuary sites, directing
residents to provide assistance to both refugees and those sheltering them, and
only forbidding local officials from direct assistance with or participation in
federal operations. The city's new resolution, which was passed on May 22,
2007, by a unanimous vote of the city council, went further.

Referencing the resolutions of 1971 (44,784-N.S.) and 1985 (55,596-N.S.),
Berkeley's 2007 resolution (63,711-N.S.) specifically mentions ICE's Operation
Return to Sender in its third paragraph. This ICE operation at least on its
face seemed innocuous; it tasked the agency's fugitive teams with a quota of
one thousand deportations annually of "fugitive aliens" whose deportation
had been ordered but were still in the United States (Bennett, 2008). A 2006
Washington Post article estimated the size of this population at five hundred
thousand, but also noted that these were not just "criminal immigrants," as this
group was typically characterized.[7]

Instead, some fugitive aliens may simply have not received their deportation
notice, and the agency's own database, which at the time they admitted
contained incomplete or inaccurate information, also meant that to meet
deportation quotas, enforcement teams would often conduct neighborhood
raids (Bennett, 2008). These raids often targeted Latino communities, meaning
that legal residents or citizens could be caught up in the net without proper
documentation and that the climate of fear they generated extended beyond
the undocumented community.

Berkeley's 2007 resolution noted that, under Operation Return to Sender,
eighteen thousand had been arrested nationwide and one-third of them
had been from the Bay Area. Condemning the operation, as well as the
tactics of ICE, the resolution claimed that parents were being separated from
young children, and that the children themselves were being incarcerated
in some cases. The resolution also stated that witnesses had reported that
ICE agents were identifying themselves as local law enforcement during
raids, and using "intimidation and harassment" to gain entry to homes
(Berkeley City Council, 2007).

Citing Berkeley's earlier sanctuary resolutions, 63,711-N.S. argued that
"the spirit and intent of Berkeley's refuge Resolutions would be violated if
City funds, facilities or staff were utilized to assist the Federal government's
inhuman immigration policies and practices." As mentioned earlier, the
resolution reaffirmed Berkeley as a city of refuge, barred local officials from
using city resources or funds to assist in federal immigration enforcement,
and forbade local officials from collecting or reporting information that could

be used to determine the immigration status of residents. It also struck any questions about immigration status from city forms that related to benefits, services, or opportunities provided by the city, unless this was required by state or federal law.

The resolution, while it was similar in spirit to Berkeley's two earlier sanctuary policies, was much more active on the city's role in standing against the federal government's aggressive immigration tactics. No longer was Berkeley simply supporting local churches that were offering sanctuary, it was taking a stance as a city on immigration policy in a way that was a much more overt challenge to federal policy writ large. This was not just about the treatment of specific groups, as it was with 1985's 55,586-N.S., but the nation's immigration policies under the Bush administration and its tactics of enforcement.

There was significant variation in the ideological component of sanctuary resolutions, though, and how specific the resolutions were in their criticism of federal policy. For example, the October 2008 sanctuary resolution of Cicero, Illinois, did not mention any specific enforcement program or federal policy, but instead noted the importance of cooperation between immigrant communities and the police. To facilitate that cooperation in a city that was, according to the resolution, 85 percent Latino, city officials could not refuse city services based on immigration status, city officials were not to inquire about immigration status, and local officials were not to participate in the enforcement of federal immigration policy (*Cicero Safe Space Resolution*, 2008). The resolution did not directly criticize federal policy and simply noted that "immigration law is a complex area and properly enforced within the authority of the federal government" (*Cicero Safe Space Resolution*, 2008).

Some cities, like Anchorage, Alaska, simply forbade local officials from participating in federal immigration enforcement, which police departments were not required to participate in but were increasingly encouraged to do so by the federal government. The Illegal Immigration Reform and Immigrant Responsibility Act (IIRIRA) of 1996 had allowed for the deputization of police officers as immigration authorities under the 287(g) program, and post-9/11 there was an increased push to get local communities to participate in these efforts (*The Illegal Immigration Reform and Immigrant Responsibility Act*, 1996).

These efforts increased fears that local immigrant communities would be alienated by the deputization of police as agents of the federal government and that this would hamper the ability of officers to do their job effectively, particularly in those communities with a large number of immigrants. Both the Homeland Security Enhancement Act (HSEA) and the Clear Law Enforcement for Criminal Alien Removal Act, introduced in the House and Senate, respectively, in 2005, would have sought to increase the role of local police in the enforcement of immigration policy, either by incentivizing it or penalizing those states that refused to do so. Some resolutions, like Cicero's, were clearly meant as pushback against this move to blur the lines between local and federal authorities.

In 2008, the Department of Homeland Security began a program known as Secure Communities, under which participating jails would transmit fingerprints to federal authorities to be checked against immigration databases to see if individuals were in the country legally. If they were not, ICE could file a detainer request, which would ask municipalities to hold the individual in question until they could be taken into custody to be processed for deportation.[8] Many sanctuary cities, counties, and states also began to implement policies dictating when immigrants would be held on an ICE detainer request, in addition to prohibiting local officials from participating in immigration enforcement operations.

San Francisco, for example, only honors ICE detainer requests for violent offenders, which was one of the criticisms leveled at the city by then-candidate Donald Trump on the heels of the Steinle shooting. San Francisco's municipal code on its status as a city of refuge forbids city officials from disseminating information to federal authorities regarding the immigration status of individuals in the city or from "assisting or cooperating" with detention or arrest procedures for undocumented immigrants. An exception to this was made for those who were arrested on certain felony charges or who had been previously convicted of a serious or violent felony (*San Francisco Municipal Code*, 2009).

California's Trust Act (AB 4), passed in 2013, specifically addressed ICE detainers, stating that local law enforcement could not hold low-level offenders on ICE detainer requests.[9] The Trust Act limited law enforcement in the state to honoring detainers only in the case of serious offenses, such as violent crimes or stalking. Misdemeanors were, for the most part, not grounds to hold someone for ICE.[10]

In the 2010s, some states moved in another direction entirely, passing laws born of a piece of legislation written by the American Legislative Exchange Council (ALEC), a public-private organization made up of conservative lawmakers from all levels of government, as well as representatives from private industry. ALEC's "No Sanctuary Cities for Illegal Immigrants Act" (NSCIIA) was a piece of model legislation that prohibited local governments from barring local officials from assisting or cooperating with ICE. In addition, the act would have allowed any official or agency of state or local governments who "limits or restricts" the enforcement of immigration policy to be brought to court and, if found guilty, to be subject to a one-thousand- to five-thousand-dollar fine for each day the policy had been in place after the filing of an action against them.[11] The goal of ALEC's model legislation is to serve as "ideal" legislation that public officials can use in crafting their own laws, which we discuss in more detail in chapter 4. As Collingwood et al. (2018) show, parts of ALEC's "No Sanctuary Cities for Illegal Immigrants" would go on to be part of anti-sanctuary legislation around the country.

Sanctuary policies have increasingly become not only a clash of federalism but are increasingly based on partisanship, as Donald Trump has turned the issue into a touchstone of his presidency. Thus, in the 2010s we have seen both pro- and anti-sanctuary legislation passed. While Donald Trump has successfully claimed this issue as his own and made it a central part of Republican politics, in the past, sanctuary policies have played a significantly lesser role in presidential politics.

The Presidential Politics of Sanctuary Cities: 1980–2015

Politically, sanctuary has waxed and waned as a subject of interest for politicians. In the 1980s Ronald Reagan never even addressed the cities that were declaring themselves as "cities of refuge" in response to the Sanctuary Movement and his administration's policy on refugees. Instead, individuals associated with the administration would try to paint refugees from Central America as economic refugees and the conflicts in Guatemala, El Salvador, and Nicaragua as necessary to prevent the spread of communism.

While the 1984 Democratic Party platform (Democratic National Committee, 1984) pledged support for the Sanctuary Movement and criticized the administration's involvement in conflicts in Nicaragua and El Salvador, the 1984 Republican Party platform would characterize the administration's involvement as necessary to limit communist influence in the region (Republican National Committee, 1984). The platform laid out the Republican Party's position in stark terms: "Today, democracy is under assault throughout the hemisphere. Marxist Nicaragua threatens not only Costa Rica and Honduras, but also El Salvador and Guatemala. The Sandinista regime is building the largest military force in Central America, importing Soviet equipment, Eastern bloc and PLO advisors, and thousands of Cuban mercenaries.... Nicaragua cannot be allowed to remain a Communist sanctuary, exporting terror and arms throughout the region" (Republican National Committee, 1984).

The platform condemned Salvadoran guerillas as communists and argued that ensuring that El Salvador remained free from the influence of communism was important because "El Salvador is nearer to Texas than Texas is to New England" (Republican National Committee, 1984). The politics of sanctuary policies were thus dominated not only by questions about how the refugees from Central America should be treated once they were in the United States, but also by questions about the foreign policy of the Reagan administration toward the region. Cities like Seattle, Berkeley, Madison, and others that declared themselves as sanctuaries in the 1980s received little public attention from the Reagan administration despite their very public opposition to its policies, with the administration instead targeting the Sanctuary Movement.

As discussed earlier, there would be a significant lull in attention to sanctuary cities in the period between the end of the 1980s and the 9/11 attacks. Bush administration policies and the immigration crackdown that followed 9/11 led new cities to declare themselves sanctuaries—and some of those that had adopted these policies earlier to revise and strengthen them to try and assuage the fears of local immigrant communities. This would lead to renewed public attention to the policies, as well as the first mentions of sanctuary cities in a presidential campaign.

In 2007, sanctuary policies emerged as an issue in the Republican presidential primary, as candidates sought to use the issue of sanctuary cities to damage former New York mayor Rudy Guiliani, who was running for the Republican nomination. At the time, many saw Guiliani as a GOP frontrunner. Giuliani's support as mayor of New York for the city's sanctuary policy was an easy target for former Massachusetts governor Mitt Romney, who also sought the GOP's nomination.

In a November 19, 2007, press release, Romney laid out his position on sanctuary policies and the actions he had taken as governor of Massachusetts. "You don't promote a lawful society by condoning illegality. As governor, I opposed driver's licenses for illegals, vetoed tuition breaks for illegals and combated sanctuary city policies by authorizing the state police to enforce federal immigration law. As president, I will secure the border and reject sanctuary policies by cities, states, or the federal government" (Romney, 2007). The release then featured a number of excerpts from public statements by Giuliani on his support for New York's sanctuary status, as well as for a path to citizenship. Romney would go on the record as pledging to cut federal support for sanctuary cities if he became president.

Another GOP contender for the Republican nomination, Fred Thompson, a former senator from Tennessee, would similarly attack Giuliani on sanctuary cities and would offer more specifics about the actions he would take as president. An October 23, 2007, press release detailed Thompson's "Border Security and Immigration Reform Proposal," which included cutting off discretionary federal grant funds to any community that restricted communications between local officials and ICE (i.e., sanctuary cities). Thompson also supported stripping federal education grants to public universities that offered in-state tuition to undocumented immigrants and the denial of federal grants to communities that offered benefits to the undocumented (Thompson, 2007).

The topic of sanctuary cities would also come up in the Republican primary debates as a means of attacking Giuliani as weak on immigration. During the Republican presidential candidate debates on January 5th and 10th, 2008, Fred Thompson, who was clearly trying to carve out space for himself as the "tough-on-immigration" candidate, criticized sanctuary policies for contributing to the problem of undocumented immigration, and Giuliani specifically for New York's policies barring local officials from collecting information on individuals' immigration status.[12]

This issue would largely drop off the political radar after the election, but was briefly revived in the lead-up to the 2012 election. In 2011, both Rick Perry and Newt Gingrich tried to revive sanctuary as a campaign issue, with Perry promising to deny federal grants to sanctuary cities in an October 18, 2011, press release, and Gingrich making a similar pledge during the December 15, 2011, Republican primary debate (Perry, 2012).[13] However, with Obama winning the presidency in both 2008 and 2012, sanctuary cities would once again became less of a matter of public and political interest.

Following the Steinle shooting, sanctuary cities would become a much more salient issue politically, with 50 percent of the total mentions of the term "sanctuary city" in the American Presidency Project's document archive coming from this period. Mentions of the term included comments by candidates during the 2015 Republican primary on sanctuary cities and the death of Ms. Steinle, as well as the frequent comments of candidate/President Donald Trump and those associated with his administration.

The rhetoric by politicians after the Steinle shooting also shifted dramatically. While Romney had frequently used New York's policies as a point of criticism directed at Rudy Giuliani, his attacks were directed at the perceived disobedience of sanctuary cities rather than the criminal narrative that would become popular in 2015. In a July 7, 2015, press release from the Trump campaign, Bill O'Reilly was cited as stating that the Obama administration was complicit in the killing of Ms. Steinle because they had not taken a harder line on immigration (Trump, 2015).

Trump would not be the only candidate to try to link sanctuary policies to violent crime. Rick Perry would criticize Trump in a July 20, 2015, press release for not speaking out earlier against the dangers posed by undocumented immigrants or sanctuary policies, citing, among other things, the shooting in 2006 of a police officer in a sanctuary city by an undocumented immigrant who had been previously deported (Perry, 2015).

An October 12 press release from the Ted Cruz campaign was titled "If I'm Elected President the Federal Government Will Stop Releasing Violent Criminal Illegal Aliens" featured an interview in which the senator from Texas pointed out that he had introduced legislation into the Senate to strip federal funding from sanctuary cities (Cruz, 2015).

Donald Trump would make his opposition to sanctuary policies a central talking point on the campaign trail and would paint these policies as endangering American citizens. At a rally on August 31, 2016, Trump would link sanctuary policies to violent crime on four different occasions, mentioning the death of Kathryn Steinle, but also the "great parents who lost their children to sanctuary cities and open borders," and the many "needless deaths" that had occurred as a result of these policies (Trump, 2016). At some of his rallies and speeches Trump would have the parents of individuals who had lost their lives to undocumented immigrants in the crowd, and was careful to point them out, as he did at the rally on August 31, 2016.

Sanctuary after Trump

Following the candidacy and election of Donald Trump, sanctuary cities came under sustained fire as Trump sought to fulfill his campaign promise to end sanctuary policies around the country. Just days after taking office, the president signed Executive Order 13768, titled "Enhancing Public Safety in the Interior of the United States," on January 25, 2017.[14] The order would have stripped sanctuary jurisdictions of federal grants for not complying with federal immigration policy, but it was quickly challenged in the courts.

A permanent injunction was issued against the order on November 21, 2017, by District Judge William Orrick after it was challenged by the city and county of San Francisco, as well as the city of Santa Clara. In his decision, Orrick stated,

> The Constitution vests the spending powers in Congress, not the President, so the Executive Order cannot constitutionally place new conditions on federal funds. Further, the Tenth Amendment requires that conditions on federal funds be unambiguous and timely made; that they bear some relation to

the funds at issue; and that they not be unduly coercive. Federal funding that bears no meaningful relationship to immigration enforcement cannot be threatened merely because a jurisdiction chooses an immigration enforcement strategy of which the President disapproves.[15]

The administration would try other tactics, such as denying the Edward Byrne Memorial Justice Assistance Grant (JAG), a federal program that assists in funding law enforcement and public safety, to sanctuary localities.[16] However, at the time of this writing this move also remained unsuccessful in defunding programs designed to benefit cities.

In addition to attempting to strip funds from sanctuary localities, Executive Order 13768 also created the Victims of Immigration Crime Engagement (VOICE) Office. The exact goal of this office was somewhat vague and its mission is not terribly clear even on the ICE website, which states that it exists to "acknowledge and serve the needs of crime victims and their families who have been affected by crimes committed by individuals with a nexus to immigration."[17] The office consisted of a hotline to provide information to crime victims, as well as information on custody changes for the perpetrator to help victims track the perpetrator's movement through the system, though the purpose of the office seemed largely symbolic.

The administration's aggressive stance on sanctuary policies also led to increasing partisanship on the issue, as we discuss in chapter 3, as well as steps by liberal-leaning states, cities, and counties to confront what was seen by many as an unjust crackdown on both the undocumented community and those localities attempting to provide them with refuge.

On September 16, 2017, California passed Senate Bill 54 (SB-54), also known as the California Values Act, which became one of the most far-reaching pieces of sanctuary legislation after Governor Jerry Brown signed it into law on October 5. The bill barred law enforcement from sharing information with federal immigration authorities, or honoring ICE detainers outside of certain crimes, providing information on release dates for individuals taken into custody, or cooperating or assisting in the enforcement of immigration policy in any way.[18]

In addition to this, Governor Brown also signed Assembly Bill 450 (AB-450) into law on October 5, 2017, which changed the labor code in California to penalize employers who allowed federal immigration agents access to non private areas. First-time offenders would pay a civil fine of between two thousand and five thousand dollars, with repeat offenses leading to a five-thousand- to ten-thousand-dollar fine. Similar civil penalties were assigned for allowing federal immigration officials to review employee records without a judicial warrant or subpoena.[19] Employees also had to be notified within seventy-two hours of any federal requests to review employment records. While the first two provisions were put on hold by District Judge John A. Mendez on July 5, 2018, the fact that they had become law in the first place signaled California's position to the administration's crackdown on sanctuary cities.

Other states would take a significantly different tack, though. On May 7, 2017, Texas governor Greg Abbott signed Senate Bill 4 (SB-4) into law. This bill was the polar opposite of California's SB-54 and AB-450, banning sanctuary legislation in the state and allowing for civil penalties for officials who did not cooperate with federal immigration enforcement. A suit could be brought by any citizen in Texas who believed a local official was not complying with the bill. The civil penalties began at $1,000 to $1,500 but any violation after the first was subject to a fine of $25,000 or more. Officials who were elected or appointed could also be removed from their position for violations of SB-4.[20]

While California's pro-sanctuary legislation (SB-54 and AB-450) was one of the most far-reaching in terms of the limits it attempted to place on the federal crackdown on the undocumented community, Texas's SB-4 was the harshest anti-sanctuary legislation ever passed. Like all sanctuary legislation in the Trump era, it was also quickly challenged in court. After the bill was initially blocked, on March 13, 2018, a federal appeals court removed the injunction and allowed the law to go into effect.[21]

Conclusion

After a brief period of notoriety in the 1980s, driven by media coverage of the Central American refugee crisis, sanctuary cities largely drifted out of the limelight for most of the 1990s. In addition to little attention being paid to the legislation that remained on the books in many cities, counties, and states that had declared themselves sanctuaries in solidarity with the Sanctuary Movement, throughout the 1990s there was also little new sanctuary legislation passed.

This changed following the September 11 attacks and the shift in immigration policy under the Bush administration. As the federal government not only sought to expand and expedite the deportation of undocumented immigrants but also took steps to increase federal surveillance of this community through programs like Secure Communities, many former sanctuary localities responded by either reaffirming their commitment to the existing policies or passing new ones to address the new reality of federal immigration enforcement. New cities also declared themselves to be cities of refuge in solidarity with their immigrant communities and to preserve or foster cooperation with local law enforcement.

The election of Donald Trump, along with the shooting of Kathryn Steinle, served as a new, and perhaps the most significant, focusing event for sanctuary policies. Trump's tough stance on immigration, as well as his use of the issue as red meat for his base, helped to keep media and public attention on sanctuary cities in a way that had simply not been the case in the past. As a result, states, cities, and counties that opposed the president's immigration agenda began passing new sanctuary laws, and ones that expanded the resistance to federal policy, with California's SB54 leading the way.

However, there was also a backlash to these policies, exemplified by Texas's SB-4. In some cities, states, and counties, anti-sanctuary legislation was passed while in others, such as Miami–Dade County, Florida, sanctuary policies were retracted or practices such as denying detainer requests were reversed.[22] Some cities, fearing the wrath of the administration, declared themselves "Compassionate Cities," "Welcoming Cities," or "Freedom Cities." It remains somewhat unclear what the future is for these policies, regardless of the name they go by, though thus far the courts have shielded most jurisdictions from any significant penalties resulting from their refusal to cooperate with federal immigration officials.

One factor that will help to determine this future is the public perception of sanctuary policies. Public opinion is strongly influenced by media coverage and elite rhetoric, particularly in those areas where individuals have low levels of knowledge about the policy in question. In the next chapter, we analyze how media coverage has shifted over the last thirty-five years, as the intended beneficiaries of these policies has changed and as the immigration debate has become both more charged and more partisan.

2

Media Coverage of Sanctuary Cities, 1980–2017

As we discussed in chapter 1, sanctuary policies were initially borne out of a desire to show solidarity with the Sanctuary Movement in the 1980s. As faith-based organizations fought a public battle to prevent the deportation of refugees from Guatemala, Honduras, and Nicaragua, some cities declared themselves as sanctuaries to support the refugees. This support was usually explicitly declared in the city's resolution, as was opposition to the Reagan administration's refusal to both acknowledge the violence many of these Central Americans faced at home or to accept their claims of asylum in the United States.

By the end of the 1980s, the Sanctuary Movement had shrunk and drifted out of the public eye as the number of Central American refugees fell. Even so, sanctuary resolutions remained on the books in many cities. At the end of the 1980s and through the 1990s, the size of the undocumented population skyrocketed from an estimated 1.9 million in 1988 to 8.5 million by 2000 (Wasem, 2012).

Because the sanctuary policies passed in many cities forbade local officials from inquiring into the immigration status of residents, many undocumented immigrants became the unintended beneficiaries of these policies, and cities benefited from having undocumented immigrants feel more secure in their communities. As Los Angeles recognized with Special Order 40, barring police from inquiring into immigration status could increase trust between immigrant communities and the police and facilitate cooperation between the two.

Following 9/11, however, many cities passed new or updated sanctuary policies that were meant to address the immigration crackdown under policies like the USA PATRIOT Act and Secure Communities program. The George W. Bush administration's aggressive enforcement of immigration policy under the guise of protecting the United States from terrorism was often cited in these cities' sanctuary policies. Post-9/11 policies were also much more explicit in highlighting the importance of cooperation between local law enforcement and immigrant communities, which remains a central part of pro-sanctuary arguments to this day. This helped to reframe the purpose of sanctuary policies from one meant specifically to protect a given population to one that also has material benefits for American citizens. This shift in the intended beneficiaries of sanctuary policies also affected how the media covered the sanctuary debate, as did the candidacy and presidency of Donald Trump. In recent years, Trump has weaponized the immigrant-as-criminal narrative in his rhetoric and specifically targeted sanctuary localities during his time as president.

The preceding chapter traced how sanctuary policies evolved as the conflicts around immigration shifted and as cities sought to facilitate cooperation between local authorities and a growing undocumented population. This chapter shifts the focus from the policies themselves to how they were covered in the media with an eye toward understanding present-day public opinion. We first examine how media agenda setting and framing has been shown to impact public opinion. We next turn to what research says about media framing of undocumented immigration. We then analyze coverage of sanctuary policies specifically across five different periods: 1980–1989, when sanctuary policies were first passed; 1990–2000, when many policies remained on the books; 2000–2010, when many policies were passed in opposition to the post-9/11 immigration crackdown; and 2010–2017, which saw a shift leftward under Barack Obama, followed by a backlash represented by Donald Trump. The 2015–2017 period receives additional attention because of the significance of the Kathryn Steinle shooting as a focusing event and the candidacy and presidency of Donald Trump (McBeth and Lybecker, 2018).

Agenda Setting, Framing, and the Media's Influence on Public Opinion

The American public tends to take its cues on public policy from media and elites, and the former is often the vehicle for the message of the latter (Zaller, 1992). In areas where the public has little expertise or knowledge, this influence can be of particular importance. Mass media in the United States can impact public opinion in numerous ways, but for the purposes of sanctuary policy we focus on two of these avenues of influence: agenda setting and framing. Agenda setting is the ability of the media, through the amount of coverage given to a particular issue, to dictate how important we judge it to be (Iyengar and Kinder, 1987; Scheufele, 2000; Scheufele and Tewksbury, 2007). This in turn will determine the amount of pressure placed on public officials to tackle a given issue (Schuck et al., 2016). In the words of Bernard Cohen, the media "may not be successful much of the time in telling people what to think, but it is stunningly successful in telling its readers what to think about" (Cohen, 1963). Agenda setting is thus likely to play an outsized role in determining how important the American public views sanctuary policies. Events such as the Sanctuary Movement of the 1980s or the shooting of Kathryn Steinle in 2015, which focus media attention on these policies, are likely to also elevate these issues onto the public agenda.

Framing Sanctuary: Media and the Pictures in Our Heads

While the media may not be able to tell us what to think, they do influence the lens through which we view any given policy. The opinion that we as individuals have of sanctuary policies will be based on the pictures we have in our heads, not only of what a sanctuary locality is or looks like, but also of the undocumented community (Edelman, 1988). Importantly, for understanding public opinion, whether this picture in our heads is accurate remains irrelevant. Media framing occurs when sources suggest what a given problem is really about, or the "essence of the issue," which in turn can influence public beliefs about the causes and potential solutions (Entman, 1990, 1992; Iyengar and Kinder, 1987; Scheufele, 2000; Scheufele and Tewksbury, 2007).

Today, sanctuary policies are inextricably linked to undocumented immigration, a group that is routinely framed negatively by the media. Print media and television have both been shown to frame undocumented immigration in terms of the threat it poses to American jobs, culture, health, or safety (Abrajano and Singh, 2009; Chavez, 2010; Cisneros, 2008; Farris and Mohamed, 2018; Kim et al., 2011; Masuoka and Junn, 2013; Ono and Sloop, 2002; Santa Ana, 2002). In addition, there is also a focus on crimes committed by undocumented immigrants, which can influence how this population is viewed. Even when there are no explicit discussions of immigrant criminality, there tends to be imagery associated with this in the form of footage of arrests or raids ("Cable News Caricatures", 2009; Kim et al., 2011; Masuoka and Junn, 2013). If sanctuary policies are tied to discussions of undocumented immigration, which is framed in terms of threat, we should expect to see sanctuary policies partly framed in terms of threat.

How the media frames sanctuary is important because media coverage has been shown to have a significant effect on public opinion. Just being a frequent consumer of television news has been shown to lead to greater belief in the immigrant-as-criminal narrative, and media framing is particularly significant for those with a low or moderate level of knowledge (Gonzalez O'Brien, 2018; Schemer, 2012). Specific frames, such as immigration reform offering amnesty, also influence public support for policies (Haynes et al., 2016). Further, media coverage helps to focus readers or viewers on particular aspects of immigration policy over others, which affects support for a given policy (Cargile et al., 2014; Domke et al., 1999).

How sanctuary policy has been framed historically can thus tell us a lot about public opinion on the issue, even if not directly since it was not until relatively recently that questions about sanctuary cities and sanctuary policies started to become a common part of public opinion surveys. In this chapter we examine the media framing of sanctuary across two different media and over five time periods. First, we begin with an examination of print coverage of sanctuary policies in the *Washington Post*, *New York Times*, *USA Today*, and *Christian Science Monitor* between January 1980 and July 2017. We then turn to an examination of television news shows to analyze how news programs were discussing sanctuary over this same period.

While crime undoubtedly features prominently in media framing of sanctuary policies today, how was this framed in the past, before Kathryn Steinle's death and Donald Trump's 2016 presidential campaign? In the 1980s, sanctuary policies targeted a different and more sympathetic group in Central American refugees. Many of these individuals were still technically breaking the laws of the United States by entering illegally, but much of the discourse by elites, both in politics and faith-based organizations, was about the morality of the policies. If the media takes its cues from elites, as past research has found, then we would expect that the framing of sanctuary in the 1980s–2000s period would be significantly different than in the post-9/11 period. To examine how media coverage has shifted, we first turn to an examination of print coverage of sanctuary policies between 1980 and 2017.

Print Media Coverage of Sanctuary

One major source of information on sanctuary policies, as well as elite positions on sanctuary, are print and online newspapers. To capture how media was framing the issue, using Lexis-Nexis Academic we selected all newspaper articles from the *Washington Post* (WaPo), *New York Times* (NYT), *USA Today* (USAT), and *Christian Science Monitor* (CSM) from January 1, 1980, to July 18, 2017, in which the word "sanctuary" appeared. These sources were chosen to include both conservative-leaning outlets (*USA Today*), centrist outlets (*Christian Science Monitor*), and left-leaning outlets (*Washington Post* and *New York Times*). We then read this corpus into our statistical software, refining our search to include at least one of the following words typically related to the sanctuary debate in the United States: city, cities, town, Central America, Mexican, Mexico, movement, police, immigrant, immigration, illegal, enforcement, alien, refugee, campus.

This produced a final corpus of 1,252 articles between January 1980 and July 2017. We then conducted a key-word dictionary search, with terms selected based on expert knowledge and a qualitative review of the corpus. The terms broadly related to three major frames in the sanctuary debate: (1) the impact of sanctuary policies on crime, (2) whether recipients are fleeing conflict in their country of origin, and (3) the religious or moral duties inherent in providing sanctuary. Additionally, we code for framing in the context of partisanship by looking at the mentions of Democratic positions or elites and Republican positions or elites. Lastly, we include references to Trump in our analysis of framing because of the president's significance in shaping the debate around sanctuary cities in the post-Steinle period. We quantify these frames in the text and then examine the frame prevalence across time. The frames and search terms are listed below:

- Crime: crime, criminal, murder, rape, kill, killed, gang(s)
- Fleeing war: flee, fleeing, fled, war-torn, war, civil, oppression, persecution, persecute
- Religion and morality: religious, religion, religiosity, moral, morality, catholic(s), church(es)
- Partisanship: Democrat: democrat(s), democratic. Republican: republican(s)
- Trump: trump

Issue Framing in Print Media Coverage, 1980–1989

Figure 2.1 shows the total number of articles from the corpus of articles (n=1252) used in our computational analysis relying on a key-word dictionary search of terms associated with religion or morality, fleeing war, or crime. As

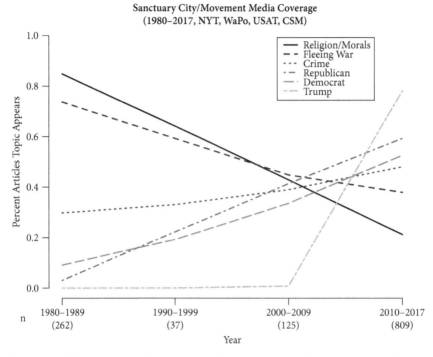

Figure 2.1 Newspaper media coverage of sanctuary cities between 1980 and 2017.

Figure 2.1 shows, when the Sanctuary Movement began in the 1980s, the issue was framed primarily as one of people escaping war, and a matter of religion and morality. The religion/morality and fleeing war themes appeared in about 80 percent of newspaper articles, but by 2017, these themes had fallen to below 50 percent. This is not particularly surprising based on the shift of the intended beneficiaries of sanctuary protections across this period. With fewer Central American refugees in the 1990s, 2000s, and 2010s, much of the debate had shifted from the moral or religious duty of sanctuary to provide safe harbor to those fleeing violence and conflict to a debate over the potential threat posed by the much-maligned undocumented population.

In the 1980s, media coverage of the Sanctuary Movement, which would inspire sanctuary city policies, tended to be very sympathetic. On January 29, 1983, writing in the *Washington Post*, Paula Herbut used the term "underground railroad" to describe the Sanctuary Movement, drawing very clear parallels between the actions of the faith-based organizations involved in the movement to those of abolitionists in the nineteenth century who set up the

Underground Railroad to help slaves flee slavery in the South (Herbut, 1983). This connection was helped by the fact that as with the original Underground Railroad, it was a Quaker, Jim Corbett, who began the Sanctuary Movement (Ingwerson, 1985).

In a *Christian Science Monitor* article published in August 1983, Jim Bencivenga explained the religious tradition of sanctuary and also linked the movement to the Underground Railroad. In the article, he noted that, "Sanctuary is an ancient tradition. It has its roots among the early Hebrews who established cities of refuge to which people under the threat of law could flee. The practice continued into the Christian era. It was recognized by English common law. The closest parallel to sanctuary in the American experience was the underground railroad that clandestinely guided fugitive slaves to Northern states and Canada in the decade before the US Civil War" (Bencivenga, 1983). Linking the Sanctuary Movement to the Underground Railroad of the pre–Civil War period was common in articles from all sources in the 1980s, with this term being mentioned fifty-seven times across thirty-seven different articles in the *New York Times, Washington Post*, and *Christian Science Monitor*.

Newspaper articles in the 1980s also commonly referred to the conditions that many Central Americans were fleeing. In a piece for the *New York Times* on April 8, 1983, a Salvadoran refugee named Miguel explained what he thought he would face if he was returned to El Salvador: "I fear that if I returned home I might be shot by government troops . . . . I know the case of a young man who was deported back to El Salvador, was arrested at the airport and was never seen again" (Volsky, 1983).

Similar themes were frequently mentioned in print coverage of the Sanctuary Movement, along with the Reagan administration's contributing role in the violence in Central America. The administration's argument was that military aid to the Salvadoran government, which many saw as contributing to violence in the country, was necessary to help defend against "Soviet- and Cuban-inspired leftists" (McCarthy, 1983).

However, the press rarely focused on the administration's claims, but instead placed a greater emphasis on the claims of refugees, missionaries, and members of the Sanctuary Movement. More than 70 percent of articles during the 1980s mentioned the political violence that refugees claimed to be fleeing in some fashion. As with the religion/morality frame, this kind of coverage painted the Sanctuary Movement in much more sympathetic terms than sanctuary cities would be portrayed after the 1980s.

In the 1980s, crime was a far less frequent topic in the coverage of the Sanctuary Movement. When this term did come up, it typically regarded the potential criminality of church members' behavior in sheltering refugees—which some antisanctuary proponents argued constituted harboring and as such would be illegal under federal law.

One exception, which would presage coverage after the 1980s, was coverage of the appointment of Harold Ezell to commissioner of the Immigration and Naturalization Service (INS). An article from March 24, 1986, notes that Ezell considered the Sanctuary Movement illegal, implied that Los Angeles may lose federal funding for declaring itself a sanctuary city, and cited studies supposedly showing that undocumented immigrants were responsible for a larger share of crimes than their proportion of the population (Mathews, 1986). This kind of coverage, while an outlier for the 1980s, would later become much more common, as would the rhetoric of criminality.

Print media coverage in the 1980s was far more sympathetic to the cause of the Sanctuary Movement than it would be in subsequent decades as the intended beneficiaries shifted from refugees to undocumented immigrants. The coverage of Harold Ezell's appointment as INS commissioner and his feelings about sanctuary policies and undocumented immigrants would become a norm of media coverage over the decades to come. Increasingly, media coverage would focus on the potential threat posed by sanctuary policies and not on the moral/religious dimension of the issue.

Issue Framing in Print Media Coverage, 1990–1999

Newspaper coverage of sanctuary policies dropped significantly in the 1990s, which reflects the evolution of sanctuary policy more generally. There were only 44 articles over the decade mentioning either sanctuary cities or the Sanctuary Movement, compared to 266 in the 1980s. This is not surprising considering that the 1980s were an important period of policy formation, with cities adopting resolutions to protect Central American refugees and the Sanctuary Movement trying to shield refugees from deportation as well as to force the Reagan administration to change its policy toward Guatemala, Nicaragua, and El Salvador.

By the 1990s the Central American refugee crisis had largely abated, and the debate had not yet shifted to undocumented immigration in the way it would in the post–9/11 period. The articles in the 1990–1999 period mostly focused on shifts in refugee policy, with mentions of the decade's conflict between faith-based organizations and the federal government over the fate of Central American refugees included for context. A 1990 *Washington Post* article, for example, chronicled the federal government's shift on refugee policy by granting temporary legal status to five hundred thousand Salvadoran and Guatemalan immigrants and noted this shift marked the most significant legal victory for the Sanctuary Movement (Mathews, 1990). Another article described Suffolk County's repeal of its sanctuary resolution because of growing resentment toward the Salvadorans and increasing conservatism in the county (Dunn, 1994).

Many of the articles during this time period mentioned the Sanctuary Movement only in passing. Because the focus of articles during this period was, for the most part, still on the Sanctuary Movement, media framing of sanctuary was similar to that seen in the 1980s. Over 60 percent of articles mentioned religion/morals or the conditions that refugees had been fleeing. There was little change in the crime framing of sanctuary over this period.

This would, of course, change significantly in the decade to come. The 9/11 attacks would lead to a significant crackdown on undocumented immigration as well as a push for increased local enforcement through 287(g) agreements, which authorized local law enforcement to enforce immigration policy, increased surveillance under the USA PATRIOT Act, and the Secure Communities Act. All of these would lead to conflict between the federal and state/local governments as the former looked to increase its power and reach in the name of greater security and the latter increasingly viewed the federal government's actions as disruptive and detrimental to local law enforcement, which relied on the cooperation of immigrant communities.

Issue Framing in Print Media Coverage, 2000–2009

There would be a significant shift in the framing of sanctuary policies in the first decade of the twenty-first century, as the 9/11 attacks led to increasing concerns about border security and undocumented immigration. The U.S. government created the Department of Homeland Security and Immigration and Customs Enforcement (ICE) to take the place of the INS. Federal policies would target undocumented communities across the United States in the name of national security, and some localities would respond to protect their undocumented residents by passing new sanctuary resolutions.

Unlike the resolutions of the 1980s, these new resolutions were not based on moral or religious arguments, but instead were repudiations of what were seen as the excesses of federal enforcement. In addition, as we discussed in chapter 1, a large number of sanctuary policies passed during this period were also meant to facilitate cooperation between local law enforcement and immigrant communities, which some state, city, and county leaders saw as threatened by the Bush administration's immigration crackdown. Many of these policies were ideological in nature, making it very clear in the text of the resolutions that these were passed both to protect undocumented residents but also as an act of protest to federal policy, something they held in common with the policies of the 1980s.

What is interesting about the coverage during this period is that many of the mentions of crime were not just related to the potential for crime among undocumented immigrants. Instead they also discussed the position of advocates that sanctuary policies facilitated cooperation between immigrant communities and local law enforcement.

An article from the *Christian Science Monitor* in 2004 demonstrates how the media could provide a more holistic picture of the reality of sanctuary policies. The article described the deportation of an undocumented immigrant from Guatemala after he served as a witness in a murder trial. This case was used to illustrate the importance of cooperation from the undocumented community as well as the potential value of sanctuary policies. Noting that many police "support confidentiality policies, which discourage them from reporting an immigrant's status," the benefits of sanctuary policies were highlighted, but a representative from the anti-immigrant Federation for American Immigration Reform (FAIR) was also quoted. David Ray, the spokesman for FAIR at the time, argued that sanctuary policies "allow illegal immigrants to establish themselves as residents and possibly commit an act of terrorism against American families. They shelter would-be terrorists from federal detection" (Miller, 2004). Print media during this period frequently mentioned the concerns of local officials that reporting the immigration status of residents would lead to a decrease in crime reporting by undocumented immigrants.

There were also increasing mentions of the confusion borne out of growing federal attempts to involve state and local authorities in immigration enforcement. Karthick Ramakrishnan of the University of California–Riverside noted that, increasingly, "smaller towns, from 50,000 to 100,000 residents, are wading into the problem. Even though California has been dealing with this for decades, its smaller cities are just beginning to wrestle with the challenges" (Wood, 2006). The two cities profiled, Maywood and Costa Mesa, took divergent paths in immigration enforcement in the post-9/11 period. In January 2006 Maywood became the first California municipality to declare itself a sanctuary city. The mayor of Maywood pointed out that the city was just trying to care for those who provided so many essential services to the community in terms of labor.

However, in Costa Mesa, the city council took the exact opposite approach, asking that police personnel be cross-designated with ICE so that they could access immigration records for those taken into custody and then hold them for federal authorities. Costa Mesa was the first municipality to ask for cross-designation from ICE under the 287(g) program.

A resident of the city would bring up crime as one of the reasons she supported the city council's actions. Clara Forsythe, who was a college senior, noted increased street crime and personal experiences of burglary and car theft that she blamed on undocumented immigration. She also characterized undocumented immigrants as a drain on social services and contributing to problems at schools because they didn't know or wouldn't learn English (Wood, 2006).

While mentions of the threat of immigrant crime were obviously not absent from print media coverage during this period, the potential positive impact of sanctuary policies on crime was raised more frequently. In 2007, even Rudy Giuliani, New York's former mayor, defended the city's policy of not reporting undocumented immigrants using city services to federal immigration authorities because, "If we didn't allow illegals to report crimes, a lot of criminals would have gone free because they're the ones who had the information" (Luo, 2007). Giuliani would go on to become a fierce critic of sanctuary policies in the post-Steinle period, but the 2000–2009 period lacked a focusing event with the power to shift the national debate on sanctuary policy.

Two events led to upticks in the crime narratives present in print media coverage. One example of the coverage, from the *New York Times* on August 11, 2007, notes that the ringleader of a group believed to be responsible for three murders in Newark, New Jersey, was an undocumented immigrant. Jose Lachira Carranza had been freed on bail despite his undocumented status, and ICE had not been notified of his arrest. The article goes on to explain that localities are not required to report the immigration status of arrestees, though some do, while others, like Newark, consider themselves sanctuary cities and do not do so (Fahim and Jacobs, 2007). The implication, of course, was that Newark's policy was at least partially responsible for the alleged murders committed by Jose Lachira Carranza.

A second case was described in a 2008 article in the *Washington Post*, where the controversy over undocumented immigration in Virginia Beach, Virginia, was linked to the death of two teenage girls in an accident that involved an undocumented immigrant who had been driving while intoxicated. The article notes that the death of the two girls had been taken up by Fox News's Bill O'Reilly as an example of the cost of sanctuary policies, something that is clear in the broadcast media coverage of sanctuary policies that we analyze later in this chapter. The article also included a mention of a website called Immigration's Human Cost, which featured descriptions of the deaths of American citizens who were linked to undocumented immigrants. Operation Body Count, which distributed posters with pictures of people that the FIRE Coalition claimed had been killed by undocumented immigrants, was also mentioned. The FIRE Coalition was an anti-immigrant group that characterized undocumented immigration as "the largest invasion in the history of the world" (Brulliard, 2007). This article mentioned crimes by undocumented immigrants more frequently than others would during this time, but would be characteristic of the print media coverage of sanctuary policy during the post-Steinle period.

As Figure 2.1 shows, while mentions of crime increased—though, as discussed, this was largely based on the potential benefits of sanctuary policies for crime reporting—the number of articles drawing on the fleeing war and religion/morality frames decreased significantly. These frames were used to give context to both sanctuary policies, as well as the New Sanctuary Movement, which took its inspiration from the original Sanctuary Movement but instead of sheltering refugees often gave refuge to undocumented immigrants with children in the United States to prevent family separations.

An article from July 9, 2007, in *USA Today* noted that the goal of the New Sanctuary Movement was to keep families together in the United States. The article then linked this goal to the religious tradition of sanctuary, stating, "Drawing on the tradition of sanctuary, in which churches declare themselves safe havens for those fleeing violence or prosecution, congregations from New York to San Diego have begun to view supporting illegal immigrants—and occasionally sheltering them from deportation—as a moral and religious duty" (Bazar, 2007).

These mentions of religious and moral duty were less common than they had been when the intended beneficiaries of sanctuary policies had been a more sympathetic group of refugees. More articles during this period featured discussions of the increasing conflict between state and local authorities and the federal government, which by the 2000s had become a far bigger issue than in the 1980s. While both the Sanctuary Movement and sanctuary cities in the 1980s had challenged federal refugee policy, they had not challenged the wider immigration policy regime in the way that they would in the 2000s.

As the first decade of the twenty-first century came to an end, media coverage of sanctuary policy continued to shift away from narratives of religion or moral reasons for sanctuary and increasingly focused on sanctuaries' effect on crime and the conflict between federal and state or local authorities. This next period can really be further divided into two smaller periods: 2010–2014, which preceded the Steinle shooting and candidacy/presidency of Donald Trump, and 2015–2017.

The Steinle shooting served as a focusing event for media attention and also helped to shape the narrative around sanctuary cities (McBeth and Lybecker, 2018). Donald Trump also made his opposition to sanctuary cities a central theme of his campaign, and the crime-narrative featured heavily in his statements on sanctuary policies. We turn to these two periods next, before moving to a discussion of the increasing partisanization of sanctuary coverage between 1980 and 2017.

Issue Framing in Media Coverage, 2010–2017

In some areas, by the early 2010s, sanctuary policies were already a campaign issue. In the Republican primary for governor of California in 2010, Meg Whitman, who would go on to challenge (and lose to) Democrat Jerry Brown, ran an ad stating her position on sanctuary policies in no uncertain terms. The ad, titled "Tough as Nails," featured a quote from Whitman, who promised, "As governor, I will crack down on so-called sanctuary cities like San Francisco who thumb their nose at our laws. Illegal immigrants should not expect benefits from the State of California (Archibold, 2010)."

The New York Times found the ad controversial enough to cover on June 19, 2010, as Whitman prepared to face Brown, who she would need Latino voters to defeat (Archibold, 2010). However, despite spending considerable funds appealing to Latinos,[1] Whitman failed to generate considerable enthusiasm among Latinos come election day, winning only 31 percent of the constituency's vote.[2]

In 2010, a fair amount of national coverage also related to a provision in Arizona's controversial SB-1070, which would have allowed law enforcement to ask for proof of citizenship during routine traffic stops. SB-1070 also would have allowed residents to sue local officials if they tried to restrict cooperation with federal immigration officials, which was meant to target sanctuary jurisdictions.

The crime framing was present in coverage in this period preceding the Steinle shooting. A 2011 *New York Times* article described a campaign ad by Rick Perry during his 2010 campaign for governor of Texas. In it, Perry featured Sgt. Joslyn Johnson, a police officer whose husband was killed by an undocumented immigrant during a traffic stop, and placed the blame on Houston's supposed status as a sanctuary city. His opponent in the race, Bill White, was the former mayor of Houston. This ad was covered in two separate pieces in the *New York Times*, on January 16 and February 27, 2011 (Ramsey, 2011a; Ramsey, 2011b). The attempts of the Texas legislature to pass antisanctuary legislation, though ultimately unsuccessful during Perry's tenure, received ample coverage in 2011 as Perry geared up for what would ultimately be a failed bid for the Republican nomination for president.

Crime would come up again in coverage of California's Trust Act, which barred law enforcement from holding undocumented immigrants for ICE unless they had been charged with serious offenses. The *New York Times* noted in 2012 that Republicans had adopted a party platform that included a statement on their opposition to sanctuary policies, which "violate federal law and endanger their own citizens" (Barnes, 2012). Indeed, negative discussions about crime were a more regular feature of articles in the 2010–2014 period than had been the case previously.

By July 2015 media coverage of sanctuary policies came to be dominated by the shooting of Kathryn Steinle in San Francisco. In a July 6, 2015, *Washington Post* article, the spokeswoman for ICE placed the blame for Ms. Steinle's death on San Francisco's sanctuary policy, arguing that "ICE places detainers on aliens arrested on criminal charges to ensure dangerous criminals are not released from prisons or jails into our communities" (Phillip, 2015).

In the *Washington Post* on July 8, 2015, Paul Waldman noted the similarities between the case of Juan Francisco Lopez Sanchez (whose name would later be corrected to Jose Ines Garcia Zarate) to Willie Horton and the role that the shooting of Ms. Steinle could play in the upcoming election. While the primary focus of the article was how Republican candidates other than Trump were trying to carefully approach the issue in order to not alienate Latino voters, the article also noted what the shooting could become. Waldman argued, "And the Lopez-Sanchez story is exactly the kind of tale that conservative media feast on: personal, vivid, tragic, just waiting to have all the outrage and anger they can muster poured into it. While the candidate says, 'Yes, this is terrible,' behind them will be the media figures Republican voters trust, screaming at the top of their lungs that everyone should be enraged" (Waldman, 2015). Waldman's statement was prescient, as the Steinle shooting would ignite a firestorm of sensationalized coverage on conservative outlet Fox News. Waldman was overly dismissive of Trump's control of the issue because at the time Trump was seen as at best a long shot for the Republican nomination and at worst as a joke. Despite this, Trump's tough rhetoric would come to dominate headlines on the shooting in the months to come.

Earlier in 2015 Trump had made his infamous comment about Mexican immigrants being "criminals" and "rapists." In an article in the *New York Times* on July 13, 2015, titled "Lost in the Immigration Frenzy," the editorial board noted that the shooting had played right into the hands of Trump. Garcia Zarate had become "the dark-skinned face of the Mexican killers that Donald Trump—in a racist speech announcing his presidential campaign, and numerous interviews thereafter—has been warning the nation about" (Board, 2015).

Trump's use of the issue not only kept attention on the Steinle shooting but also helped shape how the debate was covered in the media. A July 23, 2015, article, pointed out that, "The attention Trump brought played a central role in the Senate Judiciary Committee holding a hearing this week with testimony from Steinle's father and relatives of other victims who have been killed by illegal immigrants" (Hohmann, 2015). As Figure 2.1 illustrates, the crime framing became more common after the shooting, and Trump's candidacy and presidency helped to ensure that crime featured prominently in media coverage of sanctuary policies and undocumented immigration more broadly in the post-Steinle period.

Partisan Framing in Print Media Coverage, 1980–2017

The role played by Donald Trump in the sanctuary debate and the media's coverage thereof is also shown in the increasing partisanization of the issue over time. The number of partisan sources mentioned in the media increased substantially between 2000 and 2017, showing the increasing partisan divisions on undocumented immigration more broadly during this time, as sanctuary policies increasingly came into conflict with the immigration crackdowns of the Bush and Trump administrations.

In the 1980–1989 period, only 14 percent of articles featured a Republican source in the article; this increased to approximately 17 percent in the 1990–1999 period, 46 percent in the 2000–2009 period, and finally to 60 and 74 percent between 2010 and 2014, and 2015 and 2017, respectively. Overall, the percentage of articles featuring a Republican source increased 60 percent from the earliest to the latest time period. The representation of Democrats in articles on sanctuary cities also increased between 1980 and 2017, though this was a more modest increase of 25 percent.

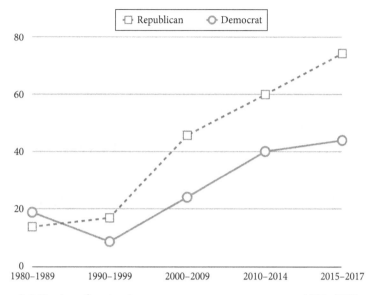

Figure 2.2 Partisan framing in sanctuary newspaper coverage, 1980–2017.

The greater increase in the mention of Republican sources in media coverage is not surprising, considering the shifts in sanctuary policy over this period. While refugees are often viewed with more empathy by both the public and the media, undocumented immigrants are often not. By 2000, sanctuary policies were solidly oriented toward the undocumented community and were coming into conflict more regularly with federal officials over their defiance.

In the post-9/11 era the Republican Party took a much more restrictionist, law-and-order approach to undocumented immigration, which meant that sanctuary cities were more often the target of rhetoric, if not also legislation. Contrast the Republican Party of the 1980s, when Ronald Reagan praised undocumented immigrants as "really honorable, decent, family-loving people," with statements made in 2015 by Donald Trump, and the difference is clear.[3]

Trump's rhetoric on undocumented immigration was the most vitriolic that had been seen in decades, at least from a president, but by 2015 it was safe language to use with the Republican base because of shifts in how the GOP approached undocumented immigration after 9/11. Members of the public tend to take their cues on policy-related issues from elites, such as party representatives and politicians (Gabel and Scheve, 2007; Iyengar and Kinder, 1987; Lenz, 2013; Zaller, 1992), and the modern GOP, particularly after 9/11, has taken policy positions that are strongly anti-immigrant

(Brader et al., 2008; Citrin and Wright, 2009; Miller and Schofield, 2008). As sanctuary policies became more associated with the undocumented population and less associated with refugees, more Republicans tried to attack these policies to show their commitment to law and order, as well as to tap into nascent nativism and racism in some segments of their base.

Democrats, however, often face a dilemma on sanctuary policy, particularly at the national level. Though it was largely Democratic-controlled cities that passed sanctuary resolutions in the 1980s, as well as later, Democrats have remained wary of the potential political costs of being seen as soft on immigration. The party has, since the 1990s, moved left on immigration to appeal to Latinos as they became a more significant part of Democrats' base (Barreto et al., 2010; Barreto and Nuño, 2011; Collingwood et al., 2014). However, at the same time, outreach to Latinos also has the potential to alienate white voters, so there is a tightrope to walk for Democrats outside of heavily Latino districts or states (Ostfeld, 2018).

Republicans have, since the election of Barack Obama, tried to link Democrats to "identity politics" and, both implicitly and explicitly, non-Whites. Brown (2016) argues that immigrants have supplanted blacks in racially divisive rhetoric used by Republicans to appeal to white voters. Trump has represented the culmination of this shift and has sought to link the Democratic Party to undocumented immigrants, as well as Democratic policies, such as sanctuary, to crime. The Steinle shooting, and more recently the case of Mollie Tibbetts, who was allegedly killed by an undocumented immigrant in Iowa, make support for sanctuary policy a difficult issue for Democrats. This likely explains the discrepancy in the number of official Democratic sources mentioned in articles on sanctuary policies and the spike in the number of Republican voices on the issue. Among Democrats, those featured in articles are more likely to be local rather than federal officials, who couch their defense of sanctuary policy in terms of their local immigrant communities.

A November 15, 2016, article illustrated these partisan differences quite clearly. Citing Trump's promise to deport millions of "criminal immigrants," it is noted that

> In the days since Trump's victory, mayors from major cities across the county, including New York, Chicago and San Francisco, have eased concerns by vowing not to coordinate with federal law enforcement to deport undocumented residents. The flood of announcements sets the stage for a major battle with Trump, who has said he will cut all federal funding to "sanctuary cities" immediately after his Jan. 20 inauguration (Scherer, 2016).

The same article went on to quote Chicago mayor Rahm Emanuel, a Democrat and the former chief of staff for U.S. president Barack Obama, as saying, "To all those who are, after Tuesday's election, very nervous and filled with anxiety ... as we've spoken to, you are safe in Chicago, you are secure in Chicago, and you are supported in Chicago. Chicago will always be a sanctuary city" (Scherer, 2016). These partisan divisions have now become a central feature of media coverage of sanctuary policies, with an increasing representation of both Republican and Democratic sources in coverage.

Policymakers have been effectively divided into two camps on sanctuary policy as the target of these policies has shifted, which now reflect divisions on the larger topic of undocumented immigration (Wong, 2017a). In the 1980s, the tactic of Republican lawmakers had been to question the validity of claims of persecution and violence in refugees' countries' of origin. In today's debate, GOP lawmakers profess that sanctuary policies reward criminal behavior and threaten the safety of U.S. citizens.

Democrats, who have become more reliant on the Latino vote as well as more vocal advocates of racial justice, argue that these policies are necessary to protect an already vulnerable population and allow them to access basic services like health care or law enforcement. The elevation of sanctuary policies onto the national agenda, the partisan nature of the debate, and the perceived threat from the undocumented population all affect the policy responses from lawmakers and how the media covers sanctuary policies.

Print media coverage has clearly shifted over the life of sanctuary policies, as both the intended beneficiaries and controversies over these policies have changed. In the 1980s, coverage tended to emphasize the religious or moral duty that many people believed they had to protect refugees who were fleeing violence that some claimed the U.S. had a hand in generating. Crime was not prominently featured in media coverage and both Republican and Democrat sources were mentioned with less frequency, suggesting that the issue was not as partisan as it would later become.

By the 2000s, however, crime became a more regular part of newspaper narratives, but this was mixed in terms of the context. More frequent were mentions of the potentially positive effects that sanctuary policies could have on crime by emphasizing their role in increasing trust and cooperation between immigrant communities and the police.

This coverage had begun to shift by the 2010s. Republican sources were mentioned with greater frequency, and the crime narrative became both more common and negatively valenced. Stories were more likely to give space to claims of immigrant crime by candidates or politicians. This tendency became particularly emphasized after the shooting of Kathryn Steinle on July 1, 2015. After this point, Republican sources and crime were both mentioned regularly, as was Donald Trump, who took ownership of the sanctuary issue in the period following Steinle's death.

While print media coverage clearly changed, by the 2000s many Americans were also getting their news not from print media but increasingly from television news. In the next section we analyze the coverage of sanctuary policies in television news to see if it parallels print media coverage over the same period.

Framing Sanctuary in Television Coverage, 1980–2017

To examine how television news and news programs covered sanctuary policies over this period we performed a Lexis-Nexis search of broadcast transcripts for "sanctuary movement" and "sanctuary city" from January 1, 1980, through October 2018. The unit of analysis is the media segment. We then narrowed the search so it was only for broadcasts from Fox News, MSNBC, PBS, CNN, and broadcast media (ABC, CBS). This returned 275 broadcast transcripts for "sanctuary city" and 91 for "sanctuary movement." As with the print media, we then applied a dictionary search for the following themes and applicable key words:[4]

- Partisan: Republican: republican, republicans. Democrat: democrat, democrats, democratic. Trump: trump
- Morality/Religion: religion, religious, church, churches, moral, morality
- Crime: crime, criminal, violence, violent, police, arrest

We then plotted the total number of thematic counts per year for the entire time period. The result is shown in Figure 2.3, which largely parallels print media coverage, particularly when applied to crime and partisan framing. In the 1980s and 1990s, broadcast media paid little attention to sanctuary policies, which was also the case with print media, though there was more coverage of the Sanctuary Movement. It must be mentioned that there were not as many transcripts for prior to the growth of cable news though, so the Sanctuary Movement may have received more coverage than is represented in Figure 2.3, but this may have been on the nightly news, for which transcripts were not available in most cases.

Figure 2.3 shows three spikes in coverage and in crime framing of sanctuary policies, which is worthy of consideration. The first period is 2007, where

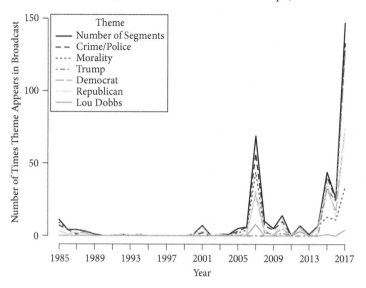

Figure 2.3 Broadcast television transcripts covering sanctuary city issues between 1984 and 2017.

there was a sudden increase in broadcast coverage. The first reason for this increase in coverage was the upcoming presidential election and the role of sanctuary in the Republican primary in 2007. As we briefly discussed in the print media section, sanctuary policies were brought up during this period. Republican candidates Mitt Romney and Rudy Giuliani were both trying to characterize the other as supportive of these policies in an attempt to win the nomination, with Fox's *Special Report with Brit Hume* on August 9, 2007, covering Romney's attack on Giuliani's former stint as mayor of New York, during which time, according to Romney, "New York was the poster child for sanctuary cities in the country." While some of the coverage was tied to the primary and upcoming election, the bulk of it was driven by instances of immigrant criminality that were used to sensationalize the threat posed by sanctuary policies.

On April 5, 2007, Fox News' *The O'Reilly Factor* led with the statement that "Once again, a sanctuary city policy has killed Americans" before detailing the deaths of Allison Kunhardt and Tessa Tranchant in a Virginia Beach car accident caused by an undocumented immigrant drunk driver. The print media had also covered this story, though using language that was significantly toned down compared to the rhetoric featured on *The O'Reilly Factor*. O'Reilly noted that the individual charged in the accident was an undocumented immigrant who had been arrested before and blamed the sanctuary policy of Virginia Beach for the deaths of the two girls. O'Reilly would return to the same topic a few days later on April 9, this time including a taped interview with the father of one of the girls, who described the difficulty of losing his daughter. The segment also featured an unidentified individual associated with the show confronting the mayor of Virginia Beach at her house after she had declined to come on the show. Near the close of the segment O'Reilly proclaimed, "Immigration anarchy affects every single American and every single migrant. The situation has reached critical mass, has misguided compassion, is leading to death and destruction," words that would mirror some of the rhetoric later used by Donald Trump in his candidacy for president.

On April 23, 2007, O'Reilly returned yet again to sanctuary cities and the deaths of the two girls in Virginia Beach, after which he would go quiet on the issue for a few months before featuring sanctuary policies on his show once again on August 13, 2007. This segment turned from the deaths in Virginia Beach to the murder of three college students in Newark. One of the alleged killers, Jose Lachira Carranza, an undocumented immigrant from Peru, had been freed on bail for rape charges and was awaiting trial for another charge of assault. Because of Newark's sanctuary status, Carranza had not been turned over to federal authorities for deportation. The segment featured Kris Kobach, who was cited as an "immigration law expert" but in reality was an anti-immigration activist and someone who would go on to have links to Donald Trump's presidency and run Trump's short-lived committee on voter fraud. Kobach would place the blame for the murder on Newark's sanctuary policy, something that would come to be characteristic of the coverage of any violent crimes committed by undocumented immigrants in sanctuary jurisdictions. The murders in Newark were also featured on Fox News's *Hannity & Colmes* that same day, where again it would be implied that the city's sanctuary policy had a hand in the deaths of the three men. On August 14, *The Big Story with John Gibson* on Fox News made the question of whether Newark's sanctuary policy led to the "execution-style murder" of the three college students and again featured Kris Kobach as a guest. Kobach stated that the city's policy led, though indirectly, to the murder of the three students.

Sanctuary policies were regularly featured on Fox News programs through-out 2007 with coverage linked to the election, the deaths in Virginia, and the three murders in Newark. These themes were combined in a segment of

Your World with Neil Cavuto, which featured Tom Tancredo, a short-lived Republican candidate for president and former representative for Colorado's Sixth District (1999–2009). Tancredo not only blamed sanctuary policy for deaths like those in Colorado but stated, "And that's why I'm saying that sanctuary cities—the people who impose these, the mayors and the city councils of all of these cities who these, they are culpable. I believe they are culpable in some of these events." Tancredo and Mitt Romney were regularly featured in Fox News programs attacking sanctuary policies in 2007.

Beginning in 2015, there was another spike in the number of segments and the narrative of crime in broadcast coverage. As with print media, the main theme of coverage was the potential threat that sanctuary policies posed to residents, with mentions of the Steinle shooting, as well as other crimes committed by undocumented immigrants commonplace. Fox News ran the largest number of segments on sanctuary policies, with 140 of the 270 total transcripts mentioning the "sanctuary movement" or "sanctuary cities" originating on the conservative media outlet. As shown in Figure 2.3, Donald Trump was also a regular feature of the coverage in the 2015–2018 period.

A segment of Fox News's *The Five* from February 22, 2017, juxtaposed Trump's position on sanctuary cities with the defense of Denver's status as a sanctuary by its mayor, Michael Hancock. The segment linked Denver's sanctuary status to the murder of a Denver resident. Leading off the segment, host Greg Gutfeld went so far as to characterize the policies as "evil." Gutfeld first described Denver's mayor as such, "Take Denver mayor Michael Hancock, who embraced the title 'sanctuary city' despite President Trump's threats to cut off his federal funding. Hancock is the type of mayor who would be portrayed saintly in movies or TV series," before turning to the murder of Timothy Cruz by an undocumented immigrant who had been in custody but was not held for ICE.

Gutfeld continued, "So off you went, free in a sanctuary city, and then may have caused the thirty-two-year-old man his life. It's the great deception in modern culture. Bad things call for noble names to cloak their evil outcomes. Sanctuary city, a heartwarming title that sounds like an oasis for the innocent except for an innocent man waiting for a train." A March 17, 2017, segment of *The Five* returned to the subject of sanctuary cities, this time including an interview with John McCain, who made his opposition to sanctuary policies clear, stating that "if you want to have a sanctuary city, then your state should secede from the union . . . . And every person who goes on television, especially every politician who defends this needs to meet with Kate Steinle's family. Needs to meet with the family of someone who had been injured or killed by an illegal immigrant in a sanctuary city." This kind of coverage was the norm rather than the exception in broadcast media coverage. Because Fox dominated the television coverage of sanctuary policies, broadcast media was far less balanced than print media in its coverage, it was far more sensational, and tended to emphasize crimes committed by undocumented immigrants. This was the case in 2007, as well as in the 2015–2018 period.

Conclusion

Media coverage of sanctuary cities, in both print and broadcast forms, has tended to frame the policies in terms of crime since the 2015 shooting of Kathryn Steinle. In the period following the shooting, media coverage regularly featured sources charging that sanctuary cities made America less safe and with lurid descriptions of the deaths of Americans allegedly at the hands of undocumented immigrants. Tragic events like the death of two girls in Virginia Beach in a drunk driving incident involving an undocumented immigrant, the murders in Newark, the shooting of Kathryn Steinle, or the killing of Timothy Cruz are used to suggest that the sanctuary policies of the cities in which they occurred were to blame. The potential benefits of sanctuary policies in the city from increasing cooperation between immigrant communities and police has been more and more drowned out, particularly in broadcast media and television news, by politicians like Donald Trump who seek to use the issue for electoral advantage and to tap into the nativism and racism that still make fear-mongering so effective in the United States.

Print media coverage has been more balanced than television coverage. In print coverage, crime is now a regular feature of the reporting, but it is not nearly as sensationalized as television coverage of sanctuary policies. Since the 2000s, broadcast coverage has leaned heavily on instances of immigrant criminality in their stories on sanctuary policies. As with print media, coverage has also become increasingly partisan as sanctuary policies were targeted by Trump and, following his lead, other members of the GOP. Democratic mayors of cities including Chicago and San Francisco have defended their city's practices, but even with their voices it seems very likely that the skewed nature of media coverage in terms of how sanctuary policies are covered has had an impact on public opinion. Research has shown that just being a regular viewer of television news increases the likelihood that someone will believe that undocumented immigrants are criminals (Gonzalez O'Brien, 2018).

Among Republicans, the heavy emphasis on sensationalized accounts of murder and death are likely to skew opinion on the issue. The increasing use of Democratic and Republican sources in media coverage, both print and broadcast, is also likely to have made the issue of sanctuary much more partisan than it was before this became a common characteristic of coverage. Since members of the public often take their cues from media coverage and elites, it is very likely that, between 1980 and 2017, and particularly in the period following the Steinle shooting, Republicans and Democrats have increasingly sorted themselves into what they believe is their party's correct position on sanctuary policies.

In the next chapter, we turn to an examination of public attitudes on sanctuary and what predicts pro- and antisanctuary positions. We analyze how these attitudes shifted from the pre- to post-Steinle period, as the media increasingly used a crime framing for stories on sanctuary policies and as the issue became more politicized and associated with Donald Trump.

3

Understanding Public Opinion on Sanctuary Cities

In the previous chapter we investigated how the media has framed the Sanctuary Movement and sanctuary cities over the past thirty-five years. In the early 1980s, media discourse largely framed the sanctuary issue on moral terms focusing on (1) Central American refugees fleeing civil war and oppression, and (2) how American churches and other religious institutions helped shield refugees from deportation. Crime was a tertiary focus at best. After the 1980s, however, sanctuary policies shifted the focus away from refugees to the protection of undocumented immigrants—a group more likely to induce antipathy (Alvarez and Butterfield, 2000; Haynes et al., 2016; Hood and Morris, 1998; Pedraza, 2014). With a rise in undocumented immigration and renewed Immigration and Naturalization Service (INS) crackdowns, the sanctuary city movement began to reflect the broader immigration debate over undocumented immigration.

With the decline of the Sanctuary Movement's focus on Central American refugees, sanctuary topics related to immigration received minimal press coverage at the national level throughout the 1990s and into the 2000s—with the exception of shows like Lou Dobbs' (who then had a program on CNN before later moving to Fox News). Because the issue was rarely discussed outside of local city politics, most Americans had little to shape and guide their views about sanctuary cities. While there was some legislative activity and Republican opposition, it was not until Kathryn Steinle's 2015 accidental shooting by an undocumented immigrant—and subsequent politicization of the event—that the topic of sanctuary cities once again burst into the political mainstream.

Since 2015, sanctuary cities have been widely debated in the media and on the campaign trail, in part because Republican candidates see the issue advantaging them (Hillygus and Shields, 2014). Indeed, following Steinle's death, Donald Trump and other GOP candidates argued vociferously against sanctuary cities as a way to flex their anti-immigrant credentials. During the 2016 presidential campaign, Trump routinely said he would go after sanctuary cities once elected. In a September 2016 stump speech in Phoenix, Trump said, "We will end the sanctuary cities that have resulted in so many needless deaths," a theme that he would return to after assuming the presidency.[1]

Since Trump took office, his administration has sued cities and states with sanctuary policies, with many cities and states countersuing, including Philadelphia, Chicago, and San Francisco. A defense of sanctuary cities from Hillary Clinton and other leading Democrats during the 2016 campaign was relatively muted, as Democratic candidates—insofar as immigration policy is concerned—tended to focus more on comprehensive immigration reform, a pathway to citizenship for undocumented residents, and a defense of Deferred Action for Childhood Arrivals (DACA), rather than on municipal-level sanctuary policies.[2] In hindsight, Trump had rearranged and reframed the immigration policy terrain, but Democrats were still playing the immigration politics of the Obama era, when many had thought comprehensive immigration reform was a realistic possibility.

Shortly after his inauguration, Trump and then—attorney general Jeff Sessions sought to withdraw federal crime-fighting funds from sanctuary cities if these cities failed to revoke their sanctuary status—targeting what is known as the Edward Byrne Memorial Justice Assistance Grant (JAG) Program. Many of these cities, such as Seattle, Chicago, New York, and Los Angeles, are Democratic strongholds with large and diverse populations. Mayors, their administrations, and immigration activists saw attacks on these cities' sanctuary status as an attack on Latinos specifically and multiculturalism generally—groups central to Democratic prospects (Collingwood et al., 2014).

Given Democratic reliance on a growing Latino voter base, many Democratic politicians increasingly cannot ignore external attacks on these communities. Thus, in the Trump era, public opinion surrounding sanctuary policy has become heavily partisan—with Democratic voters broadly supportive of sanctuary regimes and Republican voters broadly opposed.

Democratic big-city mayors, and increasingly Democratic elites across the spectrum, are now forced to defend their cities' sanctuary status; accordingly these mayors and other Democrats increasingly serve as elite opposition to Trump on the issue.[3]

Republican mayors and governors have also in some cases aligned themselves more closely with the Trump administration's approach to sanctuary cities, leading to deep partisan divisions at the state level over the proper approach to immigration enforcement and undocumented communities.

Two states, Texas and California, exemplify the split at the state and local level over sanctuary and public opinion; they can tell us a lot about how public opinion operates generally.

What Drives Public Opinion on Sanctuary Policies?

The relatively sudden rise of sanctuary cities as a salient mainstream political issue and point of controversy provokes several important questions concerning public opinion. Given that most Americans had little to shape their opinion on sanctuary cities or sanctuary policy prior to 2015, with many people likely exhibiting nonattitudes on the topic (Converse, 2006; Zaller, 1992), and given the growing elite political polarization on the issue, do public attitudes on sanctuary cities reflect a growing partisan cleavage? In other words, are voters learning to adopt their party elites' positions? Since 2015, learning may well be asymmetric, as Republican voters may well have already taken their cues from Trump and other leading Republicans that sanctuary cities are something these voters should oppose (Oskooii et al., 2018).

Because Democratic elites tended to avoid the issue until 2017, Democratic voters may have initially opposed such cities, given the one-way anti–sanctuary city information flow prior to 2017 (Zaller, 1992). As Democratic elites and key Democratic constituency groups rallied in defense of sanctuary cities, and as Democrats moved to oppose all things Trump (what political scientists call *negative partisanship*), we might expect to see Democratic voters moving sharply in defense of sanctuary cities over a relatively short period of time.

Recent research has shown that the party system may be further realigning around ethnicity and immigration (partly as a function of white status threat), much as it did around race after 1965 (Carmines and Stimson, 1989; Craig and Richeson, 2014; Jardina, 2014; Mutz, 2018; Reny et al., 2019; Schickler, 2016). Abrajano and Hajnal (2015) convincingly show that as the Latino population has grown and the Democratic Party has begun to make appeals to this group (Barreto et al., 2010; Collingwood et al., 2014), whites have begun to move into the GOP (Ostfeld, 2018).

Given that sanctuary cities are explicitly connected to immigration, and hence constitute a racialized policy domain, it is plausible that—all else being equal—whites learn to take the correct "white" position (anti–sanctuary city) and Latinos the correct "Latino" position (pro–sanctuary city). Thus, the first test in this chapter is to assess whether Americans' public opinion learning on sanctuaries/sanctuary cities/sanctuary policy is a feature of partisan learning, learning based on racial or ethnic identification, or some combination of the two. As we show below, we find strong and consistent evidence for partisan learning, but little evidence of clear racial/ethnic learning.

The second question we address in this chapter is, who supports and who opposes sanctuary cities today? While we might expect sanctuary opinion to follow opinion on pro/anti-immigration policies (i.e., conservatives oppose, liberals support, Democrats support, Republicans oppose), beyond this, our goal here is to evaluate whether the issue's framing around crime and safety actually provokes a response among people who are more likely to experience crime, or whether support or opposition to the issue is driven more by one's racial context.

Specifically, because sanctuary cities are so often connected to crime in popular discourse and media (see chapter 2), and crime is used as a justification to crack down on such city policies, people living in areas where crime risk is highest should be most opposed to sanctuary cities—all else being equal. In other words, people look around them, see that crime is high or has become worse, hear a politician or elite blaming crime in part on the sanctuary status of some cities or counties, and conclude they oppose such policies.

However, given that discussion about sanctuary cities often implicitly (and explicitly) links such cities to undocumented immigrants—specifically Mexican immigrants—we might expect people—specifically white people—living in high-Latino and high-Latino-growth areas to be precisely the people most likely to oppose sanctuary policies. Indeed, research indicates that whites often erroneously conflate neighborhood race change with crime (Quillian and Pager, 2010). In this process, whites see that their community is ethnically changing, mistakenly associate this change with increased crime, hear political elites conflating immigration (read: Latinos) with crime, and so oppose sanctuary cities.

Ample research, beginning with Blalock (1967) and Key (1949), support this latter interpretation (racial threat) over the former interpretation (criminal threat). Research indicates that whites living in high-minority areas and specifically high-minority-growth areas begin to feel threatened and therefore are more likely to support racially exclusionary policies (like opposing sanctuary cities) (Esbenshade, 2007; Hopkins, 2010; Newman, 2013; Tolbert and Grummel, 2003) and racially combative candidates (Newman et al., 2018). However, both hypotheses—criminal threat and Latino threat—are potentially plausible. Thus, beyond traditional markers of opinion variance (e.g., party and ideology), we evaluate whether opposition to sanctuary cities is driven by criminal threat or Latino racial threat.

To answer these questions, we draw on data from two states—California and Texas—that have found themselves at the center of the sanctuary debate. California has become one of the staunchest defenders of these policies, while Texas has taken the opposite position and banned sanctuary legislation entirely. These states provide insights into the broader national debate as well as the state-level characteristics that could lead to support for or opposition to sanctuary policies.

In the sections that follow we first examine the political environment in Texas and California, before turning to the extant literature on public opinion and immigration attitudes, which we use to inform our analysis of public opinion on sanctuary policies in these two states.

California and Texas: Two States, Two Very Different Approaches

After Trump's victory, in California—the nation's most populous state—Democratic governor Jerry Brown came out in strong support for sanctuary cities despite previously opposing them.[4] Leading Democrat Senate President Pro Tem Kevin de León proposed a bill to make the whole state a sanctuary for undocumented immigrants.[5] Senate Bill 54 (the California Values Act) limits state and local law enforcement's ability to cooperate with federal Immigration and Customs Enforcement (ICE) agents, amounting to a sanctuary policy for the entire state.[6] In October 2017 Governor Jerry Brown signed the bill into law, making California the second state—Oregon being the other—to declare itself a sanctuary for undocumented immigrants.[7]

The California Values Act complements the California Trust Act (AB-4), passed in 2013, which prohibited law enforcement from holding immigrants for ICE unless they were charged with certain crimes (although the list of possible crimes is long, approximately eight hundred).[8] These two policies have made California a frequent target of the Trump administration's rhetoric and one of the staunchest defenders of sanctuary policies at both the state and local levels.

At the local level, even after the Steinle shooting, San Francisco's mayor Ed Lee stated that "San Francisco is and always will be a sanctuary city."[9] In 2018, some charged that ICE raids in California were in retaliation for the state's sanctuary status and opposition to Trump's immigration crackdown.[10]

In response to rumors of a forthcoming ICE raid in the Bay Area, Oakland mayor Libby Schaaf went so far as to tweet a warning of the forthcoming raid to Oakland residents, which was immediately criticized by ICE since the planned raid wound up taking fewer people into custody than had been anticipated.[11]

The 2018 Republican candidate for governor, John Cox, strongly opposed sanctuary cities and subsequently handily lost to Democrat Gavin Newsom, who supported sanctuary in the state. The 2018 midterm elections likely will further solidify California's role as one of the most vocal and active opponents of the Trump administration's immigration policy, with the California GOP losing seats in the State Senate, State Assembly, and House of Representatives, leading some members of the state GOP to declare the party dead and call for a reorientation of the state party.[12]

In Texas—the nation's second most populous state—the situation could not be more different. Republican lawmakers and the GOP governor, Greg Abbott, moved in the opposite direction of California: attacking local jurisdictions considering adopting sanctuary policies, as well as Travis County (Austin), where ICE immigrant detainer requests were not honored for low-level offenders.

Senate Bill 4 (SB-4) was introduced to the Texas legislature on November 15, 2016, and attached Class A misdemeanor charges to noncompliance with federal immigration policies and ICE detainers by individuals, as well as civil financial penalties. It also permitted local law enforcement to inquire into the immigration status of anyone legally detained.[13] Debate over the bill recalled earlier ones on Arizona's SB-1070, which would have allowed local police to inquire into immigration status during routine traffic stops.[14] In the debate in the Texas House of Representatives, GOP proponents of the bill hewed to the crime narrative, arguing that the legislation only targeted dangerous criminals and was simply meant to ensure compliance and cooperation with federal laws. Democratic opponents pointed out that the bill could lead to racial profiling since it allows officers to inquire into immigration status and that it also would increase fear of police in immigrant communities, leading to decreased crime reporting, cooperation, and healthcare use (Pedraza et al., 2017).[15] The bill ultimately became law in Texas on May 7, 2017, and thus far has survived legal challenges.

While in California, many local lawmakers and the governor were supportive of city (and later state)-level sanctuary policies, in Texas governor Abbott was one of the harshest critics of these policies. At the time of SB-4's passage there were no formal sanctuary cities in Texas, but in Travis County, which includes Austin, the sheriff had implemented a policy stating that not all ICE detainer requests would be automatically granted.

Abbott, during the Facebook Live signing of SB-4, stated, "This law cracks down on policies like the Travis County sheriff who declared that she would not detain known criminals accused of violent crimes. Those policies are sanctuary city policies and won't be tolerated in Texas. Elected officials and law enforcement agencies, they don't get to pick and choose which laws they will obey."[16]

The governor's own webpage also included misleading information about immigrant criminality in asking Texas residents to pledge their support for SB-4. The page, titled "End Sanctuary Cities," stated, "A new report found that Immigration and Customs Enforcement (ICE) 'freed 19,723 criminal aliens, who had a total of 64,197 convictions among them in 2015. Included were 8,234 violent convictions and 208 murder convictions.'"[17] Like Abbott's statements about the policies of Travis County regarding ICE detainers, the statistics on his webpage are meant to generate support for his sanctuary ban by distorting the truth. In fact, the statistics he presents on the page have little if anything to do with sanctuary cities, since they are in reference to immigrants released by ICE, and little to do with Texas since these are nationwide statistics. They are, however, indicative of the debate in Texas where conservative lawmakers controlled the legislature and governorship. Many, such as Abbott, sought to align themselves with President Trump's tough stance on immigration, despite the large Latino population in the state.

At the level of public opinion, then, this is a tale of two similar but very different states. California and Texas both share a border with Mexico and have grappled with undocumented immigration since the hardening of the border in the 1920s. California is an increasingly blue state, with the state GOP losing even in traditional Republican strongholds like Orange County in 2018. The state has become one of the most vocal critics of the Trump administration's immigration crackdown and challenged a number of the president's executive orders in court. Texas has remained steadfastly red, despite a growing Latino population that is more closely aligned with the Democratic Party but who turns out to vote at lower rates than the state's white population.[18]

In both Texas and California, the issue of sanctuary cities—and sanctuary protection for undocumented residents in general—was dramatically thrust into the news cycle in 2015 as a result of the Steinle shooting and presidential candidacy of Donald Trump (see Figure 3.1). The political leadership of the two states would line up on opposing sides of the debate. In Texas, Abbott would sign SB-4, while in California Governor Brown signed the California

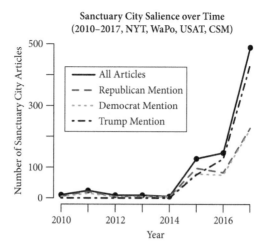

Figure 3.1 News coverage of sanctuary cities from 2010 to 2017.

Values Act (SB-54) into law. Unlike sanctuary policies in the 1980s, this time the conflict was not between the federal government and individuals affiliated with religious institutions but instead between federal and local governments over the issue of balancing immigration enforcement with the need for trust between immigrant communities and the police. This very public conflict between the Trump administration and state and local governments attracted mainstream attention once again, making the issue a highly partisan and divisive one.

Background

The political leanings of California and Texas may play a significant role in attitudes toward sanctuary policies since partisan identity has long been thought of as the main driver of political attitudes and voting behavior. Angus et al. (1960) and Lewis-Beck (2009) argued that party attachment was akin to religious identification, based on a value system developed during preadult socialization. Voters then use this partisan identification as a valuable heuristic in candidate selection even when little is known about a candidate's policy preferences (Jacoby, 1988; Lau and Redlawsk, 1997; Schaffner and Streb, 2002).

While the party system has shifted over time, invoking a massive racial and partisan realignment from the 1960s to the 1990s (Black et al., 2009; Carmines and Stimson, 1989; Schickler, 2016), parties have adopted different positions on different issues across time (Hillygus and Shields, 2014; Karol, 2009), and emerging immigrant communities seem less wedded to the party system than heretofore (Hajnal and Lee, 2011); individual-level partisan attachment nevertheless exhibits highly stable qualities (Green et al., 2004). For the most part, at least in the modern era, once voters select a party identification, they tend to stick with it.

At the same time, extant research indicates that while many voters know relatively little about American politics and policy writ large (Carpini and Keeter, 1993, 1996; Converse, 2006), elite communications (i.e., politicians, candidates, party and media elites) strongly influence citizens' attitudes on emerging topics (Gabel and Scheve, 2007; Iyengar and Kinder, 1987; Zaller, 1992). Lenz (2013) demonstrates that in many cases voters actually adopt the policy position of their preferred candidates or elected officials, as opposed to supporting candidates with whom they share identical policy preferences. In other words, voters are drawn to a candidate (and by extension party), then learn to adopt that candidate's or party's policy positions on a variety of issues.

Taken together, the literature strongly suggests that when it comes to attitudes about sanctuary cities—a topic heretofore unconsidered by the vast majority of voters—voters will rely on partisan cues to "learn" their correct position. Thus, we might expect that party will constrain attitudes on sanctuary cities much more dramatically in 2017 than in 2015, after voters had "learned" about the issue via Trump, Sessions, and Abbott on the one hand, and their Democratic opponents on the other.

Beyond party identification, however, extensive research indicates the over-whelming influence that racial attitudes and racial group membership have on constraining opinion on policy matters explicitly or implicitly connected to race and ethnicity (McClain et al., 2009; Mendelberg, 2001; Parker and Barreto, 2014; Tajfel, 2010). Dawson (2003) developed the term *black utility heuristic* to explain why blacks voting along racial lines so strongly for the Democratic Party was rational, given the overriding influence race has on the lives of most black Americans. In addition, Sanchez and Masuoka (2010) and Sanchez (2006) show that many Latinos exhibit pan-ethnic linked fate,[19] although linked fate tends to be stronger for black Americans than among Latinos.

More recent research has begun to establish the growth of white identity in American politics and how many whites now view themselves equally if not more so discriminated against than minorities (Gest, 2016; Hutchings et al., 2011; Jardina, 2014; Major et al., 2016; Schildkraut, 2017). Moreover, research indicates that whites high in racial identity were strongly supportive of Trump (Schaffner et al., 2018), and that Trump built his political base in areas that had recently undergone rapid Latino growth (Newman et al., 2018). Thus, given the competing role that racial attitudes and racial group membership play in attitude development and voting, it seems entirely plausible that whites—on average—will connect sanctuary cities with something that benefits Latinos and not themselves, whereas Latinos will see sanctuary policy as something that benefits Latinos as a whole. Thus, if racial learning is true, all else being equal, we should expect to see whites moving away from supporting sanctuary cities from 2015 to 2017, and Latinos moving toward greater support for such policies from 2015 to 2017.

The second set of hypotheses tested in this chapter inquires into who supports and who opposes sanctuary city policy. While it seems obvious that people who support sanctuary cities may be the same people who support more inclusionary immigration policy (political liberals, Latinos, Democrats, people higher in socioeconomic status) (Pedraza, 2014; Schildkraut, 2009; Walker and Leitner, 2011), and that the people who oppose sanctuary policies may be the same people who support more exclusionary immigration policy (Republicans, conservatives, nativists, and lower socioeconomic status voters) (Campbell et al., 2006; Citrin et al., 1997), we do not know that for sure, as few polls have asked voters what they think about sanctuary city status. Furthermore, beyond partisanship and ideology, we consider two hypotheses that can be directly extracted from the messaging and racist dog-whistling surrounding the sanctuary city debate: public opinion is driven more by (1) contextual experiences with crime or (2) perception of a Latino racial threat embodied by rapid Latino growth.

The crime hypothesis is relevant because immigration is often rhetorically linked to criminality (*crimmigration*) despite evidence to the contrary. The criminalization of undocumented immigration is reflected in the modern sanctuary city debate and the reliance on narratives of criminality by the Trump administration and leading Republican governors, such as Texas governor Greg Abbott, to justify crackdowns or bans on sanctuary cities. Furthermore, fear of crime has been shown to increase punitive attitudes toward crime control, even when controlling for a host of demographic factors (Costelloe et al., 2009; Dowler, 2003; Hogan et al., 2005; Stinchcombe et al., 1980). Studies have found that those who see crime as one of the most important issues facing the nation, and therefore as more salient, are more punitive (Hogan et al., 2005; Stinchcombe et al., 1980). Therefore, those who see crime as an important political issue or problem should also oppose sanctuary policies since these are narratively linked to increased criminality. That said, just because people fear crime does not necessarily mean that fear is borne out in realistic exposure to crime.

In terms of public opinion, however, little research has shown that attitudes towards immigrants or immigrant-related policy are driven by actual crime rates. Rather, past research shows that public opinion on crime is driven by media narratives, which disproportionately portray nonwhites in crime stories (Barak, 1994; Beckett, 1999; Chandler and Tsai, 2001). Offenders are often nonwhite, which can lead to a priming effect where nonwhites become associated with a higher propensity toward criminality (Iyengar and Kinder, 1987). Furthermore, programs like Secure Communities, an information-sharing initiative with ICE to identify and deport undocumented immigrants in the custody of local law enforcement, was rolled out based on the Latino population, not actual crime rates. Unsurprisingly, the rollout of Secure Communities was also found to have no impact on local crime (Cox and Miles, 2013; Miles and Cox, 2014). Thus, based on the extant literature, we doubt public opinion on sanctuary cities has anything to do with actual crime rates within residents' local geography, but may correspond to citizens' self-reported concerns about crime.

The final hypothesis we investigate in this chapter concerns racial threat. A significant body of research suggests that local populations' fear of crime is linked to shifts in the racial/ethnic composition of neighborhoods, something that fits with Hubert Blalock's theory of interracial competition and Key's theory of racial threat (Blalock, 1967; Key, 1949; Taub et al., 1984). Blalock found that dominant group prejudice tended to be higher when minority populations were larger, thus threatening the dominant group's status, something confirmed by Lincoln Quillian's study of European attitudes toward immigrants (Blalock, 1967; Quillian, 1995). Quillian (1995) found that group size and the economic conditions of the country increased the levels of prejudice directed at immigrant groups, which supports group position theory. Likewise, Key showed that racial repression by whites on blacks was highest in black belt areas (high county percent black) of the Jim Crow South (Key, 1949).

Marylee Taylor (1988) found that the local concentration of blacks had a significant impact on traditional prejudice among whites, opposition to race-targeted programs such as busing, and policy-related beliefs about blacks. Hood and Morris (1997) found that whites living in areas with large populations of Latinos or Asians in fact tended to favor less restrictive immigration policies than did whites living in racially isolated communities. However, this did not hold for California, which has a sizable Latino population but in which white participants were more likely to express a negative outlook on

Asian or Latino contributions to society and to favor reducing levels of legal immigration (Hood and Morris, 1997). Furthermore, Tolbert and Grummel (2003) found that whites living in high black and Latino areas were more supportive of California's Proposition 209, a 1996 ballot initiative designed to end affirmative action in the state.

In consideration of minority population growth specifically, more recently, Enos (2014), Hopkins (2010), Newman (2013), and others have shown that the introduction of new groups of people (e.g., Latinos) into a population can trigger outgroup backlash—although this backlash may be conditional on the preexisting size of the minority population. Nonetheless, to the extent that Latino growth stimulates backlash, and to the extent that sanctuary cities are associated with Latinos in the public's mind, local Latino growth, and Latino population size in general, may drive opinion towards sanctuary city policy. Similarly, we anticipate that voters who report immigration as the "most important problem" in the state or country will disproportionately oppose sanctuary city policy.

The foregoing discussion lends itself to four broad hypotheses and several subhypotheses. The first is that we anticipate that party identification will cleave sanctuary city opinion more in 2017 compared to opinion in 2015. Specifically, Democrats will become dramatically more supportive of sanctuary cities from 2015 to 2017. This partisan-learning hypothesis is pitted against a racial-learning hypothesis. We expect that racial/ethnic group identity will cleave sanctuary city opinion more in 2017 compared to opinion in 2015. Specifically, whites will become more opposed to sanctuary cities in 2017 than in 2015, and Latinos more supportive in 2017 than in 2015.[20]

A second set of hypotheses examines whether ethnic context shapes attitudes about sanctuary cities. The Latino growth threat hypothesis states that respondents living in counties undergoing rapid Latino growth will be more opposed to sanctuary cities relative to respondents living in low Latino-growth counties. Our Latino population threat hypothesis maintains that respondents living in high-Latino areas will express greater opposition to sanctuary cities compared to respondents living farther away from such areas. Finally, on racial threat, we develop an individual-level measure of immigration threat: Respondents who say immigration is the most important issue facing the state or country will be more opposed to sanctuary cities than will respondents who do not say immigration is their most important issue.

Finally, a third set of hypotheses addresses issues related to crime. Our physical crime threat (murder) hypothesis states: Respondents living in areas where the murder rate has increased over time will be less supportive of sanctuary cities than will respondents living in areas where the murder rate has not increased over time.[21] A second physical crime threat hypothesis investigates whether respondents living in areas where the total crime rate has increased over time will be less supportive of sanctuary cities than will respondents living in areas where the total crime rate has not increased over time. Finally, we anticipate that respondents who say crime/drugs are the most important issue will be more opposed to sanctuary cities than will respondents who do not say crime/drugs are the most important issue.

Evaluating Partisan Learning vs. Racial Learning

We rely on four surveys, two fielded in California and two fielded in Texas, to evaluate our first two hypotheses.[22] While these two states are not necessarily generalizable to the full U.S. adult population, they are the two largest states—with exceedingly diverse populations, many large cities, and opposing political environments in terms of sanctuary policy, as we explained earlier.

California

In August 2015 the Institute for Governmental Studies at University of California, Berkeley, fielded a representative poll of California adults, which included several questions about sanctuary cities, along with a host of other questions and demographic items.[23] The survey was fielded online by Survey Sampling International (SSI), and was weighted by gender, race/ethnicity, education, and age to match adult census proportions within the state. The total sample size was 1,098 respondents, producing a margin of error of +/− 2.5 percentage points. Importantly, the survey came shortly after the shooting of Kathryn Steinle.

The second California survey was fielded March 13–20, 2017, and included a sample of $n = 1000$ respondents with a margin of error of +/−3.6 percentage points. The data were collected by YouGov, an online sampling and interviewing platform, that employs propensity score sample matching to ensure a representative sample of California voters. The two surveys were then pooled to create an overall dataset of 2,090 respondents (2015 n = 1,098; 2017 n = 992). We have included detailed information about the survey in the chapter's appendix.

We present our results in Table 3.1. Column 1 presents results from a baseline (noninteractive) pooled logistic regression model. The results suggest that attitudes towards sanctuary cities are guided by party identification, age, gender, and possibly by race, as blacks report greater overall opposition to sanctuary cities than do whites.[24] However, education does not appear to weigh on sanctuary city attitudes—at least in California. Finally, the year 2017 dummy variable reports large substantive and statistically significant effects— indicating the presence of significant overall attitude change from 2015 to 2017. Specifically, people's sanctuary policy attitudes became more favorable in 2017 relative to 2015.

To evaluate our first two hypotheses, we interacted party identification and Latino, respectively, with year 2017. Essentially, these model specifications let us pit hypothesis 1 (partisan learning) against hypothesis 2 (racial-identification learning). The results from Column 2 clearly demonstrate support for the partisan-learning hypothesis as the product term is statistically significant and substantively large. In particular, Democrats in 2017 are much more strongly supportive of sanctuary policy than were Democrats in 2015. We do not, however, produce any statistical evidence in support of the racial-learning identity hypothesis (given the white-Latino dyad). That is, Latinos and whites do not become more polarized on the issue in 2017 versus 2015.

To more cleanly evaluate the partisan-learning hypothesis, we simulated expected probability outcomes on support for sanctuary policy as a function of changes to partisan identification. Figure 3.2 presents the results of this post regression Monte Carlo simulation: in 2015 party identification barely constrained public opinion on the topic, as strong Democrats were marginally more positive on sanctuary policy than were strong Republicans. As we discussed in chapters 1 and 2, sanctuary policies received little attention between the 1990s and 2015, and because the issue was relatively new to most individuals in 2015, Democrats did not have much information to guide their policy views (Oskooii et al., 2018).

However, by 2017—as chapter 2 reveals—the issue had become extremely partisan in the press, with President Trump attacking sanctuary cities and Democrats defending them. Public opinion data mirror these changing media patterns. In 2017, our results show that strong Democrats now supported sanctuary policy by a probability of over 0.75, whereas fewer than 10 percent of Republicans expressed support for sanctuary cities. This smaller shift for Republicans is not terribly surprising, considering that Republican voters likely had already developed a position on sanctuary prior to the Steinle shooting since it was an issue in the 2008 Republican primary and had already been

Table 3.1 Predictors of public opinion on sanctuary cities in California, 2015–2017 Pooled Model. DV: "Do you believe that local authorities should be able to ignore a federal request to hold an illegal immigrant who has been detained? Yes, local authorities should be able to ignore these federal requests (1). No, local authorities should not be able to ignore these federal requests (0)."

	Dependent variable:	
	Sanctuary Support	
	(1)	(2)
Party Identification 7-point (Dem-Rep)	−0.363***	−0.105***
	(0.027)	(0.037)
Female	−0.324***	−0.329***
	(0.106)	(0.109)
Education (low-high)	0.053	0.055
	(0.057)	(0.059)
Age	−0.263***	−0.276***
	(0.039)	(0.040)
Latino	0.185	0.339*
	(0.142)	(0.191)
Black	−0.465**	−0.549**
	(0.233)	(0.249)
Asian	−0.043	−0.072
	(0.174)	(0.178)
Race: Other	0.122	0.157
	(0.197)	(0.201)
Catholic	−0.121	−0.091
	(0.127)	(0.131)
Income: Medium	−0.062	−0.014
	(0.128)	(0.132)
Income: High	−0.227	−0.207
	(0.158)	(0.164)
Income: Missing	−0.219	−0.202
	(0.187)	(0.194)
B Split 2015 (Steinle mention)	−0.321**	−0.291**
	(0.149)	(0.145)
B Split 2017 (Sanctuary specified)	0.238*	0.297*
	(0.140)	(0.152)
2017 Year Dummy	1.178***	2.703***
	(0.145)	(0.231)
Party ID X 2017 Dummy		−0.489***
		(0.055)
Latino X 2017 Dummy		−0.361
		(0.259)
Constant	0.920***	0.140
	(0.277)	(0.297)
Observations	2,090	2,090
Log Likelihood	−1,148.551	−1,106.306
Akaike Inf. Crit.	2,329.102	2,248.612
Pseudo R2	0.168	0.199

Note: *p<0.1; **p<0.05; ***p<0.01

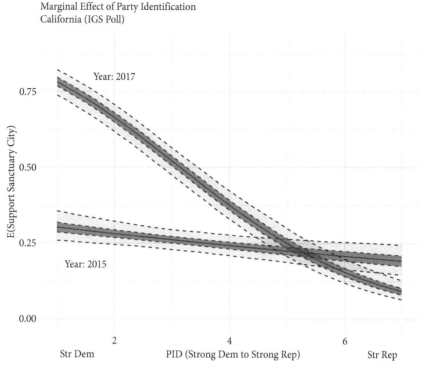

Marginal Effect of Party Identification
California (IGS Poll)

Figure 3.2 Simulations predicting support for sanctuary cities, marginal effect of party identification in 2015 versus 2017, California, based off results from Table 3.1.

featured on Fox News on multiple occasions in relation to other immigrant-related crimes.

Our findings provide strong evidence for a partisan learning model, given how debate of the issue—and the media coverage thereof—shifted between 2015 and 2017. Democrats "learned" the correct position as the fight over sanctuary policies increasingly became associated with resistance to the Trump administration's policies, while there was a smaller shift for Republicans, some of whom were already likely somewhat familiar with the issue because of conservative media coverage and its use as an electoral issue in 2012.

While the results in Table 3.1 do not support a racial learning model, we nevertheless conducted a similar simulation evaluation as with the partisan learning approach. Figure 3.3 presents the findings from this analysis (because the dependent variable is binary, we do not simulate a range). To show effects for racial learning, we would anticipate whites to drop in support of sanctuary

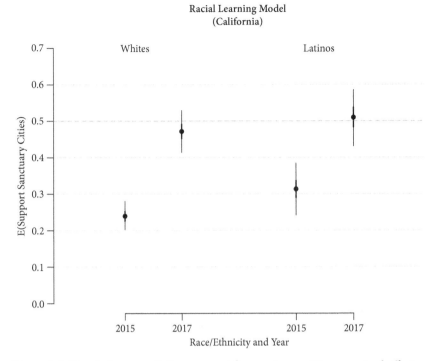

Figure 3.3 Simulations predicting support for sanctuary cities, marginal effect of white versus Latino identification in 2015 versus 2017, California.

policy/cities from 2015 to 2017, and for Latinos to show above mean increases in support from 2015 to 2017. However, as the graph demonstrates, Latinos and whites *both* move in support of sanctuary cities in almost uniform slopes. These results are inconsistent with a racial learning model. While Latinos "learned" to support sanctuary cities, they did not do so any more than any other group, so we cannot conclude with these data that their learning was inherent to racial/ethnic identification.

Texas

To provide greater generalizability and reliability to our California findings, we replicated our analysis with two publicly available polls in Texas fielded by the *Texas Tribune* / University of Texas in 2015 and 2017, respectively. The first poll was in the field between October 30 and November 8, 2015, and surveyed $n = 1,200$ adults, with a margin of error of $+/-$ 2.83 percentage points. The second survey fielded February 3–10, 2017, with an overall $n = 1,200$.

The surveys were both online opt-in panels fielded by YouGov, a firm that uses a well-established and reliable propensity score matching algorithm that balances the sample on age, gender, education, ideology, party identification, and race/ethnicity to create a representative sample (Vavreck and Rivers, 2008).

Between the two fielding periods, a raucous debate on sanctuary cities emerged in Texas, with the Republican governor, Greg Abbott, supporting a bill (SB-4) designed to void any and all sanctuary city policies in the state (even though there weren't any), and Democrats fighting back during debates on the House floor. Thus, it seems reasonable that significant amounts of mass partisan learning occurred in Texas from 2015 to 2017.

For Texas, we follow an identical analytic strategy as pursued in the above analysis using California data. We present our main regression findings in Table 3.2. Column 1 presents our baseline estimates: party identification, ideology, age, and race (Latino) are strongly predictive of sanctuary attitudes. Democrats and liberals report stronger support for sanctuary cities, whereas Republicans and conservatives express high levels of opposition to sanctuary cities. As with California, older voters are more anti-sanctuary than are younger voters. We do see evidence—consistent with extant research on anti-immigrant attitudes (Walker and Leitner, 2011)—that better-educated Texans are more favorable on sanctuary cities than are less-educated Texans, all else being equal. Finally, the coefficient for Year 2017 is positive and statistically significant, indicating that support for sanctuary cities in 2017 is greater than support in 2015. These results are broadly consistent with the California findings.

Column 2 in Table 3.2 adds product terms for Party Identification X Year 2017, and Latino (with white as comparison group) X Year 2017. If the two learning models are correct we should see a negative coefficient for partisan learning, and a positive coefficient for racial learning. The partisan-learning model is confirmed, whereas the racial-learning model is not confirmed. The coefficient on Latino X Year 2017 is statistically significant, but the sign is in the opposite direction. While these effects are hard to interpret, Figure 3.5 demonstrates why the racial-learning model is falsified. The statistically significant effect is due to whites increasing their support for sanctuary cities at a pace faster than Latinos, who began with a higher starting point in 2015.

As with the California analysis, Figure 3.4 replicates the postestimation Monte Carlo simulation plots. While the trends are the same in Texas as in

Table 3.2 Predictors of public opinion on sanctuary cities in Texas, 2015–2017 Pooled Model. "In so-called 'sanctuary cities,' local law enforcement officials do not actively enforce some federal immigration laws. Do you approve (1) or disapprove (0) of city governments that choose not to enforce some immigration laws?"

	Dependent variable:	
	Sanctuary Support	
	(1)	(2)
Party Identification 7-point (Dem-Rep)	−0.430***	−0.347***
	(0.043)	(0.056)
Female	−0.098	−0.108
	(0.131)	(0.132)
Education (low-high)	0.149**	0.148**
	(0.070)	(0.070)
Age	−0.299***	−0.300***
	(0.051)	(0.051)
Latino	0.870***	1.119***
	(0.150)	(0.204)
Black	−0.250	−0.251
	(0.196)	(0.199)
Asian	0.508	0.447
	(0.713)	(0.716)
Ideology (lib-conserv)	−0.559***	−0.561***
	(0.048)	(0.049)
Income	0.066	0.066
	(0.047)	(0.047)
No Income Dummy	0.140	0.127
	(0.258)	(0.259)
Year 2017	0.867***	1.504***
	(0.131)	(0.265)
Party Identification X Year 2017		−0.150**
		(0.068)
Latino X Year 2017		−0.508*
		(0.283)
Constant	2.959***	2.649***
	(0.347)	(0.362)
Observations	2,015	2,015
Log Likelihood	−779.188	−774.671
Akaike Inf. Crit.	1,582.377	1,577.342
Pseudo R2	0.428	0.432

Note: *p<0.1; **p<0.05; ***p<0.01

California (asymmetric learning for Democrats), the shift in support among Democrats is not as extreme. One potential reason for this could be the different political environments of the two states. In California, public officials from mayors to the governor had publicly spoken out in favor of sanctuary cities.

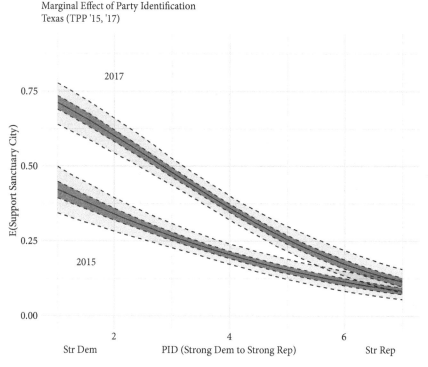

Marginal Effect of Party Identification
Texas (TPP '15, '17)

Figure 3.4 Simulations predicting support for sanctuary cities, marginal effect of party identification in 2015 versus 2017, Texas, based off of results from Table 3.2.

In Texas, Democrats opposed SB-4 but did not publicly defend sanctuary policies. Even the mayor of Austin, which is situated in Travis County, went out of his way to make it clear that Austin was not a sanctuary city.[25] Thus, Democratic voters in Texas may not have developed the same partisan identification with the sanctuary issue. Still, overall, these findings, and the findings presented in Figure 3.5 are entirely consistent with the California findings. Thus, in both California and Texas, we confirm the partisan learning hypothesis but do not find evidence to support racial learning in either state.

Evaluating Immigrant (or Racial) Threat versus Criminal Threat

Our second analysis evaluates the two final sets of hypotheses: Latino racial threat versus physical criminal threat. Latino racial threat builds off the

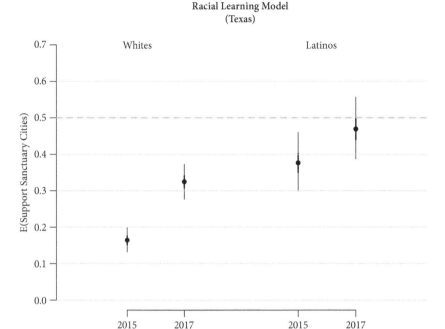

Figure 3.5 Simulations predicting support for sanctuary cities, marginal effect of white versus Latino identification in 2015 versus 2017, Texas.

concept—initially proposed by Key (1949) in his observation of white-black political relations in the Jim Crow South—that whites tend to be most punitive in their racial politics in locations with relatively higher shares of minorities. This logic has subsequently extended to the study of Latino politics and immigration politics. We would thus expect that attitudes toward sanctuary policies would be more negative in areas of high Latino growth or high Latino population.

We also examine the role played by crime, since this is part of the GOP's narrative in opposition to sanctuary cities. In areas with high murder rates or high crime rates, if crime is driving sanctuary opposition, we should find that support is lower. Furthermore, those who rank crime high in their list of concerns should also be less supportive of sanctuary policies.

To evaluate these hypotheses, we draw on two Texas polls that include the geographic information needed to evaluate the role of the Latino population or crime on sanctuary attitudes. Unfortunately, the same geographic data was not available for the California polls and thus we are unable to make the same comparisons between the two states that we could in the preceding section.

The Texas polls asked about sanctuary city attitudes, include items inquiring into the importance of crime and immigration, and have geographic indicators such as county Federal Information Processing Standards (FIPS) or zip code. The polls fielded in February[26] and April 2017. Both polls include many of the same variables that serve as controls and come with geographic indicators, which lets us evaluate our hypotheses.[27] For each respondent, we merge county-level crime data from the Uniform Crime Reporting (UCR) agency and racial demographics from the U.S. American Community Survey. Thus, we have both the individual- and contextual-level data to test our hypotheses.

We pool the two datasets because they represent the same universe of Texas registered voters. The first survey is the *Texas Tribune* / University of Texas statewide poll, which fielded February 3–10, 2017, with an overall $n = 1,200$. The second survey is the Texas Lyceum poll, a telephone statewide survey of $n = 1,000$ respondents fielded between April 3 and 9, 2017. The two surveys asked many of the same questions. Any variance due to data collection is captured with a dummy variable for one of the surveys, which we include in all analyses.[28]

Table 3.3 presents initial tests of our two hypotheses and subhypotheses. If our contextual hypotheses are to be confirmed, we should see a statistically significant negative coefficient for our two Latino context variables (growth and size), and our two crime variables (murder change and total crime change).

Turning to our results, we find strong support for hypotheses that the size and growth of the local Latino population affects opposition to sanctuary policies and no support that crime plays a role in sanctuary support/opposition. Both Latino growth and the size of the population are statistically associated with decreases in support for sanctuary cities. That is, respondents who live in areas that have undergone rapid Latino change over the past fifteen years— and areas that have sizable Latino populations—tend to most strongly oppose sanctuary cities.[29]

Despite the crime narrative associated with sanctuary cities, we find that public opinion—at least in the state of Texas—is influenced by on-the-ground Latino population size and rapid Latino growth and *not* by actual on-the-ground crime rates, murder rates, and crime statistics more generally. Real on-the-ground experiences with crime are statistically unrelated to sanctuary city attitudes. These results are broadly consistent with literature in political science, communications, and sociology that shows attitudes about crime are driven more by media coverage of crime than actual crime; and that whites tend to draw illusory correlations between minority populations and crime.

Table 3.3 DV: Do you support or oppose "sanctuary cities"?

	Dependent variable:
	sanc_approve
Party ID (Dem-Ind-Rep)	−1.031***
	(0.098)
Ideology (Lib-Mod-Cons)	−1.067***
	(0.083)
Black	−0.425**
	(0.176)
Hispanic	0.483***
	(0.169)
Female	0.036
	(0.120)
Age	−0.016***
	(0.004)
Education (low-high)	0.217***
	(0.061)
Geo: Urban	0.186
	(0.132)
Income: 40–150K	0.178
	(0.140)
Income: 150K+	0.286
	(0.218)
Income Missing	−0.062
	(0.202)
Pct. Latino Growth: 2000–2014	−0.010**
	(0.004)
Pct. Latino 2014	−0.010**
	(0.005)
Change in Murder Rate 2000–2015	−0.115
	(0.096)
Change in Total Crime Rate 2000–2015	0.037
	(0.270)
Immigration Most Important Issue	−0.919***
	(0.175)
Crime/Drugs Most Important Issue	−0.841*
	(0.459)
UT-Poll Dummy	−0.457***
	(0.124)
Constant	4.719***
	(0.479)
Observations	2,042
Log Likelihood	−918.882
Akaike Inf. Crit.	1,875.763
Pseudo R2	0.359

Note: *p<0.1; **p<0.05; ***p<0.01

Next we evaluate whether individual-level concern about immigration or crime is associated with support for sanctuary policies. Remember, these items are based on whether respondents think these issues are the most important in the state. The results in Table 3.3 indicate that both variables are statistically significant and negative, meaning that relative to respondents who do not think either of these issues are important, voters who think either immigration or crime, respectively, are the most important issues in Texas are less supportive of sanctuary cities. This suggests that fear of crime, irrespective of actual crime rates, plays a significant role in tamping down support for sanctuary policies. Since conservative politicians regularly claim that sanctuary policies increase crime, it is not surprising that those who see crime as a significant issue for the state would be more opposed to these policies. Similarly, it was expected that those who thought immigration was one of the biggest issues facing the state of Texas would also be less supportive of sanctuary policies, and that is in fact what we find.

To ease interpretation we present four postestimation Monte Carlo simulation plots of our main contextual independent variables in Figure 3.6 and our two main individual-level variables in Figure 3.7. The two left panels in Figure 3.6 assess hypothesis 1. Moving along the x-axis from left to right, as Latino growth increases, respondents shift from a .47 probability of supporting sanctuaries to a 0.08 probability. On Latino population size, the effects shift from a probability of 0.41 (minimum Latino population) to a probability of 0.22 (maximum Latino population). These effects are very dramatic and provide very clear evidence that Latino growth and Latino population size negatively influence opinion on sanctuary city policy.

The two rightmost panels in Figure 3.6 evaluate the criminal threat hypotheses. The top-right plot shows no statistical or significant relationship between change in county murder rate and sanctuary city attitude, despite a downward association. The bottom-right plot (change in total crime rate) clearly reveals no relationship between actual change in county crime and attitudes about sanctuary cities. Taken together these findings reject the idea that actual crime rates drive sanctuary opposition.

Figure 3.7 presents the simulations for the individual-level most important issue variables. The top panel shows the effects for immigration as the most important issue, whereas the bottom panel shows the effects for crime as the most important issue. As respondents move from the issue not being important to being important, their expected support for sanctuary cities moves from .37 to .19 for immigration and .33 to .19 for crime. While these support

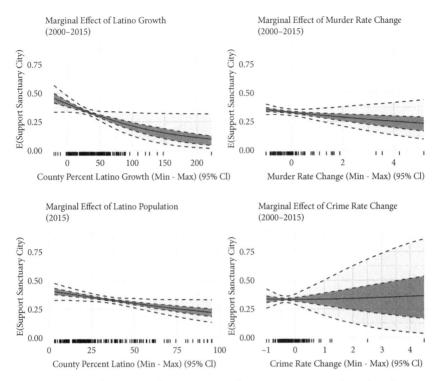

Figure 3.6 Simulations predicting support for sanctuary cities, based on four county-level predictors: Latino growth, Latino population size, murder rate change, total crime rate change. Models control for party ID, ideology, education, race/ethnicity, gender, age, income, and survey house. DV: Thinking about your own view, do you support or oppose "sanctuary cities"?

both that immigration and crime concerns drive sanctuary opposition, the relationship is more uncertain for the crime variable.

Conclusion

Sanctuary cities are now a major divisive mainstream issue in the United States, despite being mostly off the national political and media agenda prior to 2015. Kathryn Steinle's death sparked a massive public backlash against sanctuary cities, with the most vehement opposition coming from conservative Republicans such as then-candidate Donald Trump. Our findings from chapter 2 support this claim, as we observed a large growth in newspaper articles and

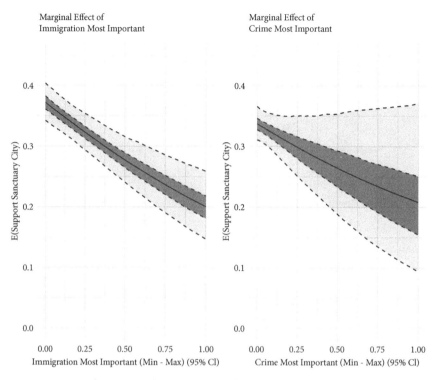

Figure 3.7 Simulations predicting support for sanctuary cities. Models control for party ID, ideology, education, race/ethnicity, gender, age, income, and survey house. DV: Thinking about your own view, do you support or oppose "sanctuary cities"?

television broadcast stories about sanctuary cities starting in 2015. Unlike the 1980s, sanctuary cities are no longer associated with a sympathetic group like refugees, and the debate around these policies is now much more closely linked to the broader debate around undocumented immigration. The criminality narrative that has been pushed by conservative politicians from Greg Abbott to Donald Trump mirrors the increasing criminalization of undocumented immigration in the United States more broadly (Gonzalez O'Brien, 2018).

As a result, public attitudes about sanctuary cities have polarized in recent years reflecting contours somewhat consistent with public attitudes about immigration policy more generally (Casellas and Wallace, 2018). This polarizing process is a relatively recent phenomenon, though, as sanctuary cities, particularly among Democrats, have received little attention from Democratic politicians or media. Our research shows that in 2015, a majority of both Republicans and Democrats opposed policies barring local law enforcement from working with the federal government to enforce immigration policy. That is, the mass public as a whole opposed sanctuary policy. We contend that public opinion at this point was massively uninformed on the issue—which is consistent with much public opinion research on policy attitudes (Converse, 2006; Zaller, 1992).

However, attitudes, especially among Democrats and liberals, began to change in 2017 as Trump continued his attack on sanctuary policy and elite Democratic opposition emerged as a counterweight, with big-city mayors and blue-state governors providing strong arguments in support of sanctuary policy. The massive change in media coverage on the issue increased public attention, thereby elevating the issue as more important in the minds of the public. In 2015 and 2016 Trump and Republicans had largely framed the issue around crime, but counternarratives in 2017 began providing Democratic voters and liberals with alternative arguments that sanctuary cities do not have more crime and that if anything they might reduce crime (Gonzalez O'Brien et al., 2017; Lyons et al., 2013; Wong, 2017a). Scholars have since shown these elite-driven arguments are important to driving support for sanctuary policy, particularly among Democrats and liberals (Oskooii et al., 2018).

In this chapter we have demonstrated that voters now view sanctuary policies through highly partisan lenses. Our findings show that voters employed partisanship to "learn" how to adopt sanctuary policy attitudes. We argued that Democrats in 2015 really had little to guide their sanctuary opinion. As Democratic mayors and governors opposed Trump over the emerging sanctuary conflict, public opinion cleaved on party identification. The governors of Washington (Jay Inslee), Oregon (Kate Brown), and California (Jerry Brown) took very public positions in support of sanctuary policies with all three states adopting or strengthening sanctuary state legislation in 2017. While partisan learning did play a role in sanctuary attitudes, we found little support that these attitudes were driven by race. Racial learning—the idea that one's self-identified race will act as a heuristic to facilitate policy attitude change regarding sanctuary policy—did not appear to explain sanctuary attitude shifts from 2015 to 2017, at least for Latinos and whites.

Beyond explaining attitude change, we analyzed two 2017 public opinion surveys in Texas to better understand correlates of sanctuary policy attitudes. Public opinion today is shaped largely by partisanship, with self-identified Republicans opposing sanctuary cities and self-identified Democrats supporting sanctuary cities. We found very similar results among self-identified conservatives and liberals. Further, older respondents tend to oppose sanctuary policy more so than do younger respondents. We also demonstrate that—perhaps not surprisingly with an issue rife in misinformation—better-educated people tend to support sanctuary cities more so than do less-educated people. Finally, we found that Latinos are more supportive of sanctuary cities than are members of other racial/ethnic groups.

Beyond the individual voter demographic characteristics, we further investigated measures of racial and criminal context. Racial threat (particularly among whites)—here conceptualized as percent Latino and percent Latino growth at the county level—was found to play an outsized role in public opinion. Specifically, respondents living in high-Latino-growth counties respond much more negatively to sanctuary city policy than do voters not living in such high-growth areas. Despite the elite narrative conflating sanctuary cities with crime, voters living in high-crime areas were no more or less supportive of sanctuary cities than were voters who did not live in such geographic spaces. Thus, people's claims that they oppose sanctuary cities because they are legitimately worried about crime are based not on actual realistic crime threats, but rather more likely based on media imagery leading to illusory and inaccurate correlations between Latinos and crime. Support for this is shown by the negative relationship between concerns about crime and support for sanctuary policies. Lastly, as mentioned earlier, support for sanctuary policies is linked to broader concerns about immigration, with those who see this as an important issue more likely to oppose sanctuary legislation than those who do not see this as one of the top problems facing their state.

These findings are largely in line with the expectations one would have based on both the evolution of sanctuary policies and media attention. As sanctuary legislation shifted in terms of its intended beneficiaries after the 1980s from refugees to undocumented immigrants, it increasingly became the target of politicians on the right. As immigration restriction increasingly became part of the Republican agenda, politicians tried to seize on the issue in order to attract voters. Both Mitt Romney and Fred Thompson tried to make sanctuary an issue in the 2008 Republican primary, though this did not catch on as it would in 2016. While it did not become an issue at the forefront, sanctuary policies played a larger role in Republican politics prior to the Steinle shooting than they did in Democratic politics. This, combined with the significant increase in media coverage following the Steinle shooting, helps to explain the effect of partisan learning on sanctuary attitudes after 2015.

In chapter 4 we examine the legislative dynamics of sanctuary policy at the state level, which would increasingly become driven and representative of the increasing partisan divides over the issue that have been detailed in the preceding chapters.

4

Legislative Expression: Sanctuary Policymaking in the U.S. States

As discussed in previous chapters, sanctuary policies emerged in the 1980s to protect unauthorized Central Americans fleeing civil war, oppression, and conflict in their home countries. In the 1990s and especially after 9/11, though, sanctuary policies were reinvented to facilitate the political and social incorporation of the undocumented population residing in the United States, with the specific aim of engendering trust in the local police force and city government among immigrant communities. While Republicans occasionally railed against such policies as a way of flexing their anti-immigrant credentials to appeal to their conservative base (Hughey and Parks, 2014; López, 2015; Mendelberg, 2001), especially during the 2008 presidential primary contest, the issue was largely moot at the national and state levels until the summer of 2015.

The murder of Kathryn Steinle in 2015 focused the nation's attention on sanctuary cities and sanctuary policies. Many conservative politicians and members of the public argued that San Francisco's sanctuary city policy was responsible for her death and that such policies needed to end. Similar incidents have since cropped up, including the 2016 death of Iowan Sarah Root, who was killed by a drunk driver and undocumented immigrant, nineteen-year-old Eswin Mejia. After Root's death Mejia was released on bond after ICE declined to issue a detainer request, which led to criticism of the agency by both the president and congressional Republicans.[1]

President Trump and conservative lawmakers similarly seized on the murder of Mollie Tibbetts in Iowa in 2018 to emphasize the dangers posed by undocumented immigrants. Her killer, Cristhian Bahena Rivera, was an undocumented immigrant, and her death was once again used as a rallying cry for increased immigration restriction, though Tibbetts's family pushed back on this narrative in their public comments.[2] Legislatively, the battle over sanctuary cities did not really begin until 2017 (see Figure 4.1), when the number of both anti- and prosanctuary bills introduced for consideration in state houses around the country increased dramatically, driven by both

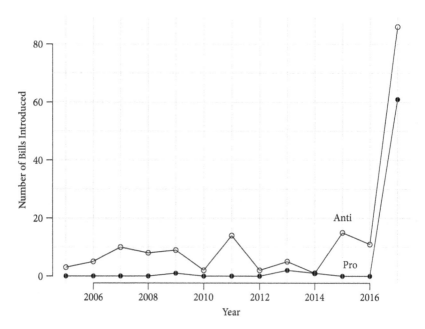

Figure 4.1 Frequency of bill introductions related to sanctuary cities/
movements over time.
Source: Lexis-Nexis Legislative Database/NCSL

President Trump's rhetoric on the issue and the increasingly high profile of
cases where an American was killed by an undocumented immigrant.

Seizing upon Donald Trump's victory, in which the candidate campaigned
strongly and consistently against sanctuary cities, many Republicans came to
see attacking sanctuary cities as a possible winning strategy. Once Trump
took office, his administration began suing cities over their sanctuary policies
and looking for ways to strip federal funding from sanctuary localities.[3]
Many cities responded with countersuits. In a multilayer federalism response
(city, state, national), state legislatures took up the issue with gusto—with
Democrats introducing prosanctuary legislation and Republicans introducing
anti-sanctuary legislation. In this chapter we analyze the precise determinants
of why states introduced both anti- and prosanctuary legislation in 2017.

In early 2017, as the Trump administration began the legal battle with
cities over their sanctuary policies, the press largely overlooked how state
legislators had joined the fray by dramatically expanding the introduction of
new legislation on sanctuary cities.[4] The most draconian bill signed into law
was Texas's Senate Bill 4—a law that essentially banned sanctuary cities in the
state, which we discussed in the preceding chapter. On the other hand, the
California legislature enacted Senate Bill 54, effectively making the entire state

a sanctuary.[5] These bills typify the sanctuary debate that played out across the country as state and local leaders increasingly took sides in the conflict (Collingwood et al., 2018). However, scholars know very little about why states are likely to propose punitive or welcoming sanctuary measures. While it may be that sanctuary policymaking in the states mirrors state-level dynamics of immigration policymaking, there has been little research examining whether this is indeed the case.

Although just a few states actually implemented sanctuary-related laws in 2017, many states saw dramatic increases in legislative bill proposals, including in states like Iowa, where both Sarah Root and Mollie Tibbetts had been born, that eventually enacted an anti-sanctuary law in 2018.[6] Outlawing sanctuary cities within a state is simply another avenue that anti-sanctuary proponents could pursue, as—relative to the federal constitution—some state constitutions may make it easier to pass and implement such laws.

This chapter assesses the politics behind the introduction of sanctuary policy proposals at the state level in 2017 to understand how state policy on the issue is likely to be shaped in the coming years as the battle over immigration federalism continues (Ramakrishnan and Gulasekaram, 2012). Proposals, or bill introductions, are important to examine because they demonstrate the emergence of an issue that directly affects a large portion of society (Bratton and Haynie, 1999; Gonzalez O'Brien et al., 2017; Gonzalez O'Brien, 2018), tell us something about legislator signaling or position taking (Grimmer, 2013; Jones, 2003; Koger, 2003), and let us assess the extent that public opinion and the recent push for immigration restriction by the Trump administration is driving the policy agenda in the states (Baumgartner and Jones, 2010; True et al., 1999).

Relying on literature that divides state-level immigration policy proposals and legislation into two categories (restriction/control versus pro-immigrant/integrative) (Boushey and Luedtke, 2011; Chavez and Provine, 2009), in this chapter we analyze two models of sanctuary legislative proposals: anti-sanctuary legislative proposals and prosanctuary legislative proposals. Our goal is to develop a better understanding of what predicted the introduction of pro- or anti-sanctuary legislation at the state level and to determine whether this was primarily driven by either crime or the economic status of the state in the way that some theories may anticipate.

We also examine whether bill introductions are driven by state-level voter ideology (as measured by Percent Trump and ALEC legislative membership within the state), state institutional variation on competition and professionalism, or characteristics of the Latino population. We expect to find that crime and the economic status of the state play little role in whether or not pro- or antisanctuary legislation is introduced. Instead, we anticipate finding that state-level voter ideology will play the biggest role in whether sanctuary legislation is introduced, with more conservative states being the most likely to introduce legislation. As we discussed in chapter 3, at the level of public opinion it is partisanship that plays the largest role in public attitudes, and we expect ideology to perform similarly in terms of bill introductions.

Background

Many scholars have investigated the U.S. state policymaking process, but scholars have only relatively recently begun to unpack why states pass or propose restrictive or inclusive immigration legislation. Chavez and Provine (2009) investigate four broad factors that predict why states enact restrictionist or pro-immigrant legislation: race/ethnicity, economic anxiety, criminal threat, and ideology. These scholars find that restrictionist legislation is primarily determined by a state's citizen ideology—as measured by Jacobs and Carmichael (2002). In particular, states with more conservative citizens (i.e., more Republicans) were more likely to enact restrictionist legislation. However, these scholars found that states with large Latino and growing foreign-born populations were more likely to enact pro-immigration legislation. Furthermore, more liberal state governments were more inclined to enact pro-immigrant legislation. Notably, the passage of immigration legislation was unrelated to both economic and criminal anxiety.

Noting a recent rise in state-level immigration policy highlighted by Arizona's passage of the anti-immigrant SB 1070 bill, Boushey and Luedtke (2011) conduct a similar analysis as Chavez and Provine (2009) by examining whether economic conditions, immigrant growth, state demographics, party control, and state political institutions (i.e., legislative professionalism) are associated with integrationist versus control/restrictionist laws and proposals. Looking at a variety of pro- and anti-immigrant legislation—such as driver's licenses for undocumented immigrants, in-state tuition for undocumented immigrant students, bilingual education, and denying access to state employment and social services—these scholars find that ethnic factors (i.e., the size of the Latino population) are associated with both integration and control bills, as are state ideology, legislative professionalism, and some state economic factors.

Most recently, Ybarra et al. (2016) examine anti-immigrant state laws enacted between 2005 and 2012. Their research finds that increases in the state Hispanic population (and likewise decline in white/Anglo population) and economic anxiety are most strongly linked to punitive immigrant state laws. Likewise, Marquez and Schraufnagel (2013) show that the most consistent predictor of restrictive legislation between 2008 and 2012 is the change in the size of the Latino population since the previous census. Examining data from a similar time period, but using a structural model with a latent variables approach, Monogan (2009) finds that citizen ideology—as measured by presidential vote, congressional vote, and self-reported ideology— is the primary mover of immigrant legislation. Other scholars show that the presence of undocumented populations influences immigration legislation (Nicholson-Crotty and Nicholson-Crotty, 2011), as does state unionization levels (Marquez and Schraufnagel, 2013). Finally, Zingher (2014) argues that conservative Republican-controlled states are more likely to pass exclusionary immigrant laws, although this is tempered by the size of the Latino electorate.

Taken as a whole, these findings support the notion that "racial threat" may be a key influential variable in the development of state-level immigrant restrictionist legislation (Blalock, 1967; Hood and Morris, 1997; Key, 1949; Newman and Johnson, 2012; Newman et al., 2012). That is, the greater the Latino or foreign-born population within a state, the greater the likelihood at least some states will introduce anti-immigrant legislation. However—and this is crucial—citizen and state ideology also play key roles, and to a lesser degree so do state institutions and economic considerations (Citrin et al., 1997).

However, it seems unlikely that actual crime rates within the state will play much of a role in driving whether and the degree to which states introduce sanctuary legislation. Finally, we also think that interest groups— particularly the American Legislative Exchange Council (ALEC)—will play a role in the introduction of anti-sanctuary legislation. That is, states with more ALEC-affiliated legislators will be more likely to introduce anti-sanctuary legislation.

Threat, Ideology, State Institutions, and Economic Anxiety

Racial/Latino Threat

Blalock (1967), Key (1949), Tolbert and Grummel (2003), and countless others have consistently shown that the white public and white elected officials are most punitive in attitude and policy when minority populations are large and/or growing, although a liberal political culture of inclusiveness can temper "racial threat" (Elazar, 1994; Erikson et al., 1987; Johnson, 1976; Wells, 2004).[7]

Specifically, locations with larger shares of minority residents (Key, 1949), and locations that are undergoing rapid immigrant growth tend to produce white backlash (Abrajano and Hajnal, 2015; Matsubayashi and Rocha, 2012) and white panic, and therefore, we should expect more punitive and restrictive legislation in states exhibiting such characteristics. We therefore expect that states with larger Latino populations will be more likely to introduce anti-sanctuary bills. Similarly, states experiencing rapid Latino growth should also be more likely to introduce prosanctuary bills.

We should note, though, that this hypothesis should play out up to a point. Once the Latino population is large and politically incorporated, Latinos may have enough power within a given jurisdiction to begin pressuring whites to cede some political power. This, of course, depends on the racial attitudes held by whites in a particular state or jurisdiction (Bishin, 2009; Collingwood, 2012).

Political and Ideological Orientation

Past research has demonstrated that political ideology and party drive mass public opinion and state-level immigration policy outcomes (Monogan, 2009; Ramakrishnan and Gulasekaram, 2012). Ramakrishnan and Gulasekaram (2012) and Wallace (2014) show that even states with relatively low Latino populations pushed "show me your papers" laws after Arizona implemented SB-1070 in 2010. Rather, party control and ideology appeared to be powerful drivers.

Given that sanctuary city policy became a nationally contested issue largely due to Trump's media agenda-setting (Scheufele and Tewksbury, 2007; Weaver, 2007), we think that the Trump 2016 state vote share will serve as a powerful predictor of anti-sanctuary legislation. Clearly, Trump's main 2016 campaign theme—from his announcement all the way through Election Day— was stopping illegal immigration. His opposition to sanctuary cities—along with building a wall between the United States and Mexico—was central to his immigration policy agenda. Throughout the 2016 campaign he continually castigated sanctuary city policy, stating that he would "end sanctuary cities" and claiming that they "breed crime."

Trump's very explicit denigration of these cities, in combination with his victory, may have sent strong cues to GOP voters and legislators alike that opposition to sanctuary cities could be a potentially winning wedge issue and a means of winning favor with the White House (Hillygus and Shields, 2014;

Hutchings and Valentino, 2004). Under this situation, we expect that legislators in Trump-heavy states will disproportionately introduce anti-sanctuary bills; whereas Democrats should pivot to oppose all things Trump. At the same time, the converse should be true for low-Trump states.

We also include a count measure of legislator membership in the highly conservative American Legislative Executive Council (ALEC).[8] This measure is highly correlated with state liberalism, but we choose to include the ALEC measure because the organization has grown in recent years, and significant state legislation is a result of ALEC's efforts. Indeed, ALEC's "No Sanctuary Cities for Illegal Immigrants Act" (which is readily available from ALECexposed.org) has been shown to have directly influenced Arizona's infamous SB-1070 (Jackman, 2013). It has also been shown that this piece of model legislation served as a template for a number of anti-sanctuary bills nationwide (Collingwood et al., 2018). We build off of this analysis later in the chapter.

From this, we therefore expect that state percentage vote for Trump (2016) will positively associate with anti-sanctuary legislation and negatively associate with prosanctuary legislation. Based on ALEC's role in drafting anti-sanctuary legislation, we also predict that states with larger numbers of ALEC members will be more likely to introduce anti-sanctuary legislation and less likely to introduce prosanctuary legislation.

State Institutions

Existing research shows that various components of state government and institutions influence the state immigration policymaking process. Given how Trump's elevation of sanctuary cities connotes threat and racial competition to his base voters (Newman and Johnson, 2012; Parker and Barreto, 2014), we think variables that measure state competition are highly relevant to predicting state sanctuary bill introductions. In particular, states with divided governments and an underlying competitive electoral environment might induce legislators to look toward advantageous wedge issues on the one hand (anti-sanctuary bills) (Hillygus and Shields, 2014). At the same time, legislators might look to appeal to a growing electorate in highly competitive states as an attempt to reshape the composition of the electorate (Alamillo and Collingwood, 2016; Barreto and Collingwood, 2015; Barreto et al., 2010; Fraga and Leal, 2004; Reny, 2017).

We also include a measure of legislative professionalism (King, 2000). Legislators in more professionalized states have greater access to resources in terms of compensation, staff, and length of legislative sessions and therefore can introduce more bills in general—whether anti- or prosanctuary. Thus, we anticipate legislative professionalism will positively covary with bill introductions of all kinds. These expectations lead to the following expectations: states with divided government should have more anti- and prosanctuary legislation; states that are competitive at the legislative level should have more anti- and prosanctuary bill introductions; relative to less professionalized states, more professionalized states will be more likely to introduce anti- and prosanctuary bills.

Criminal Threat

Despite overwhelming evidence that shows a negative or noncorrelation between immigration and crime (Cohen, 1931; Gonzalez O'Brien, 2018; Lyons et al., 2013; Reid et al., 2005), anti-immigrant politicians generally, and opponents of sanctuary city policies in particular, frequently say they oppose sanctuary cities because of crime. These arguments have been echoed by both President Trump and then–Attorney General Jeff Sessions, both of whom have suggested on numerous occasions that sanctuary policies lead to increased crime.[9]

On February 5, 2017, in an interview with Bill O'Reilly, Trump claimed that sanctuary policies "breed crime," a claim he had made frequently both on the campaign trail and in the first months of his presidency.[10] On March 27, 2017, the attorney general claimed, "Countless Americans would be alive today and countless loved ones would not be grieving today if these policies of sanctuary cities were ended."[11] Furthermore, nearly 50 percent of the introduced anti-sanctuary legislation contains at least one reference to the terms "crime/criminal" (see Figure 4.2). Thus, despite evidence from Chavez and Provine (2009) showing that state crime rates are unrelated to immigration policymaking, we nonetheless test a crime hypothesis as it relates to the introduction of anti–sanctuary city bills.

Economic Anxiety

A frequent argument made to explain the results of the 2016 presidential election is that white voters cast their ballots for Trump due to so-called

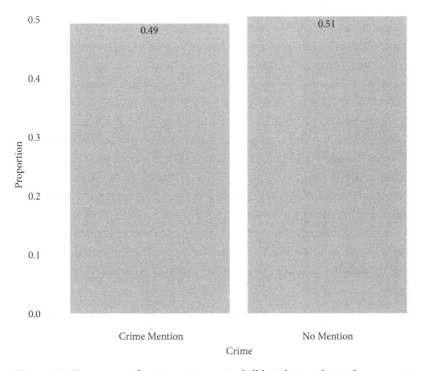

Figure 4.2 Frequency of anti-sanctuary city bill legislation that references crime.

economic anxiety.[12] Despite evidence that shows white Trump voting—or even vote switching from Democrat in 2012 to Republican in 2016—was largely a function of racial anxiety and not economic anxiety (Reny et al., 2019; Sides et al., 2016, 2017), some evidence does suggest that states are more supportive of anti-immigrant legislation when residents in the state are struggling financially (Ybarra et al., 2016). Therefore, it seems reasonable to think that states that contain disproportionately larger numbers of unemployed and low-income residents might move to legislatively punish sanctuary cities, all else being equal. If this is true, we would expect to find that states with lower median income or higher unemployment will be more likely to introduce anti-sanctuary legislation.

Data and Methods

Treating the state as the unit of analysis, we gathered every introduced bill from 2017 that pertained specifically to sanctuary cities. This produced approximately 150 bills using a combination of the National Conference of State Legislatures (NCSL) database on sanctuary legislation, and the Lexis-Nexis State Net bill search database. On the former, NCSL recently released a database that compiled sanctuary city legislation in the states during the 2017 sessions.[13] However, we augmented these data with a search on the term "sanctuary" in the Lexis-Nexis legislative bill database. We then applied a search algorithm to ensure some bills from our search were not really about sanctuary marshes for birds, animals, or some other unrelated topic.[14]

Following Boushey and Luedtke (2006, 2011), we separate our sanctuary legislation analysis into two types: policies designed to punish immigrants (anti-sanctuary legislation), and policies designed to integrate immigrants (prosanctuary legislation). We then read and coded each bill as either prosanctuary or anti-sanctuary. The text of the language of these bills is almost always obviously pro or anti, leading to an inter-item correlation between coders of 100 percent. Below we list the title and some excerpts of a few anti and pro bills.

Antisanctuary

California SJR 4
"Harboring violent criminals protected by the policies of sanctuary cities has contributed to the problem of many citizens of the United States suffering great bodily harm, including death."

Rhode Island H 5394
"This act would require the division of sheriffs to verify the immigration status of each incarcerated person presented to the court for any hearing, to notify ICE as to any such person lacking legal immigration status, and to cooperate with ICE relative to any deportation proceedings regarding any such individual."

Prosanctuary

Vermont HJR 2
"Joint resolution commending Vermont municipalities that have adopted or are considering adopting sanctuary status."

California SR 22
"The Trump administration has justified its vast expansion of those targeted for deportation by falsely portraying the United States as a country under siege by

Figure 4.3 Distribution of antisanctuary legislation across the U.S. states, 2017.

a flood of undocumented immigrants who threaten public safety, giving rise to anti-immigrant fervor and a nativist desire to preserve our nation's historically dominant Euro-Christian culture."

In total, n = 89 (59 percent) bills are coded as anti-sanctuary, and n = 61 (41 percent) bills coded as prosanctuary. Figure 4.3 and 4.4 display the pro- and antisanctuary proposal distribution across the U.S. states, respectively. Clearly, Texas and Virginia introduced the most anti-sanctuary bills within their respective state legislatures, but several other states, including Iowa and Mississippi, contended with multiple anti-sanctuary bills. On the prosanctuary side, Democratic states with large and diverse populations, like New Jersey, New York, Illinois, and California, lead the way.

We craft two dependent variables: state count of anti-sanctuary bills proposed in 2017 and state count of prosanctuary bills proposed in 2017. Thus, our unit of analysis is the state (not the bill). Because these variables are counts, we estimate two negative binomial count models to investigate determinants of different types of proposed sanctuary legislation.[15]

We include a host of explanatory variables to evaluate our hypotheses. To investigate our first two hypotheses concerning racial threat we include

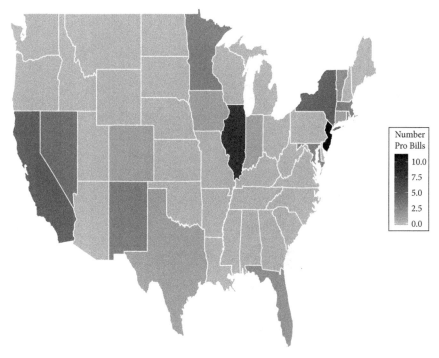

Figure 4.4 Distribution of prosanctuary legislation across the U.S. states, 2017.

a measure for the percent Latino within the state and state percent Latino growth (2000–2015). These data are gathered from the 2012–2015 American Community Survey (ACS) and the 2000 Census.

To measure political and ideological orientation, we include measures for Trump percent vote share within the state as recorded by the U.S. Federal Elections Committee. Our measure for legislature ideology is a count of ALEC members per state, collected in 2017 by the Center for Media and Democracy. We use this measure because ALEC provides model legislation that conservative legislators can easily copy and introduce in their own state. A model piece of legislation even exists for policy related to immigration federalism and sanctuary cities.[16]

We utilize NCSL documentation on state legislative seats to develop two variables: a measure of state competition (a simplified Ranney index) and divided control of state government (1 = yes, 0 = no). States where at least one house of the legislature and the executive are controlled by different parties are denoted as divided. Following Bentele and O'Brien (2013), we also include a measure for institutional competition. Our simplified Ranney index was constructed based on the formula in equation 4.1:

$$\text{Ranney Index} = 100 - abs\left(\left(\frac{\text{Senate Dem}}{\text{Total Senate}} * 100\right) + \left(\left(\frac{\text{House Dem}}{\text{Total House}} * 100\right) - 100\right)\right) \qquad (4.1)$$

We also include a measure for legislative professionalism as measured by King (2000). This measure incorporates days in session, legislator salary, and state expenditures on legislative operations and services. State legislatures similar in professionalism to the U.S. Congress—like California—will approach a score of 1, whereas states with little professionalism (e.g., Wyoming) will score closer to 0).

We include three variables to measure crime and economic explanations. For crime, we include the violent crime rate from the Federal Bureau of Investigation's (FBI) Uniform Crime Reporting Program 2014 database, which collects and aggregates crime rates by state. For economic anxiety, we include the state's median household income (logged), and the percentage of adults who are unemployed—both from the 2015 American Community Survey (ACS).

Finally, as a control, we include a measure of immigration public opinion in the state, which is a state-level aggregate calculation from the 2016 Cooperative Congressional Election Studies (CCES) on several immigration policy questions (see Appendix B for coding).

Analysis

We present our results in two ways, separated by predictors of anti-sanctuary legislation and prosanctuary legislation. Each analysis includes a table of regression results and a plot of standardized rope-ladder coefficients. Positive coefficients suggest that variable is positively related to pro/anti (depending on the model) bill introduction counts, whereas the converse is the case for negative coefficients. The rope-ladder point estimates are postestimation simulated standardized coefficients are useful in demonstrating the relative impact of one variable against another.

We begin with an analysis of our racial threat variables—percent Latino and percent Latino growth within the state. Table 4.1 presents our anti-sanctuary (column 1) and prosanctuary (column 2) findings. In the anti-sanctuary model, percent Latino is positive and statistically significant, meaning—all else being equal—that as states' Latino population rises, states are more likely to introduce anti-sanctuary legislation. However, Latino growth is not significant in the anti model but is significant in the

Table 4.1 Predictors of count of sanctuary city bill introduction in state legislatures, 2017.

	Sanctuary Bill Count	
	Anti (1)	Pro (2)
ALEC Legislator Count	0.026**	−0.019
	(0.013)	(0.025)
Percent Trump 2016	0.069*	−0.120**
	(0.037)	(0.057)
Public Opinion: Anti-Immigration Attitudes	−4.226	13.609
	(7.957)	(12.248)
Percent Latino 2015	0.045*	0.002
	(0.023)	(0.026)
Percent Change Percent Latino	0.007	−0.019*
	(0.007)	(0.010)
Percent Change HH Median Income (2000$)	−0.024	−0.037
	(0.025)	(0.038)
Percent Adult Unemployment Rate 2016	−0.325*	0.132
	(0.194)	(0.239)
Violent Crime Rate 2014	−0.001	−0.001
	(0.001)	(0.002)
Divided State Government	0.986**	1.294***
	(0.383)	(0.451)
State Legislative Competition Index	0.012	−0.003
	(0.010)	(0.012)
Legislative Professionalism	2.853**	1.247
	(1.187)	(0.985)
Constant	−2.550	−0.969
	(2.833)	(4.725)
Observations	50	50
Log Likelihood	−81.587	−50.177
θ	4.764 (3.521)	8.625 (11.367)
Akaike Inf. Crit.	187.175	124.354
Pseudo R^2	0.108	0.297

Note: *p<0.1; **p<0.05; ***p<0.01

prosanctuary model, though the coefficient is negative. This means that a state's Latino growth correlates with a lower count of prosanctuary bill introductions, though not with the introduction of anti-sanctuary legislation. Both findings correspond to previous racial threat research, confirming our general expectations regarding the role of both the size and growth of the Latino population on the introduction of pro/anti-sanctuary legislation.

Furthermore, we can assess the relative influence of our racial threat variables against all other covariates' influence with an examination of

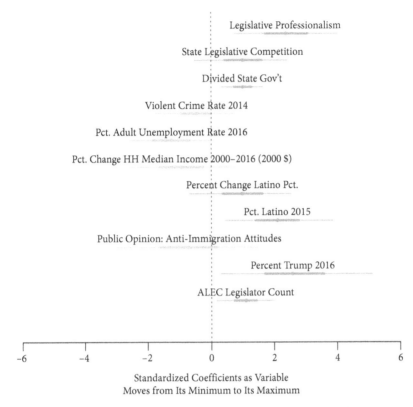

Figure 4.5 Standardized predictors of anti-sanctuary city bill introductions within U.S. state legislatures, 2017.

simulated standardized predictors in Figures 4.5 and 4.6. Each point represents a standardized effect on the number of anti-sanctuary bills introduced in a state based on simulating a change from the independent variable's minimum to maximum then taking the difference in predicted number of introduced bills between the two (minimum, maximum) expected outcomes. The dashed lines include confidence intervals for 95 percent (thick) and 99 percent (thin). Points to the right of the dotted line at 0 indicate a positive effect on the likelihood of introducing a bill proposal. However, if the confidence band crosses the center line, we cannot say with absolute certainty that the effect is statistically significant at either the 95 or 99 percent confident level.

Our measure of Latino size rivals several other state institution and ideology variables in terms of relative impact on predicting anti-sanctuary legislation. Indeed, the standardized effect is about 2. That is, as we move from states with

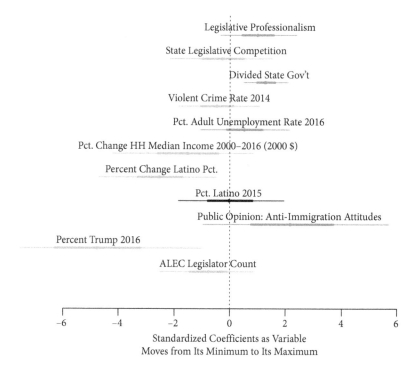

Figure 4.6 Standardized predictors of prosanctuary city bill introductions within U.S. state legislatures, 2017.

the smallest share of Latino population to the largest share, we can expect to observe two anti-sanctuary bill introductions in 2017.

For predictors of prosanctuary legislation, only Percent Trump has greater relative influence than does Latino growth. That is, as we move from states with little Latino growth since 2000 to states with high observed Latino growth in 2015, we can expect to observe two fewer prosanctuary bill introductions. Thus, these findings present strong evidence for the hypothesis that racial threat plays a significant role in driving the introduction of anti-sanctuary legislation in 2017 and reduces the likelihood that prosanctuary bills will be introduced. The fact that these rival other explanatory variables in terms of influence highlights the racialized nature of the sanctuary debate and mirrors our findings in chapter 3, where the size and growth of the local Latino population both reduced public support for sanctuary policies.

Our second category of hypotheses investigate measures of state citizen and legislator ideology. Our measures include Percent Trump and a numerical count of ALEC state membership in both models. If our hypotheses are correct, the presidential vote variable will statistically and positively associate with the introduction of anti-sanctuary legislation but negatively correlate with the introduction of prosanctuary legislation. In addition, ALEC membership will take on a positive coefficient in column 1 of Table 4.1 and a negative coefficient in column 2.

The findings in both the table and the rope-ladder figures broadly support each of these hypotheses. States where Trump did well are much more likely to instigate anti-sanctuary legislation. Specifically, as we move from states where Trump did the worst to states where he did the best, we can expect to observe more than two anti-sanctuary bill introductions. The converse is especially the case with respect to the introduction of prosanctuary legislation. Specifically, moving from states where Trump did poorly (but where Clinton did well) to where he did well (but Clinton did poorly), we can expect to observe more than four fewer prosanctuary proposals.

Finally, ALEC membership rivals other variables in terms of its predictive power of anti-sanctuary legislation. As we move from states with few ALEC legislators to states with the most, we can expect to observe at least one additional anti-sanctuary bill introduced into a state's legislature. At the same time, states with large shares of ALEC members are no more or less likely to introduce prosanctuary bills.

The third set of hypotheses inquire into the influence of several components of state institutions, including divided government, legislative competition (simplified Ranney index), and state legislative professionalism. First, we hypothesized that states with divided government are essentially more competitive in the moment and so should see both more pro- and anti-sanctuary legislation as legislators (and presumably executives) jockey for the support of different constituencies to either shore up their base, push an ostensibly advantageous wedge issue, or reach out to growing constituencies. The tables and figures both provide strong empirical support for this hypothesis. Specifically, as we move from states without divided government to states with divided government, we should expect to see about 1 anti-sanctuary bill introduced and 1.2 prosanctuary bills introduced.

However, we find no statistically significant evidence that the Ranney index—a more intricate measure of state competition—influences the introduction of sanctuary legislation, once we control for divided government. We also theorized that legislative professionalism should lead to an overall increase in legislative activity; however, the results only partially support this hypothesis. Professionalized states are statistically more likely to introduce anti-sanctuary bills. Specifically, we can expect to observe more than two anti-sanctuary bills introduced when we move from states with no professionalized legislature to states with highly professionalized legislatures. However, this variable has no statistically significant impact on the introduction of prosanctuary bills. Greater resources thus translate into more anti-sanctuary activity on the part of legislators, but not more prosanctuary activity.

If concerns about crime on the part of legislators is what drives the introduction of pro/anti-sanctuary legislation, then states with higher crime rates should be more likely to propose anti-sanctuary legislation. Table 4.1, column 1, reveals that the violent crime rate 2014 measure is statistically insignificant thereby invalidating the idea that legislators are responding to crime in their communities in introducing anti-sanctuary legislation. Furthermore, Figure 4.5 shows the variable is—if anything—negatively related to the introduction of anti-sanctuary legislation. While no firm conclusions can be drawn with this finding, we would be remiss to note the irony that legislators whose bills often connect sanctuary cities with crime are not themselves living in states that actually do have a crime problem, at least relative to other states. These findings are broadly consistent with our public opinion results observed in chapter 3.

Finally, we find no evidence for either economic anxiety hypotheses. Specifically, we tested the argument that states that got richer from 2000 to 2015 should be less likely to introduce anti-sanctuary legislation and more likely to introduce prosanctuary legislation. The coefficient on this variable for both anti- and prosanctuary models is negative but not statistically significant. Furthermore, as a state's unemployment rate rises, that state is actually less likely to introduce anti-sanctuary legislation (which is the opposite of an economic anxiety prediction). Finally, our economic anxiety measures are statistically unrelated to the introduction of prosanctuary laws.

Despite how often concerns about crime or the economic burden posed by undocumented immigrants is referenced in pushing to eliminate sanctuary policies, neither crime rates, the median income of the state, nor the unemployment rate affect the likelihood of sanctuary legislation being introduced.

ALEC Case Study

Our state-level regression results reveal a central role for legislators affiliated with the American Legislative Exchange Council (ALEC), even after accounting for presidential election results. Founded in 1973 around principals of federalism, free markets, and limited government, ALEC is a venue where legislators can work with private entities and the organizations' corporate sponsors to craft model legislation in a public-private process. This model legislation can then be introduced directly or serve as a template for legislator's own bills (Anderson and Donchik, 2016; Jackman, 2013).

ALEC claims that its members represent more than 60 million Americans, and their membership includes 20 percent of Congress, eight governors, 25 percent of state legislators, as well as two hundred corporate and nonprofit members (ALEC, 2016). ALEC-affiliated legislators have introduced bills on immigration, energy and environment, guns and prisons, health and pharmaceuticals, voting rights, tort reform, consumer rights, schools and higher education, and tax and budgets (Hertel-Fernandez, 2014; Jackman, 2013). In immigration, ALEC has been active in drafting anti-immigrant model legislation, with research by National Public Radio (NPR) in 2010 finding that Arizona state senator Russell Pearce, who played a significant role in drafting SB-1070, was an ALEC member (Sullivan, 2010). When Pearce was drafting what would become SB-1070, representatives from the Corrections Corporation of America (CCA, now CoreCivic) were also in the room (Sullivan, 2010). The private prison industry benefits from immigration detention, with Geo Group and CoreCivic both in charge of a network of private immigrant detention facilities around the country.

Our finding that states with more ALEC-affiliated legislators are disproportionately likely to propose anti-sanctuary legislation is worth further examination, considering the role ALEC has played in the push for tough immigration policies at the state level. We buttress our earlier regression analysis with a key case study, specifically by examining ALEC's influence on the diffusion of anti-sanctuary legislation across state legislatures.

As it turns out, ALEC was hacked around 2010, with over eight hundred model bills leaked to the Center for Media and Democracy in 2010–2011. Of these bills, at least one addressed sanctuary cities directly.

On the heels of SB-1070's passage in Arizona, ALEC sponsored model anti-sanctuary legislation beginning in 2010—with a bill called "No Sanctuary Cities for Illegal Immigrants."[17] This shared textual similarities with both SB-1070 and earlier legislation introduced by Russell Pearce, ALEC member and Arizona state senator. To assess ALEC's direct influence over anti-sanctuary legislation diffusion, we compare "No Sanctuary Cities for Illegal Immigrants" against all sanctuary bills introduced in state legislatures between 2010 and 2017. We are particularly interested in how much of ALEC's ideas percolate into the lawmaking process. We employ a plagiarism detection strategy to examine whether text from ALEC's model bill diffuses to bills introduced around the United States after 2010–2011.

We assess bill similarity to ALEC model legislation via plagiarism software that lets us generate a numeric measure of similarity/influence between the ALEC model legislation and all sanctuary-related bills (Burgess et al., 2016; Huang, 2008; Mihalcea et al., 2006; Wilkerson et al., 2015). We use the count of overlapping words as our measure of diffusion, which is basically interchangeable with the percentage overlap between two documents but provides slightly more measurement granularity.[18]

Using the plagiarism software Wcopyfind and the R package RCopyFind (DeMora and Collingwood, 2018), we can see how much text from one document matches exact passages from another document. We generate a similarity measure for each bill in our corpus. The measure is simply a count of the number of overall words that match ALEC's model legislation, where the low number of matches in the search algorithm is eight consecutive words.[19] We prefer this measure to a relative percentage measure because we are interested in the total amount of copied text. For instance, a bill might have one thousand overlapping words of text but could be a part of an omnibus bill, so a relative measure would show this bill has only limited connection to ALEC's model legislation. That said, either measure—total word overlap or percentage overlap—produces nearly identical findings.

Figure 4.7 reports all bills in the corpus (n = 26), scoring over one hundred overlapping words. In other words, each of these bills has segments in them directly lifted from ALEC's model legislation. Bills introduced around the same time as SB-1070 and/or bills from Arizona are obviously the most related to ALEC's model legislation; however, several bills even in 2017 (i.e., in Maine and Mississippi) directly lift passages from ALEC's model legislation.

While the influence of the No Sanctuary for Illegal Immigrants Act diminished somewhat by 2017 in terms of overlapping text, as bill language began to more directly address the issue of sanctuary cities specifically, we still see clear evidence of the lingering influence in text similarity when we compare the ALEC model legislation to all anti-sanctuary bills introduced in 2017. While over 50 percent of all anti-sanctuary-related bills introduced in 2017 are unrelated to the No Sanctuary for Illegal Immigrants Act, about 20 percent of all anti-sanctuary bills have text directly lifted from the ALEC-backed bill. Figure 4.8 presents an ordered dot-plot of bills with at least some matching text in 2017. Overall, these findings corroborate the finding from our regression analysis that ALEC has played a central role in the diffusion of anti-sanctuary legislation around the U.S. states.

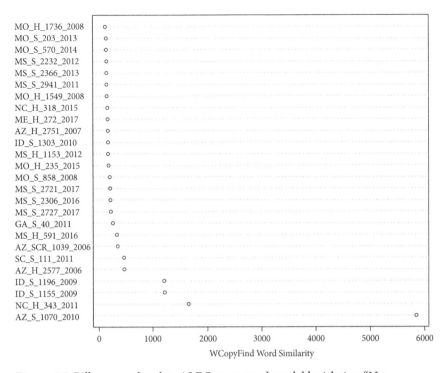

Figure 4.7 Bills most related to ALEC-sponsored model legislation "No Sanctuary of Illegal Immigrants Act."

Conclusion

In this chapter, we investigated the determinants of state-level sanctuary policy-making. We focused primarily on the year 2017 because the number of bill introductions spiked that year. While state legislators had introduced some sanctuary-specific legislation during the preceding decade, 2017 stands alone as a critical year for sanctuary policymaking. This reflects the importance of both the Steinle shooting and the candidacy and presidency of Donald Trump for driving the introduction of state-level sanctuary legislation nationwide. We specifically examined the determinants of pro- and antisanctuary bill proposals in the U.S. states. Was the sudden rise of sanctuary bill proposals a consequence of and response to Trump's victory? If yes, are determinants of the sanctuary policymaking process reflective of what we already know about the contours of the immigration policymaking process?

We found that the contours determining sanctuary bill introductions in the U.S. states are (broadly defined) racial threat (alternatively conceptualized as

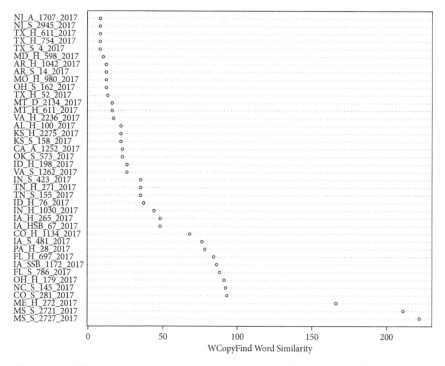

Figure 4.8 Bills most related to ALEC-sponsored model legislation "No Sanctuary of Illegal Immigrants Act," introduced in 2017.

white panic to an increase in minority population), state and voter ideology (i.e., of legislators as well as the mass public), and the structure of state political institutions (i.e., legislative professionalism and structural political competition). We did not find evidence consistent with an interpretation that states introduce sanctuary legislation due to concerns about the economy (i.e., states might be more likely to pass punitive immigration laws during times of economic downturn) or crime. This latter finding is consistent with our public opinion findings surrounding crime. Neither legislators nor the public appear to respond to actual crime threats when introducing legislation or shaping their public attitudes.[20]

Rather, the results of the most recent presidential election were clearly predictive of how states would later respond to the emerging sanctuary city issue. As we demonstrated, very few sanctuary city proposals were introduced before the 2017 legislation. In the 2016 presidential campaign, the Republican candidate strongly criticized sanctuary cities specifically and sanctuary policy more generally, linking these cities to crime, undocumented immigration, and thereby to Latino (and Mexican) cultural threat (López, 2015). Given the candidate's electoral success, it comes as little surprise that legislators in pro-Trump states would emulate Trump's strategy by waging an attack on these cities and introducing anti-sanctuary legislation. However, our data do not allow us to test whether state representatives introduce legislation because they believe sanctuary policies really enhance crime rates or because they think taking a stance against sanctuary cities is simply good politics.

However, our results make sense when we consider that some Republican and ideologically conservative legislators saw an opportunity to further squeeze an emerging Democratic constituency (Latinos), and signal position-taking to conservative constituencies (Box-Steffensmeier et al., 1997; Highton and Rocca, 2005). Republican legislators across the country—but particularly those in states with relatively large and growing Latino populations (i.e., Texas)—introduced anti-sanctuary legislation. At the same time, some Democratic state legislators came to the defense of sanctuary cities, but primarily those in places where Clinton performed well and where public opinion was more favorable on matters concerning immigration policy (i.e., California). For example, Democrats came to the defense of these cities primarily in Democratic stronghold states with relatively large Latino populations, including California, New Jersey, New York, and Illinois.

These competing dynamics broadly speak to the finding that state partisanship/ideology (both citizen and legislature) plays a central role in determining the sanctuary (and immigration) policymaking process. While this is not especially surprising, it is notable that conservative organizing entities like ALEC provide ready-made legislation and that the count of ALEC members in a state is positively associated with anti-sanctuary proposals. Indeed, ALEC's success at porting model legislation around the U.S. states does not bode well for states that want to protect their undocumented immigrant population via sanctuary laws. That said, ALEC-backed bills are most likely to succeed in GOP-controlled states. While ALEC's model legislation likely makes the task of introducing anti-sanctuary legislation easier, many of these states would probably introduce some version of this legislation anyway considering the current political environment in regard to immigration.

The last thing to note is that the size and growth of the Latino population are extraordinarily important in understanding how conservative white panic leads to anti-sanctuary legislative activity. It is worth underscoring that this trend appears in both legislative activity and in public opinion, as we showed in the preceding chapter. This finding is consistent with research documenting white fragility amid growing minority populations. No doubt, these competing dynamics will only continue into the future, as the United States and its state legislatures continue to diversify. In this sense, sanctuary politics is clearly encapsulated within the broader immigration debate.

5

Sanctuary Cities, Crime, and Incorporation

The preceding chapters have shown that public opinion and legislative activity on sanctuary cities are little affected by actual crime rates, despite the claims made by opponents of sanctuary cities that sanctuary policies lead to increases in crime. The public has developed sanctuary policy attitudes based on partisanship and "racial threat," rather than on objective contextual crime rate measures. Similarly, sanctuary city legislative activity at the state level is also clearly linked to state partisanship, as well as the size and growth of the Latino population. These findings indicate that actual crime plays little role in formulating the basis of public opinion or legislative activity.

However, the crime connection remains perhaps the primary narrative promoted by those who oppose sanctuary policies in the post-1980s period. What should we make of this claim, and of the counterclaim by proponents that sanctuary policy actually facilitates a more democratic and responsive government? Are sanctuary policies associated with more crime or are opposition responses to sanctuary policy based more on the anecdotal occurrence of crimes committed by immigrants that are then highlighted by the media? While anecdotal incidents of crime might generate media coverage, to understand policy impact and to be able to make generalizable claims about a policy (i.e., "sanctuary cities cause crime"), we must look at rates of change and trends around key sanctuary moments.

This chapter explores whether sanctuary policies as a general rule produce negative and/or positive outcomes for residents living in sanctuary localities. By negative outcomes, we specifically investigate whether cities that become sanctuaries subsequently see an increase in their crime rate. Does a change from no sanctuary policy to a sanctuary policy somehow increase crime within a jurisdiction? Additionally, we examine data on crime outcomes in counties that recently underwent an ICE-detainer policy change. For both analyses, we focus on violent crime.

We also examine 911-call data in the city of El Paso, Texas, before and after the passage of SB-4, a law that banned sanctuary cities within the state. El Paso is on the Texas-Mexico border and has a large foreign-born and Latino population. Specifically, we investigate what happens to 911-call behavior in disproportionately high foreign-born and noncitizen parts of the city in response to statewide restrictive immigration policy and the signaling that the passage of these policies entails.

By positive outcomes, we examine whether cities that implement sanctuary policy subsequently experience Latino incorporation as a result of sanctuary policy. Specifically, we focus on changes in Latino turnout and Latino police force representation. Thus, in this chapter we implicitly evaluate a sanctuary spillover effect. That is, we argue and show that the benefits of sanctuary policy extend beyond the undocumented population, which is disproportionately Latino, into the citizen population.

To foreshadow our results, we find that sanctuary policies have no statistically significant generalizable effect on violent crime, contrary to what certain politicians and elected officials continue to argue. These results are actually unsurprising, given extant research that demonstrates undocumented immigrants tend to commit less crime than do the native born (Lee et al., 2001; Lyons et al., 2013; Ousey and Kubrin, 2009; Wadsworth, 2010; Wong, 2017a). We show that several counties that decline ICE detainer requests, if anything, experience a drop in violent crime rates although our results produce generally mixed findings. And we estimate that the causal effect of SB-4 enactment in Texas led to twenty-two fewer 911 calls in parts of El Paso, Texas, with a large foreign-born noncitizen population.

We also demonstrate that sanctuary policies have incorporating benefits. To our knowledge, this is the first empirical demonstration of such findings. We show that registered Latinos residing in a city that subsequently becomes a sanctuary are more likely to turn out to vote in later elections. Additionally, our results indicate that a city's police force becomes more Latino upon passage of a sanctuary policy.

First, in this chapter we critique the supposed (and made-up) link between criminality and immigration (Gonzalez O'Brien, 2018). Second, we place sanctuary cities into contemporary political context and lay out the claims as to whether sanctuary policy is "good" or "bad" policy for the residents of a city or county. We next present our hypotheses, data/methods, and results for the crime analysis (which we call negative outcomes). We then proceed to our analysis of ICE detainers and the effect that declining these requests has on counties. We then turn to a case study of 911 calls in El Paso and the effect that the passage of Texas's SB-4 had on call volume. We close this chapter with our hypotheses, data/methods, and results for political incorporation in sanctuary localities, which we call *positive outcomes*.

The Myth of Immigrant Criminality and Sanctuary Policy

The idea that sanctuary policies drive up crime rates is premised to a large extent on the notion that undocumented immigrants tend to offend and break the law at higher rates, an assertion that has been disproven time and again. The logic goes something like this: if people are willing to break the laws to get into a country, they are more prone to criminality in general.

This narrative is fed by a highly negative and stereotypical portrayal of immigrants by the media. Farris and Mohamed (2018) show that the media persistently frame immigrants as undocumented, imply criminality by drawing attention primarily to immigrant arrests and detention, and focus on the border. Given the scholarship reviewed in Chapter 2, there is little doubt that this framing drives many Americans to conflate immigration with crime, and to think of the issue in highly episodic ways.

One of the earliest comprehensive investigations of immigrant criminality dates to a 1931 report by the National Commission on Law Observance and Enforcement—also known as the Wickersham Commission—on crime and the foreign-born. One volume of the report specially examined the relationship between Mexican immigration and crime, something that had helped to drive the criminalization of undocumented Mexican immigration under S. 5094, which attached criminal charges to illegal entry and reentry for the first time (Gonzalez O'Brien, 2018).

The report acknowledged that historically the immigrant-as-criminal narrative was part of the United States since the colonial period, arguing, "The theory that immigration is responsible for crime, that the most recent wave of immigration, whatever the nationality, is less desirable than the old ones, that all newcomers should be regarded with an attitude of suspicion, is a theory almost as old as the colonies planted by Englishmen on the New England coast" (NCLOE, 1931). In regard to Mexican immigration specifically, the commission reviewed data from multiple locations and found that when it came to Mexican immigrants, criminality varied significantly by location. In some cities, Mexicans were arrested and convicted at a higher rate than the native-born population, while in others this was the inverse. The report concludes its section on Mexican immigrants with the following statement: "Is the Mexican really criminally inclined? Without hesitation, the conclusion is that he can not be consigned to such a category any more than any other nationality or race .... While numerous arrests and frequent convictions of Mexicans tend to make it appear that they are inclined to be delinquent, it is quite likely that such things rather point to misfortune, the lack of ingenuity and resources, and, in some instances, perhaps some discrimination against them" (NCLOE, 1931). Ultimately the authors found no support for the foreign-born generally, or Mexicans specifically, being more inclined toward criminality. Indeed, many of the arrests of Mexican immigrants were linked to differences in culture and laws surrounding alcohol, as well as some allusions to the deliberate targeting of Mexicans for arrest by local police—a process documented by Michelle Alexander (2012) and others.

Despite the Wickersham Commission's findings, criminalization has been the default response of the federal government (and both major political parties) to the "problem" of undocumented Latino immigration. In 1929 undocumented entry was formally made a criminal offense, with illegal entry deemed a misdemeanor and reentry after deportation a felony under Senate bill 5094. During debate over the bill, the potential criminality of Mexican immigrants was referenced frequently (Gonzalez O'Brien, 2018). The passage of this bill helped to define how the federal government would respond to undocumented entry in the decades to come by linking the long-standing rhetoric of immigrant criminality, which as the Wickersham Commission acknowledged was as old as the country itself, to the formal legal treatment of the undocumented for the first time (Gonzalez O'Brien, 2018).

The 1996 Illegal Immigrant Reform and Immigrant Responsibility Act (IIRIRA) furthered these linkages by increasing the militarization of the southern border and focusing on crime-control tactics as the primary response to undocumented immigration, which would only be exacerbated on the heels of 9/11. This program of criminalization has helped to turn Latino immigrants into a racialized threat, justifying extreme measures to control them, leading to programs like Donald Trump's proposed border wall with Mexico and family separation (Provine and Doty, 2011). Criminalization has proven to be ineffective at actually reducing undocumented immigration, but like "broken windows" policing it *can* be a popular response. Even when increased militarization does not reduce immigration, its failure can simply be sold as a result of a need for greater enforcement and militarization. If a triple fence isn't working, for instance, build a wall; if deportation is not dissuading people from entering unlawfully, threaten to charge them as criminals and separate them from their children.

While criminalization has largely been the default federal response, studies have found no support for the idea that immigrants are responsible for more crime. Lee et al. (2001) examined homicide rates in three border cities with large immigrant communities and high levels of immigration between 1985 and 1995. Examining 352 neighborhood census tracts in Miami, El Paso, and San Diego, the authors found that the percentage of new immigrants in these tracts had no relationship to homicide rates, with the exception of El Paso, where there was an inverse relationship between the two. Rather than immigration, the only consistent predictor of homicide in the three cities was, unsurprisingly, poverty. In a longitudinal study of homicides in San Diego from 1980 to 2000, Martinez et al. (2010) found that neighborhood homicide rates in San Diego were, as was the case in El Paso, negatively associated with the percentage of foreign-born who were present in the community. In 2010 Tim Wadsworth expanded on these studies by drawing on homicide and robbery data for 459 cities nationwide. A pooled cross-sectional time series model demonstrated that the size of the new immigrant population had an inverse relationship to rates of both robbery and homicide between 1990 and 2000 (Wadsworth, 2010).

Indeed, if anything, undocumented immigrants may actually be more likely to be victims of crime given their vulnerability, rather than perpetrators of crime (Kittrie, 2006). Furthermore, regardless of legal formalities, many undocumented immigrants may fear that turning to local police will result in deportation. Thus, punitive enforcement strategies may actually generate the exact opposite outcome (lawlessness) pursued by supporters of strict crime enforcement. For example, multiple studies indicate that undocumented women are reluctant to call the police in cases of domestic violence due to fear that either they or their partner will be deported (Crenshaw, 1995; Menjivar and Bejarano, 2004; Menjivar and Salcido, 2002). In addition, the immigrant population—especially the undocumented—may experience cultural and language problems interacting with the state, leading some to remain in the shadows as victims (Davis and Erez, 1998). Indeed, research shows that Hispanics are less likely than Anglos, blacks, American Indians, and Asians to report violent crime perpetrated against them (Rennison, 2007).

These studies suggest that immigrants tend to offend at lower rates than the native-born population, which we would expect to apply to the undocumented community as well. Sanctuary policies could help with incorporation, which Lyons et al. (2013) argue could lead to lower crime rates in sanctuary cities. However, the positive benefits associated with greater Latino incorporation could be hidden insofar as crime rate is concerned, as cooperation could lead to a concomitant rise in crime reporting—regardless of actual changes to crime levels.[1] Therefore, in our sanctuary "benefits" analysis, we examine "positive" outcomes such as voting and minority police-force representation.

The literature therefore suggests that an increase in the size of the immigrant population in a city should decrease crime even if incorporation is not assisted by sanctuary policies. Because the presence of immigrants is likely positively related to lower crime rates, one expectation is that unless sanctuary cities draw in a larger number of immigrants, there would be no relationship between sanctuary policies and crime. However, we do evaluate inmigration in both sanctuary and non-sanctuary cities in our data and do not find a significant difference of people moving into sanctuary cities more so than people moving into non-sanctuary cities.

Since sanctuary policies do not seem to increase the number of immigrants in a city, the logical deduction is that such policies should have little effect on crime rates. Research to date suggests that this is the case. Lyons et al. found that crime rates in neighborhoods in cities designated as sanctuaries were actually lower than in non-sanctuary cities when they looked at eighty-nine cities nationally with a population of more than one hundred thousand. Similarly, Wong (2017a) found that sanctuary counties were associated with positive socio-economic outcomes and lower crime rates.

Both of these findings suggest that sanctuary cities may actually reduce crime rates, or at the very least not lead to the increases their opponents claim they do on the heels of tragedies like the Kathryn Steinle shooting. Here, we put this debate to a rigorous test using causal inference matching techniques and cities as the unit of analysis (as opposed to neighborhoods or counties), since cities bear the political brunt of the charge. We then follow up our city-level analysis with two additional, largely confirmatory analyses of counties and ICE-detainer policies, and 911 calls following on the heels of the enactment of Texas's SB-4 anti-sanctuary law.

Potential Negative Outcomes

The claim that sanctuary cities are disproportionately associated with crime is important to investigate because much of the push to undo sanctuary policy rests on this connection between sanctuary policy and crime. If sanctuary policy is systematically related to a rise in crime, then critics' claim may have merit and thus banning sanctuary policy should be considered a viable policy solution based on scientific evidence. However, despite the claim that sanctuary policy "breeds" crime, the majority of scientific evidence to date suggests that, if anything, sanctuary policy might reduce crime rates.

That said, to walk through the logical pathways in which sanctuary cities might be associated with increases in crime, we could consider that sanctuary cities might attract undocumented immigrants after policy enactment. Especially with high-profile local enactments, word may get out that a certain city is safer for those without papers. If this is in fact the case, however, we would actually anticipate a drop in violent crime and homicide because immigrants tend to commit less crime than the foreign-born.

Second, some sanctuary policies are premised on the idea that the policy will lead to greater cooperation with the police and incorporation of the existing undocumented population. The latter is expected to decrease crime as a result of greater opportunities, as Lyons et al. found in their 2013 study. However, any potential decrease in crime may also be counterbalanced by an increase in crime reporting precisely because of increased cooperation, which is often cited as one reason to enact sanctuary policies.

However, it is possible—as President Trump has claimed—that sanctuary cities by virtue of their unique status raise crime rates. This claim rests on two possibilities. First, this argument might be true if undocumented immigrants do commit more crime relative to the native-born and then move into sanctuary cities postpassage. This premise, though, is not rooted in existing available evidence, which, as noted above, strongly suggests that the foreign-born have lower crime rates. Second, to date, there does not appear to be a significant difference in in-migration into sanctuary cities relative to similarly situated non-sanctuary cities (Gonzalez O'Brien et al., 2017). We might see more crime as a result of sanctuary policy if undocumented residents already living in a city begin to commit more crime or report more crime because they feel more secure. Again, the former premise holds little weight as the vast majority of research on foreign-born crime indicates that the foreign-born commit less crime than the native-born or that no difference exists (Miles and Cox, 2014). But, given the design and motivation of most sanctuary policies, it is possible that greater cooperation between city officials and undocumented immigrants could emerge. This could lead to an increase in crime reporting, not necessarily an increase in crime per se. However, this possible link has not been tested or established in the literature. Thus, the claim as to whether sanctuary cities/policy are associated with variation in crime needs assessment.

In the analysis that follows, we isolate the effects of sanctuary policy itself by employing a statistical technique known as matching. This technique allows us to control for a city's Latino population size as well as a city's Latino noncitizen population size (i.e., those most likely to be undocumented immigrants). This procedure also makes possible a comparison between similarly situated cities on the aforementioned variables, and other relevant factors that might distinguish cities that choose to pass sanctuary ordinances from cities that do not period.

Employing a matching statistical strategy is important due to the possibility of selection bias. More specifically, cities that choose to become sanctuaries may be systematically different from those cities that do not. And these systematic differences—not the sanctuary policy—might be driving observed differences in crime between the two types of cities.

Thus, in this analysis, sanctuary cities—on average—will not have more undocumented immigrants in them compared to their matched city, so the above logic that cities with larger shares of undocumented residents should experience lower crime rates is not applicable. Instead, we demonstrate there is no net effect on crime as an outcome from a sanctuary city policy. The next section then evaluates sanctuary cities' myriad positive benefits.

Sanctuary City Crime Analysis

To begin, we first empirically evaluate whether sanctuary cities reveal higher crime rates, lower crime rates, or no discernible difference between the two city types. Specifically, based on a review of the literature, we think that sanctuary cities—as policy—do not have higher crime rates than they otherwise would had they not issued a sanctuary policy. Compared to other similarly situated cities, we find it unlikely that sanctuary cities will have more crime. However, again, in comparison to similarly situated cities, we doubt that enough undocumented immigrants move to cities, because of that city's sanctuary status, thereby reducing the crime rate. Many costs are associated with moving (Amundsen, 1985; Carrington et al., 1996), and it is unclear whether undocumented immigrants or the public more generally are broadly aware of the sanctuary status of any given city.[2] We therefore hypothesize that sanctuary policies will not be related to either an increase or decrease in local crime rates.

To evaluate the above hypothesis, we collected data on all sanctuary cities in the United States, relevant census data, and crime data from the Federal Bureau of Investigation (FBI). Our list of sanctuary cities is taken from a list generated by the National Immigration Law Center (NILC). All sanctuary cities in the study passed sanctuary laws after or during 2002 and before 2015. We time-bound our analysis for a variety of reasons: first, 9/11 changed the tenor and nature of immigration-related politics, as we showed in chapter 1. The tone and tenor of sanctuary policies in the post-9/11 political environment shifted from one that emphasized the plight of refugees to open resistance to the immigration policies of the George W. Bush administration. Cities that became sanctuary cities prior to 9/11 were often responding to different crises (e.g., those in Central America) and received far less publicity and negative attention than did cities post-9/11, as we discussed in chapter 2.

Second, Immigration and Customs Enforcement (ICE) was created as part of the Department of Homeland Security shortly after 9/11 and has generally been much more aggressive in enforcement via workplace and neighborhood raids than its precursor, Immigration and Naturalization Services (INS). The effect of sanctuary policy may have differed under the INS, and thus we confine our analysis to those cities whose policies were specifically created in reaction to ICE immigration tactics in the post-9/11 period.

The first analysis is a simple difference of means t-test at the individual sanctuary-city level. The question here concerns whether, on average, cities that pass sanctuary policies demonstrate higher crime rates in the year immediately following passage or not. Taking crime data from all fifty-five cities in our dataset that passed sanctuary city laws post-9/11, we compare crime rate in the year following implementation of a sanctuary policy to the crime rate in the year preceding the implementation of a sanctuary policy. This is simply a first cut to assess the claim that sanctuary policies lead to crime; if they do, then we should see a statistically significant crime increase after policy passage.

The second analysis employs a matching causal inference strategy to test the claim that sanctuary cities are associated with more crime than are non-sanctuary cities. This approach lets us control for—and thereby rule out—a variety of confounding factors that might lead to the making of a sanctuary city in the first place. Because we want to know the effects of a sanctuary-city-as-policy we want to compare similarly situated cities (treatment = sanctuary; control = non-sanctuary) where everything is the same across the cities prior to the enactment of the sanctuary policy. Differences between the treatment and control in crime rates following the enactment can then be attributed to the policy—as opposed to economic conditions or other characteristics that might explain a city's crime rate.

This approach is sensible because sanctuary cities—on their face—are quite distinct from non-sanctuary cities, which are most cities. According to Table 6 in Appendix C, sanctuary cities are larger, less white, more racially and ethnically diverse, have lower median incomes, have higher levels of poverty, have larger foreign-born populations, and are more Democratic than are non-sanctuary cities. Specifically, the Latino population (year 2000) in our pool of sanctuary cities was 17.3 percent, whereas in non-sanctuary cities it was 14.08 percent. Among the foreign-born population in sanctuary cities,

40.08 percent were from Latin America, whereas in non-sanctuary cities this percentage was 35.36 percent. Thus, a simple comparison of sanctuary cities to non-sanctuary cities is unbalanced, and so a comparison between the two entities without taking into account possible confounders might lead to a conclusion about crime rates that is about the city, not the policy.

Because we look at a variety of data by year (across time), the total number of sanctuary cities varies depending on the availability of crime data from the FBI. On an independent basis, city police departments provide the FBI with annual crime reports for most or all categories of crime. Therefore, due to incomplete, missing, or inaccurate data, matching analysis of crime between sanctuary and non-sanctuary cities was conducted on an annual basis by crime type in order to maximize the amount of observations per year. Only those cities that had crime data listed before and after passing sanctuary-city legislation were used for our analysis in each year, in order to accurately test the before-and-after effects of sanctuary legislation.

Given the aforementioned restrictions, analysis of crime data was maximized between forty-eight and fifty-five sanctuary city observations annually. In total, we matched the sanctuary cities against roughly four thousand non-sanctuary cities across twenty states and the District of Columbia. Figure 5.1 maps out the geographic location of the sanctuary cities that we analyze. The geographical distribution of cities reveals that most are clustered in specific regions, including the Northeast to Mid-Atlantic corridor, around the Great Lakes, and along the West Coast, which largely mirrors the distribution of sanctuary sites at the height of the Sanctuary Movement. However, there are also a few sanctuary cities in the Southwest and in Alaska.

In total, sanctuary cities (in our data) exist in just twenty states. For our crime data match, we therefore gather data on all other cities in these twenty states and the District of Columbia so that we can compare cities in similarly situated locations. We use the genetic matching algorithm from the MatchIt package as specified in Ho et al. (2007). This algorithm matches treatment to control using a series of propensity scores and weights to find the most similar control city to the treatment city.[3]

With our list of cities and key variables outlined, we built up the dataset with relevant census data. Because we are interested in examining all cities after 2002, we use data from the 2000 census as our baseline comparison. The variables included in the match are total population,[4] percent white, percent black, percent Asian, percent Hispanic, percent unemployed, median household income, percent poverty, percent college degree (twenty-five-years-old-plus), percent foreign-born, percent foreign-born not citizen, percent foreign-

Sanctuary Cities Analyzed

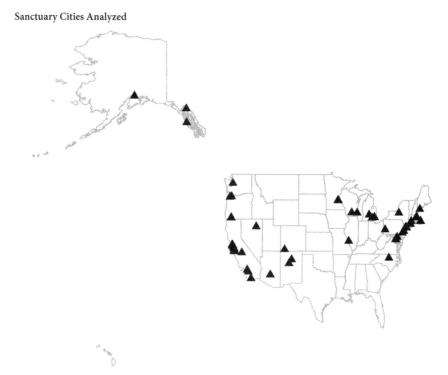

Figure 5.1 The geographical distribution of sanctuary cities in our dataset reveals that most cities are clustered in specific regions, including the Northeast to Mid-Atlantic corridor, around the Great Lakes, and along the West Coast.

born from Latin America, percent Latina/o noncitizen, and percent new city residents (mobility). Race/ethnicity is important to account for in the match because racial characteristics may influence cities to implement sanctuary policies. Likewise, economic indicators such as median household income, unemployment, and poverty are all important control variables (Cantor and Land, 1985). Finally, a measure of ideology (percent Gore 2000) is included to guard against the possibility that more Democratic cities may be more prone to passing sanctuary laws. The appendix includes our coding procedure for the aforementioned variables.[5]

Violent crime rate is our outcome variable of interest; we gathered violent crime rate data between the years of 2000 and 2013. These data are gathered by year so that we can assess whether there is any change in crime over time, possibly because the effects of a sanctuary policy may be delayed. In addition, sanctuary cities come into being at different points in time across our spectrum of analysis. Again, the motivation behind gathering these data is that they are statistics that opponents of sanctuary cities purport to be caused by sanctuary policies.

Beginning with our pre-post city-level analysis, recall that our hypothesis is that there are no systematic differences on crime rates following the passage of a sanctuary policy within a city. If we are correct, we will observe two possible sets of outcomes: (1) there will be no change whatsoever at the city level; or (2) there will be some change after sanctuary implementation, but some cities will experience higher crime, other cities lower crime. Figure 5.2 plots each city's change in violent crime rate following adoption of a city sanctuary policy.[6] For clarity and by example, if a city passed a sanctuary ordinance in 2006, our measure subtracts that city's crime rate in 2005 from that city's crime rate in 2007. Dots that are to the right of 0 show increases in crime, whereas dots to the left of 0 show decreases in crime following implementation of a sanctuary policy.

Figure 5.2 clearly reveals that some cities experience mild increases in violent crime, whereas other cities experience drops in crime in the years following the passage of a sanctuary ordinance or the implementation of a sanctuary policy. It is important to note that the results for a single city experiencing increases or decreases in crime pre/post sanctuary implementation is not evidence that that crime change is a result of the policy change. Assessing single cities, without including confounders, is anecdotal and tells us little about the actual effects of a broad policy. Overall, there is no clear generalizable pattern (some cities experience more crime, whereas others less crime)—but what is clear is that the individual city-level plots are supportive of our hypothesis that sanctuary policy as a general rule does not lead to more crime. If sanctuary policies did truly "breed crime," then we should see higher crime rates in a far larger number of cities than we do.

To buttress these findings, we conducted a difference of means t-test where one group is all city crime rates before sanctuary implementation, and the other group is all city crime rates after implementation. This test is designed to assess whether crime rates change, as a rule, after sanctuary implementation. The results of the t-test show that for violent crime (t-stat $= -0.133$, p-value $= 0.894$) there is no statistical difference across the two groups. Indeed, the mean difference for violent crime is nearly 0.

We begin our second analysis with an examination of crime data by year. Recall that, in contradistinction to public claims that sanctuary cities cause crime to increase, our hypotheses suggest no such effects. If we are correct, then there will be no statistically significant evidence that sanctuary cities look dif-

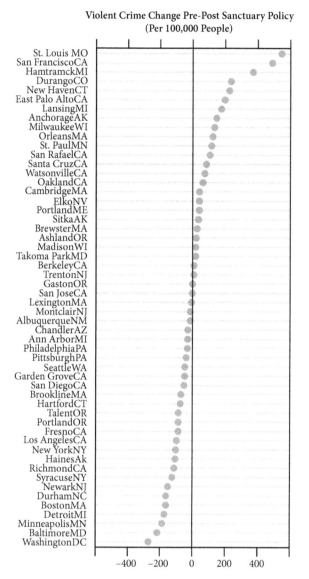

Violent Crime Change Pre-Post Sanctuary Policy
(Per 100,000 People)

Figure 5.2 City-level violent crime pre/post passage of post-9/11 sanctuary policy. Dots indicate an annual decrease (left of 0) or increase (right of 0) in crime rates post-passage sanctuary policy enforcement.

ferent than non-sanctuary cities in crime-related statistics after the sanctuary policy has been implemented. Based on previous research and existing data, we believe undocumented immigrants are less likely to commit crime because they do not want to be deported. Thus, to the extent that sanctuary cities may

Sanctuary Cities

Figure 5.3 The geographical distribution of sanctuary cities with indication as to the change in rate of violent crime (per city) after passing sanctuary city legislation.

draw in more undocumented immigrants precisely because of their sanctuary policies, if anything, crime rates should drop.

However, we doubt such movement occurs, as the process of intercity moving can be taxing, and people tend to follow jobs as the primary motivator for moving (however, we do control for mobility). In addition, as we noted earlier, we find no difference in noncitizen Latino immigration rates between matched sanctuary and nonsanctuary cities, providing evidence that sanctuary cities in and of themselves do not attract undocumented immigrants.

We conduct difference of means t-tests discretely for each year between 2000 and 2014 to assess whether average crime rates exist between our matched treatment (sanctuary) and control (non-sanctuary) groups. In each year, we find no statistically significant difference in crime rates across the two groups.

However, while the match is designed to alleviate differences between treatment cities on variables that may induce sanctuary status, the postmatch balance table (in the appendix) showed that our two treatment groups are not perfectly balanced. This is one slight limitation of matching—that is, the matching procedure and balancing process are never perfect, and there are possibly unobservable differences between our treatment and nontreatment cities. Following Ho et al. (2007), we conduct multivariate regression analyses postmatch for each year analyzed. Theoretically, multivariate regression will hold constant any unbalanced variables emerging from the match, letting us get an even more accurate test of our hypotheses. Therefore, we also conducted a regression analysis of our matched data where our dependent variable is crime rate. Table 5.1 in the appendix confirms our expectations for year 2012. As with our t-test analyses, we do not find a statistically significant coefficient for our treatment variable (sanctuary city). Thus, with each test, we observe the same pattern: no statistically significant differences on crime rates between sanctuary and non-sanctuary cities.

ICE Detainers and Crime

In the debate surrounding sanctuary policy, the media often conflates sanctuary cities and counties. While there are some important distinctions between the two geographical units in how they interact with the federal government in terms of sanctuary politics, in the broad scope of our analysis, counties can be thought of as sanctuaries when they choose to decline ICE detainer requests and put a policy on the books. An *immigration detainer* is an ICE-issued request to a law enforcement agency (LEA) that ICE plans to take over custody of an individual presently under LEA protection. With any detainer request comes background information about the individual's criminal record. Under very harsh immigration regimes, ICE would detain, then deport any undocumented immigrant, whereas under more welcoming regimes, ICE might aim to detain and deport only undocumented immigrants with violent criminal records.

After 9/11, ICE began working closely with county jails across the country to hold people suspected of being undocumented immigrants beyond their release date. Arrangements between the federal government and local governments brought cash benefits for counties. However, over time, some counties implemented policies to break with ICE to no longer honor detainer requests, except in the case of certain, often violent crimes. Many observers consider these counties de facto sanctuaries, including both ICE and various anti-immigrant organizations because the counties are refusing to cooperate with federal requests to hold undocumented immigrants in jail past their release date.

Table 5.1 Regression analysis post-match, modeling violent crime for year 2012.

	Crime Type Violent
Sanctuary (Treatment)	89.909
	(54.809)
Population Size	−0.00005
	(0.00003)
Percent White	−18.984***
	(2.943)
Percent Black	−11.151***
	(3.189)
Percent Asian	−8.573
	(7.538)
Percent Hispanic	−10.593**
	(4.474)
Percent Unemployed	−44.123***
	(14.922)
Median Income	−0.001
	(0.004)
Poverty (Over 18)	27.660**
	(10.891)
BA or Greater (25+)	−3.206
	(3.692)
Percent Foreign-Born	−15.989
	(14.094)
Percent Foreign-Born w/o Citizenship	−2.309
	(22.433)
Percent Foreign-Born Latin American	2.364
	(1.995)
Latino Not Citizen	−1.235
	(11.893)
Mobility	−16.287***
	(5.046)
Gore Vote (2000)	3.688
	(3.128)
Percent Male 15–19	61.505*
	(32.800)
Percent Male 20–24	−32.965
	(20.593)
Percent Male 25–29	38.817
	(35.862)
Percent Male 30–34	34.145
	(43.098)
Constant	1,809.181***
	(567.625)
Observations	110
R^2	0.775
Adjusted R^2	0.725
Residual Std. Error (df = 89)	259.575
F Statistic (df = 20; 89)	15.368***

Note: *$p<0.1$; **$p<0.05$; ***$p<0.01$

Through a variety of FOIA requests conducted by media organizations and county-level datasets, we secured monthly crime data from five counties that changed immigration policy vis-à-vis ICE somewhere between 2009 and 2017. These data include counts for *part 1 crimes* (overall and violent), which include murder, rape, robbery, aggravated assault, larceny, arson, and burglary.[7] Thus, in our analysis, crime occurrence is our dependent variable. Depending on data availability, we discretely analyze part 1 crime and part 1–violent crime.

All five counties reported a change in ICE-detainer policy during this time. To assess the effects of these detainer policy changes on crime reporting, we employ a statistical estimation strategy known as interrupted time series analysis. Essentially this analysis targets a point in time (i.e., day, month, year) as an interruption that might then effect changes in observed outcomes (in this case, crime).

A dummy indicator for the date of the county's ICE detainer policy change becomes our interrupting variable ($\beta_2 X_t$, below). Before the policy was enacted, the variable takes on a value of 0, whereas once the policy is enacted, the variable scores a 1. In the model, the variable's coefficient estimates the immediate effect of the policy change, although because the time series is monthly as opposed to daily, we can be less certain that change in crime is attributable to the policy shift as opposed to some other confounder, or that any one county's results are generalizable to other counties.

The interrupted time series design calls for a running "time elapsed" variable ($\beta_1 T$), which takes on the value $1:n$, where n = length of the time series. This variable's coefficient can be interpreted as the series' trend before the interruption. Finally, we interact the interrupting variable with the time-elapsed measure, which we call "Interruption X Time" ($\beta_3 TX_t$). This variable's coefficient represents the slope effect of one unit change in time on crime occurrence *after* the interruption. In other words, while there might be an initial interruption effect, this variable will let us tell if the effect of the interruption attenuates or enhances over time and how rapidly.

Finally, we include fixed effects for month to control for seasonal variation in crime. For instance, it might be that more crime happens in the summer months when the weather may be more amenable to criminal activity (McDowall et al., 2012). We estimate the following specified model with a linear form. We include ARIMA models in the appendix (Tables C.5 and C.6).[8] The results are substantively similar.

$$Y_t = \beta_0 + \beta_1 T + \beta_2 X_t + \beta_3 TX_t \qquad (5.1)$$

With these data, we can begin to assess whether counties that formally change their relationships with ICE—specifically in regards to detainer requests—also experience shifts in crime rates following these changes. The counties examined include four in California: Santa Clara, Los Angeles, Alameda, and San Diego; and one New York county: Queens. In October 2011 Santa Clara County passed an ordinance to facilitate working with ICE in which the jail system would hold someone up to twenty-four hours after they would normally have released an individual. However, these individuals had to have been convicted of a serious felony for which they are currently in custody, or had been convicted in the previous ten years. This policy change is actually a pro-ICE move because the county now could theoretically hold people longer than they would have otherwise.

In July 2014 Los Angeles County's sheriff imposed a policy to "require a judicial determination of probable cause or a warrant from a judicial officer [in order to hold someone]." In November 2014 Queens County (NY) passed a local law stating the county would no longer honor ICE detainer requests. In May 2014 both Alameda and San Diego Counties' sheriffs enacted policies stating their offices would no longer honor ICE detainers unless warranted by a judge. These policies all made the release of undocumented immigrants back into the community more likely to occur. If anti-sanctuary proponents' claims are correct, then at the very least we would expect to see crime rates increase in these counties immediately after the counties stopped granting ICE detainer requests.

Did any of these changes to ICE detainer policy correlate with changes in crime within the counties? If yes, did that change persist or eventually regress toward the mean? And if yes, is there a clear pattern in that working with ICE associates with increases or decreases in crime, or vice versa? Mixed results would be suggestive of no generalizable trend and thus call into question anti-sanctuary proponents' claims that sanctuary policy causes crime.

While this design does not let us infer causality, as with our match or difference in difference analyses, we can test various hypotheses about whether changes in detainer policy are associated with changes in crime/crime rate. If sanctuary opponents' claims that sanctuary policy leads to increases in crime are true, then we should expect to see Santa Clara crime drop immediately following the sanctuary policy intervention (negative $\beta_2 X_t$ coefficient), then continuing to drop after the intervention (negative $\beta_3 TX_t$ coefficient). Likewise we would expect to see Los Angeles, Queens, San Diego, and Alameda Counties' crime rising immediately after the policy change (positive $\beta_2 X_t$ coefficient), then continuing to rise afterward (positive $\beta_3 TX_t$ coefficient).

Table 5.2 presents our main results. We also include all models with lagged dependent variables in Table 5.3, to adjust for possible autocorrelation not captured in the initial model (this is further addressed with our ARIMA models). As noted, the key coefficients to pay attention to are labeled "Post Interruption" and "Interruption X Time." The former measures the immediate time relationship between ICE detainer policy and crime. A negative and statistically significant coefficient indicates the county policy shift is associated with an immediate drop in crime, whereas a positive coefficient is indicative of an immediate rise in crime. The later coefficient measures the trend post-interruption.

The first two columns in Table 5.2 present results for Santa Clara County—the one county that shifted policy in an ostensibly more "pro-ICE" direction, in the sense that the county now would turn over immigrant felons to ICE. The interruption coefficient is negative but not statistically significant, whereas the "Interruption X Time" coefficient is positive. This suggests, if anything, Santa Clara County's immigrant detainer policy shift is associated with a rise in crime. In Los Angeles County, we observe a pattern that again is inconsistent with anti-sanctuary proponents' arguments. The policy shift interruption is initially associated with a drop in crime, although the "Interruption X Time" covariate is positive, suggesting that over time, crime rates move back to whence they came.

In Queens County, New York, we see the opposite pattern from Los Angeles, with the results suggesting that crime initially increased but then dropped back down again. No statistically reliable findings emerge for violent crime in Queens. In Alameda County, for both part 1 crime and part 1 violent crime, the interruption is associated with an initial drop in crime, but again a positive interaction term suggesting that gradually crime rose back toward the series' initial levels before the interruption, finding that are more or less replicated in San Diego County. These inconsistent findings are also more or less replicated in the lagged models below and the ARIMA models found in Appendix C.

Overall, these findings suggest that across the five counties analyzed, no clear pattern emerges. These findings do not support anti-sanctuary proponents' arguments that sanctuary policy (here, in the form of limiting interaction with ICE detainer requests) leads to crime. Rather, these results are more consistent with the findings presented in Figure 5.2, which shows that crime increased in some cities after they became sanctuaries whereas crime decreased in other cities after those cities implemented sanctuary ordinances. The most likely conclusion from these findings is that shifts in county ICE detainer policy has broadly little influence on crime within the county.

Table 5.2 Interrupted time series models. Outcome variable = Crime; Independent variable = Change in ICE detainer policy. Santa Clara, Los Angeles, Queens, Alameda, and San Diego Counties.

	Dependent variable:								
	Santa Clara Crime (1)	Sana Clara Violent (2)	Los Angeles Crime (3)	Queens Crime (4)	Queens Violent (5)	Alameda Crime (6)	Alameda Violent (7)	San Diego Crime (8)	San Diego Violent (9)
Post Interruption	-41.144	-13.533	-1,398.084***	129.504*	-7.318	-52.805*	-33.516***	-970.589**	-188.522***
	(39.932)	(11.057)	(236.558)	(74.660)	(36.309)	(27.395)	(8.140)	(408.837)	(54.037)
Time Elapsed	-4.101***	-0.429**	-17.826***	-6.299***	-2.930***	-1.308***	-0.312**	-2.948	-0.384
	(0.753)	(0.208)	(3.792)	(1.369)	(0.666)	(0.439)	(0.130)	(6.554)	(0.866)
Interruption X Time	3.460***	0.499*	41.109***	-4.208**	0.632	1.235*	0.650***	7.299	2.579**
	(1.039)	(0.288)	(5.380)	(1.981)	(0.964)	(0.623)	(0.185)	(9.297)	(1.229)
February	-44.463*	-10.654	-913.229***	-244.576***	-103.449***	-40.144**	-1.179	-721.868***	-79.239**
	(23.380)	(6.474)	(139.281)	(44.611)	(21.695)	(16.130)	(4.792)	(240.716)	(31.816)
March	-9.092	0.192	-536.125***	-103.551**	-34.099	-14.454	5.808	-447.903*	13.188
	(23.397)	(6.479)	(139.366)	(44.646)	(21.712)	(16.140)	(4.795)	(240.862)	(31.835)
April	-3.888	-6.795	-507.521***	-88.560**	-32.862	-20.764	-0.871	-419.771*	13.949
	(23.427)	(6.487)	(139.507)	(42.860)	(20.844)	(16.156)	(4.800)	(241.107)	(31.868)
May	20.150	-4.782	-191.583	108.010**	59.585***	-2.880	4.013	-285.067	53.894*
	(23.468)	(6.498)	(139.705)	(42.879)	(20.853)	(15.570)	(4.626)	(232.361)	(30.712)
June	-7.479	-2.770	-427.145***	70.247	49.032**	21.338	7.921	-314.755	40.508
	(23.520)	(6.513)	(139.959)	(42.921)	(20.873)	(16.286)	(4.839)	(243.051)	(32.125)
July	10.392	0.410	-219.786	234.189***	106.172***	11.694	9.409*	-23.790	92.935***
	(23.585)	(6.531)	(134.650)	(44.749)	(21.762)	(16.244)	(4.826)	(242.421)	(32.041)
August	2.325	-1.110	-354.855**	245.371***	102.049***	-4.116	8.730*	-30.159	94.196***
	(24.706)	(6.841)	(139.959)	(44.766)	(21.771)	(16.208)	(4.816)	(241.886)	(31.971)

(continued)

Table 5.2 Continued

					Dependent variable:				
	Santa Clara Crime (1)	Sana Clara Violent (2)	Los Angeles Crime (3)	Queens Crime (4)	Queens Violent (5)	Alameda Crime (6)	Alameda Violent (7)	San Diego Crime (8)	San Diego Violent (9)
September	−12.958	−12.680*	−545.584***	151.754***	52.926**	−15.426	8.217*	−345.527	41.957
	(24.770)	(6.859)	(139.705)	(44.806)	(21.790)	(16.179)	(4.807)	(241.448)	(31.913)
October	4.857	0.659	−265.979*	294.737***	54.603**	−14.736	6.204	−102.729	42.051
	(24.605)	(6.813)	(139.507)	(44.867)	(21.820)	(16.156)	(4.800)	(241.107)	(31.868)
November	−0.118	−11.611*	−576.542***	93.120**	8.080	−14.380	3.525	−539.930**	−43.355
	(24.600)	(6.812)	(139.366)	(44.952)	(21.861)	(16.140)	(4.795)	(240.862)	(31.835)
December	−40.893	−7.882	−113.938	183.976***	16.849	1.310	1.346	122.535	24.073
	(24.607)	(6.814)	(139.281)	(44.611)	(21.695)	(16.130)	(4.792)	(240.716)	(31.816)
Constant	411.758***	41.666***	6,672.082***	2,112.026***	703.362***	299.020***	52.921***	6,789.575***	933.387***
	(20.607)	(5.706)	(125.218)	(40.091)	(19.497)	(14.773)	(4.389)	(220.466)	(29.139)
Observations	67	67	73	63	63	73	73	73	73
R^2	0.456	0.258	0.719	0.932	0.859	0.504	0.448	0.555	0.579
Adjusted R^2	0.309	0.058	0.652	0.912	0.818	0.385	0.315	0.448	0.477
Residual Std. Error	40.485 (df = 52)	11.210 (df = 52)	241.193 (df = 58)	70.518 (df = 48)	34.294 (df = 48)	27.932 (df = 58)	8.299 (df = 58)	416.847 (df = 58)	55.096 (df = 58)
F Statistic	3.111*** (df = 14; 52)	1.291 (df = 14; 52)	10.619*** (df = 14; 58)	47.142*** (df = 14; 48)	20.952*** (df = 14; 48)	4.217*** (df = 14; 58)	3.369*** (df = 14; 58)	5.176*** (df = 14; 58)	5.690*** (df = 14; 58)

Note: *p<0.1; **p<0.05; ***p<0.01

Table 5.3 Interrupted time series models. Outcome variable = Crime; Independent variable = Change in ICE detainer policy. Santa Clara, Los Angeles, Queens, Alameda, and San Diego Counties. Includes lagged dependent variable.

	Dependent variable:								
	Santa Clara Crime (1)	Sana Clara Violent (2)	Los Angeles Crime (3)	Queens Crime (4)	Queens Violent (5)	Alameda Crime (6)	Alameda Violent (7)	San Diego Crime (8)	San Diego Violent (9)
Post Interruption	−46.977 (41.462)	−17.941 (11.156)	−552.687* (289.538)	100.092 (68.861)	−6.002 (36.853)	−31.333 (26.952)	−30.968*** (9.379)	−499.972 (371.255)	−161.770*** (57.601)
Time Elapsed	−4.577*** (0.972)	−0.578** (0.222)	−9.040** (4.112)	−3.579** (1.566)	−2.402*** (0.834)	−0.986** (0.458)	−0.271* (0.145)	−7.222 (5.922)	−0.809 (0.891)
Interruption X Time	3.879*** (1.189)	0.663** (0.298)	18.176** (7.276)	−2.489 (1.895)	0.496 (0.996)	0.850 (0.617)	0.589*** (0.209)	7.816 (8.137)	2.553** (1.251)
February	−35.190 (25.394)	−10.362 (6.797)	−971.448*** (123.988)	−146.243*** (49.881)	−100.723*** (22.000)	−39.529** (15.163)	−1.099 (4.860)	−655.004*** (207.229)	−74.405** (31.292)
March	−6.144 (24.773)	−2.032 (6.717)	−116.378 (157.939)	125.201 (78.647)	−14.485 (28.050)	1.217 (16.040)	5.957 (4.871)	−5.005 (229.773)	33.327 (33.949)
April	3.971 (25.125)	−6.410 (6.796)	−283.368** (134.201)	72.875 (61.111)	−25.305 (23.125)	−14.520 (15.322)	−1.211 (4.901)	−114.546 (218.009)	16.813 (31.220)
May	28.674 (25.259)	−6.039 (6.709)	18.895 (133.135)	253.899*** (58.145)	67.729*** (22.231)	9.144 (15.472)	3.553 (4.881)	105.895 (217.407)	69.196** (31.263)
June	4.361 (26.117)	−3.523 (6.726)	−380.332*** (124.344)	112.925*** (41.087)	42.026* (21.955)	20.384 (15.319)	7.623 (4.963)	−197.652 (210.974)	31.052 (31.893)
July	18.277 (25.210)	0.160 (6.757)	−43.340 (130.467)	271.461*** (42.235)	101.026*** (22.416)	3.483 (15.498)	9.031* (4.970)	179.866 (213.995)	88.219*** (31.445)
August	12.537 (26.741)	−0.828 (7.080)	−342.160*** (123.906)	219.509*** (41.470)	87.403*** (25.557)	−8.614 (15.304)	8.239 (4.998)	27.055 (208.340)	79.797** (32.568)

(continued)

Table 5.3 Continued

	Dependent variable:								
	Santa Clara Crime (1)	Sana Clara Violent (2)	Los Angeles Crime (3)	Queens Crime (4)	Queens Violent (5)	Alameda Crime (6)	Alameda Violent (7)	San Diego Crime (8)	San Diego Violent (9)
September	-3.732	-12.507*	-424.850***	120.790***	38.919	-13.917	7.761	-281.374	27.584
	(26.554)	(7.076)	(126.872)	(41.814)	(25.279)	(15.222)	(4.970)	(208.025)	(32.554)
October	10.181	-2.131	-44.428	314.160***	48.593**	-8.893	5.771	127.763	37.858
	(25.906)	(7.036)	(134.024)	(41.259)	(22.634)	(15.322)	(4.950)	(213.968)	(31.276)
November	9.709	-11.061	-499.688***	37.654	1.760	-8.666	3.217	-431.034**	-47.299
	(26.567)	(7.086)	(124.633)	(44.110)	(22.738)	(15.298)	(4.902)	(208.432)	(31.243)
December	-31.826	-10.238	126.287	230.616***	18.735	7.018	1.209	460.618**	36.602
	(26.393)	(7.003)	(135.578)	(42.899)	(21.928)	(15.285)	(4.865)	(220.770)	(32.350)
Part 1 Lagged DV	-0.141		0.522***	0.529***		0.372***		0.516***	
	(0.137)		(0.123)	(0.156)		(0.125)		(0.118)	
Violent Lagged DV		-0.238*			0.164		0.068		0.190
		(0.137)			(0.146)		(0.133)		(0.130)
Constant	459.269***	52.297***	3,252.088***	903.116**	584.341***	190.443***	48.769***	3,343.276***	762.580***
	(56.859)	(8.006)	(813.440)	(359.306)	(107.854)	(39.896)	(8.526)	(826.497)	(127.573)
Observations	66	66	72	62	62	72	72	72	72
R²	0.440	0.305	0.786	0.946	0.863	0.574	0.440	0.683	0.610
Adjusted R²	0.271	0.097	0.728	0.929	0.818	0.461	0.290	0.598	0.506
Residual Std. Error	40.771	11.041	213.389	64.226	34.560	26.255	8.410	357.939	53.912
	(df = 50)	(df = 50)	(df = 56)	(df = 46)	(df = 46)	(df = 56)	(df = 56)	(df = 56)	(df = 56)
F Statistic	2.615***	1.465	13.698***	53.813***	19.300***	5.041***	2.933***	8.038***	5.849***
	(df = 15; 50)	(df = 15; 50)	(df = 15; 56)	(df = 15; 46)	(df = 15; 46)	(df = 15; 56)	(df = 15; 56)	(df = 15; 56)	(df = 15; 56)

Note: * $p<0.1$; ** $p<0.05$; *** $p<0.01$

To be sure, the interrupted time series design does not let us make causal inferences about whether detainer policy caused a drop in violent crime. The analysis simply lets us test—and rule out—a hypothesis promoted by anti-sanctuary proponents. At least with these data available to us, we find little evidence that not honoring ICE detainers is associated with increases in violent crime. This squares with work conducted by Wong (2017a). The next section, however, employs a design that better lets us test precise behavioral outcomes as a response to the rollout of anti-sanctuary policy.

Senate Bill 4 and 911 Calls in El Paso, Texas

On May 7, 2017, Texas governor Greg Abbott signed Senate Bill 4 (SB-4), a sweeping law that banned sanctuary cities across the state, which we discussed in chapter 3. Perhaps no state received as much media attention in 2017 for its anti–sanctuary city stance than did Texas. The Texas GOP staunchly opposes sanctuary policies and has taken an increasingly tough stance on immigration, emphasizing enforcement, deportation, and greater border security. Many observers have suggested that these policy moves have led to an overall chilling environment for undocumented residents in particular but for Latinos more generally.

SB-4 bans sanctuary policies in the state and attaches criminal penalties to noncooperation with ICE by local officials. SB-4 also allows local police to inquire into immigration status, which some have argued could lead to racial profiling. In this way, SB-4 fits the "show me your papers" laws that were enacted in several states following Arizona's infamous SB-1070. SB-4's purpose is to take decision-making related to law enforcement away from local government entities. Given that much of Texas's undocumented population resides in large Democratic cities like El Paso, Houston, San Antonio, McAllen, and even Austin, many observers and scholars have argued that this law is not only worse for the targeted communities but actually worse for public safety as a whole.

In fitting with previous discussion in earlier chapters, the argument on the other side is that sanctuary policies aim to create trust between undocumented residents and local government. This is particularly relevant in the context of law enforcement, where police rely upon witnesses to testify in court, people to call 911 when they experience or see a crime, or call the fire department when a house is burning down. It is worrisome at best and extremely detrimental to civil society at worst if enacted laws reduce residents' willingness to interact with their local government or even call 911—regardless of an individual's immigration or citizenship status. One can easily imagine a scenario where someone commits a crime, no one calls 911 because of fear the caller or a family member might be deported, and then the criminal commits another crime.

However, despite growing scholarship showing attitudinal and reported health outcomes in response to punitive immigration legislation, so far, little actual behavioral evidence has been brought to bear on whether punitive immigration laws actually produce deleterious behavioral and community effects. We test the specific case of SB-4's causal effect on 911-call behavior among residents living in El Paso, Texas. Specifically, we hypothesize that SB-4's original enactment on May 7, 2017, caused residents living in disproportionately high-foreign-born/undocumented areas to reduce their likelihood of calling 911 in the days immediately following the law's enactment. We provide strong evidence in support of our central hypothesis.

Data and Methods—SB-4 and Behavioral Outcomes
We gathered individual-level 911-call records from the city of El Paso, from January 1, 2016, until August 28, 2018. Each call comes with address as a matter of public record. We then geocoded these data to extract latitude and longitude coordinates. We overlaid each record with an El Paso census tract shapefile to pinpoint each call's census tract. We next merged in relevant tract-level characteristics from the 2015 American Community Survey five-year estimates, notably percent Hispanic, percent foreign-born, and percent non-citizen. We then split the 911-call data by above and below percent non-citizen, and conduct two discrete analyses. We aggregate all 911 calls to the day; thus our unit of analysis is the day. Our expectation is that we will observe a greater reduction in calls in areas above the mean percent non-citizen than in areas below (i.e., places that have fewer non-citizen).

We employ a regression discontinuity in time (RDiT) design to causally assess the effect of SB-4 on 911-call behavior in both of our time series. The model takes on the following form:

$$Calls_i = \gamma_m + \rho_w + \tau SB4_i + \beta_1 d_i + \beta_2 SB4_i \times d_i + Calls_{i-1} + \varepsilon_i \qquad (5.2)$$

where $Calls_i$ = #911 Calls in a Day (the outcome variable); $d_i = days$ (the forcing variable); and $SB4_i$ = treatment. To mitigate the effects of temporal autocorrelation, we incorporate a dependent variable lagged term. Finally, we include fixed effects for month (γ_m) and day of the week (ρ_w) to control for the possibility that people might make more 911 calls on Friday, for instance.

Analysis

Figure 5.4 presents our main findings. Each panel plots the regression slope with error bands on either side of the discontinuity. The left panel comes from 911 calls among residents in census tracts below the median percent non-citizen, whereas the right panel presents results from residents in census tracts above the median percent non-citizen. The left panel reports overlapping confidence bands on either side of the cut-point. While the area appears to have witnessed a reduction in 911 calls on account of SB-4 enactment, the results are not statistically significant. This is not the case for the right panel, where a clear statistically significant reduction in 911 calls is shown. We estimate that the enactment reduced 911 calls by twenty-two.

The Regression Discontinuity Design (RDD) framework is a technique that allows analysts to infer causality between treatment and outcome variables even though the data are observational. The RDD analysis conceptualizes observational data into a treatment (i.e., post SB-4 enactment) and control (i.e., prior to SB-4 enactment) framework. That is, the design conceptualizes observational data in an experimental framework. But in order to make the leap

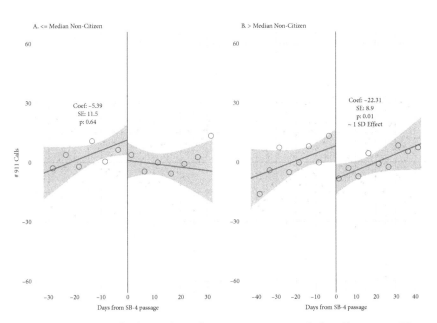

Figure 5.4 Estimated effects of SB-4's enactment on 911 daily call count in El Paso, Texas.

from observational to quasi-experimental it is essential to conduct a variety of robustness checks. These include optimal bandwidth selection (Calonico et al., 2015), anticipatory effects, evaluating the possibility of discontinuous 911-call jumps at the cut-point, whether the outcome is a function of other unrelated features of that day (i.e., weather), and statistical randomness. All of these tests ensure the identification of our causal strategy and let us assume a control/treatment arrangement.

However, to examine scope conditions, we also gathered 911-call data from Tucson, Arizona, with the anticipation that we should not see a drop in 911 calls as a result of SB-4 enactment. Tucson is in a different state, and so individuals there are less likely to pay attention to Texas politics, or if they do, they know they are unaffected by SB-4 within their own state. Therefore, we should not anticipate SB-4 to influence 911-call behavior in the manner that we observed in El Paso. Figure 5.5 presents these placebo results, which show no 911-call behavior change as a function of SB-4 enactment.

Thus, our results in this section provide causal evidence that implementing anti-sanctuary policies likely produces the exact opposite result as anticipated (fighting crime). If the policy is designed to combat crime, then policies that lead to decreases in 911 calls are hardly the way to combat criminal activity. Still, much research needs to be completed before we can conclude

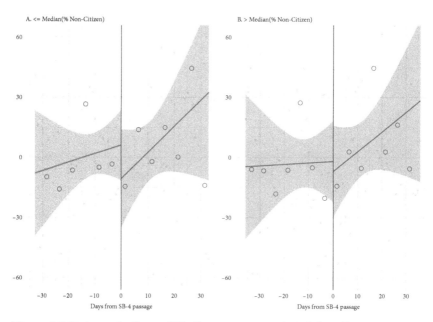

Figure 5.5 Estimated effects of SB-4's enactment on 911 daily call count in Tucson, Arizona.

with absolute certainty that punitive immigration laws ostensibly designed to combat crime actually empower the opposite outcome. In this case, future research needs to more fully engage the particular types of calls that drop as a result of anti-sanctuary laws to more precisely assess how noncitizen communities are affected.

Positive Outcomes

The chapter thus far has examined and debunked claims about sanctuary cities' association with crime. Missing from the discussion is an empirical investigation of possible upsides to sanctuary policies. If little evidence can be produced that shows sanctuary policies tend to produce positive outcomes, then why bother passing such ordinances in the first place other than as a mere symbolic gesture?

As we discussed earlier in the book, cities pass sanctuary policies with the hope that local residents—particularly undocumented immigrant residents—become more trusting of and willing to work with the police and other city personnel. The argument is that once undocumented immigrants become more trusting, they are more likely to report crimes in their neighborhood so that the city overall becomes safer. In other words, sanctuary policies are implemented with the goal of enhancing public safety and increasing the political incorporation of affected communities.

This section assesses whether positive (incorporating) outcomes emerge as a result of sanctuary implementation. Specifically, we examine whether sanctuary cities achieve some sort of incorporation for communities directly affected by sanctuary policy by looking at Latino political participation and Latino police force representation. We select these two issues for two reasons. First, if sanctuary policy is incorporating we might anticipate a sanctuary spillover effect among Latino voters—voters most directly affected by changes in sanctuary policy. This is because Latinos are disproportionately likely to know people who are undocumented or live in a mixed-status household. A city that changes its policy to be clearly welcoming to the undocumented population might stimulate enhanced trust with the broader Latino community, thereby increasing engagement in public affairs, including voter participation.

Second, minority representation on the police force is important to establishing trust with residents living in high-density minority communities. Just as Latino voters are more likely to vote when canvassers are bilingual and

Latino (Michelson, 2003; Ramírez, 2013), Latino police force representation might be important to facilitating trust in local government broadly speaking.

We hypothesize that, in general, sanctuary policy should promote a greater political incorporation of Latinos (and not just foreign-born undocumented Latinos) both in the voting booth (increased political participation) and in governmental representation (police). Our analyses—presented below—support these hypotheses. We find two positive outcomes to sanctuary policy: (1) cities that become sanctuary cities experience higher Latino turnout in subsequent elections; (2) cities that become sanctuary cities increase Latino police-force representation. The next section reviews the data and methods employed to support these claims. We then present our results.

Data and Methods

First, to investigate whether sanctuary policy contributes to the political incorporation of Latinos, we gathered voter files containing every single Latino registered voter in the United States as of June 2012. This file contains individual records for voter turnout in the 2006 general election, the 2008 general election, and the 2010 general election. In addition, like all voter files, the data include geolocation information, notably city and state.

We then aggregate turnout to the city level, summing up the total number of Latino voters by city for each year. We then added an indicator variable for whether the city became a sanctuary between 2006 and 2010. This indicator variable is now thought of as our treatment. We then stacked the data such that each city appears in the data twice. This technique controls for invariant city-level characteristics because we compare cities against themselves over a relatively short time span.

To assess whether cities that became sanctuaries during our treatment time period influenced Latino voter turnout, we estimate a difference in difference regression model where our outcome measure is voter turnout at the city level, and our treatment variable is a dummy measuring whether the city became a sanctuary city during the specified time frame. We include a time variable ($0 = 2006$, $1 = 2010$), then interact time and treatment in our specification. The coefficient on this product term can be interpreted as the average causal treatment effect on Latino voter turnout attributed to the change in sanctuary status. A positive coefficient indicates that sanctuary policy increases political incorporation, whereas a negative coefficient reveals the converse.

The second source of data we analyze comes from the Justice Bureau's Law Enforcement Management and Administrative Statistics (LEMAS) survey. Every few years, this survey collects data from all law enforcement agencies across the country in cities and localities with populations greater than one hundred thousand. The survey asks agencies to report a variety of statistics, including a count of total officers and their race/ethnicity. Thus, our outcome measure is the percentage of the police force in each city that is Hispanic relative to the percentage of the city that is Hispanic. Increasing Latino representation on the police force is seen as incorporating because Latinos—on average—may be better equipped than non-Latinos to address various concerns in the Latino community and immigrant community writ large.

We compiled the data from the 2000 and 2012 LEMAS surveys. Any city that became a sanctuary during this time is conceptualized as treated. Like our voter turnout analysis, we estimate a difference in difference regression model where we interact time and treatment to estimate the causal effect of sanctuary city status on Latino police force representation. If our hypothesis that sanctuary cities are politically incorporating is correct, we should observe a positive and statistically significant coefficient on our interaction term.

Analysis

Table C.7 in Appendix C reveals our difference in difference Latino voter turnout estimates. The main numbers to examine can be found in the Treatment X Time row. The coefficient is 0.03 (p = .10), which indicates that Latinos living in cities that became sanctuaries between the 2006–2010 elections were 3 percentage points more likely to vote in 2010 than they would have been had those cities not become sanctuaries. These findings present initial evidence that sanctuary policy can produce an incorporating effect—here in the form of enhanced voter turnout.

To better visualize these effects, Figure 5.6 plots Latino turnout in different contexts, based off the numbers from Table C.7. Points on the left side of the x-axis show 2006 turnout rates for Latino voters living in cities that later became sanctuary cities (open square) versus cities that had no status change (open circle). Latinos living in cities that did not change status had higher baseline turnout rates to the tune of 5.6 percentage points. However, by 2010, this difference dropped to 2.7 percentage points. The key comparison, though, is the 2010 sanctuary voter turnout (black line) versus the counterfactual turnout sketched by the dotted gray line. This is what the

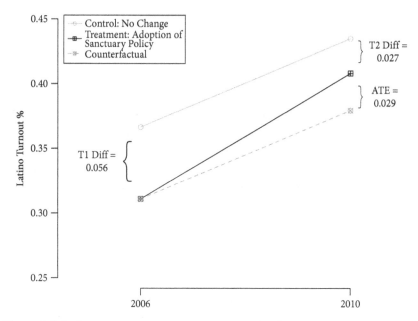

Figure 5.6 Latino voter turnout increase as a result of sanctuary city status change.

expected Latino turnout would have been in these cities that became sanctuaries had they not done so. In comparing these two points in 2010, we thus estimate the sanctuary treatment effect on Latino turnout at 2.9 percentage points.

Our second analysis produces somewhat similar results. Before we turn to our difference in difference analysis for Latino police force representation, first we conduct a placebo test of sorts. Since the majority of undocumented immigrants in most U.S. cities are Latino,[9] we might expect changes to sanctuary status to have disproportionate incorporating effects upon Latinos but not other racial minorities. To assess this, we examined the simple change in sanctuary city police force representation by race from 2000 to 2010 using a difference of means t-test.

Cities that became sanctuaries during this time improved their Latino police force representation nearly 5 percentage points (Mean = 4.77, t = 3.43, $p < 0.001$). However, this representation does not extend to other minority populations, with black (t = .65, $p > .10$) and Asian (t = 1.28, $p > .10$) police force representation not changing between 2000 and 2010 in sanctuary cities. Thus, right off the bat, we observe that sanctuary policies disproportionately affect members of the group most directly tied to the policy.

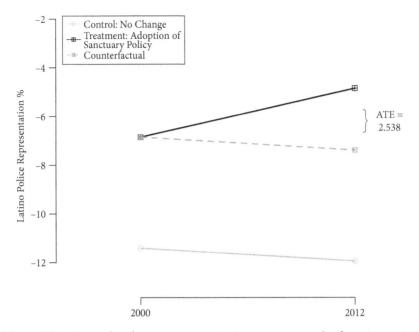

Figure 5.7 Latino police force representation increase as a result of sanctuary city status change.

Turning to our more robust analysis, Table C.8 in Appendix C reports regression results estimating the effect of sanctuary status on Hispanic police force representation. The Treatment X Time row estimates the causal relationship between sanctuary status and Latino police force representation. The results suggest that sanctuary status increases Latino police force representation by 2.54 percent. So, for every 100 officers, sanctuary cities are estimated to have an additional 2.5 Latino police officers than they would have had they not become sanctuary cities.

As with the voter turnout analysis, we also plot out the coefficients based on Table C.8's analysis, presented in Figure 5.7. Beginning on the left side of the x-axis, cities that did not become sanctuaries between 2000 and 2012 had Latino police forces more underrepresented relative to cities that later became sanctuaries. By 2012, however, the gap in Hispanic police force representation had grown by an estimated additional 2.5 percentage points. Taken together, our analyses of both voting and policing suggests that sanctuary policy produces effects in ways that promote the incorporation of the Latino population.

Conclusion

This chapter began by investigating the claim put forth by some political candidates, commentators, and elected officials that sanctuary cities and by implication sanctuary policy lead to higher crime. This argument is often brazenly made by political elites and believed by many people in the mass public. However, this claim is premised on at least two logical fallacies.

First, even if sanctuary cities had higher crime rates than did non-sanctuary cities, the crime rate disparity could be due to other features of cities that eventually become sanctuaries. In other words, the sanctuary policy does not come first in the chicken-and-egg causal pathway. The sanctuary policy could occur precisely to address a city's problems with crime. If this were the case, the claim that sanctuary cities cause crime is based on an observed correlation, not on a causal relationship, leading to fallacious reasoning.

Second, the mechanism people often assert to explain why sanctuary cities cause more crime is that foreign-born undocumented immigrants come to a sanctuary city and know they can get away with crime, thereby increasing crime rates. However, this specified theoretical process flies in the face of study after study showing that foreign-born residents tend to commit less crime.

Nevertheless, we compiled data on sanctuary cities and investigated this claim in two ways: (1) difference of means on crime rate pre/post city passage, and (2) difference of means and regression analyses on crime rate on a matched sample of sanctuary and non-sanctuary cities. In every single test we posed in this chapter, we found no discernible difference in crime rates between sanctuary and non-sanctuary cities.

We also investigated the relationship between county change in ICE detainer policy and crime outcomes in Los Angeles County, Santa Clara County, San Diego County, and Alameda County, California, and Queens County, New York. We found no consistent pattern demonstrating that counties that shift to pro- or anti-ICE positions are more or less likely to experience increases or decreases in crime.

In our final examination of the possible downsides to sanctuary policy, we inverted the analysis by examining what happens to 911 calls from high percent non-citizen areas immediately following a major anti-sanctuary policy enactment. We found strong evidence that Texas's SB-4—a punitive anti-sanctuary city measure—reduced 911 calls primarily from areas of El Paso with concentrations of non-citizens.

The latter part of the chapter examined the possible incorporating benefits of sanctuary cities. Our results indicate that sanctuary policy can increase both Latino voter turnout and Latino police force representation. Specifically, cities that became sanctuaries during our data endpoints (i.e., 2006–2010; 2000–2012) reported greater levels of incorporation than they would have, had they not become sanctuaries.

Our findings suggest that sanctuary policies themselves do not affect crime rates, which contradicts the primary narrative for their repeal, and instead are broadly beneficial for democracy and political incorporation. The positive benefits of sanctuary policy—that is, immigrant incorporation—could disappear based on little more than fear-mongering if Congress does manage to pass a bill like the Enforce the Law for Sanctuary Cities Act, which would have stripped federal funds from sanctuary cities, or more states pass laws like Texas's SB-4. The justification for the Enforce the Law for Sanctuary Cities Act and SB-4 relied heavily on the narrative of criminality despite having no empirical support for claims that sanctuary cities increased crime, and our findings suggest that the reason for this lack of supporting evidence is simply because it does not exist.

Sanctuary cities were initially designed to provide aid to and then incorporate people into American life from war-torn Central American countries, as well as to show solidarity with the Sanctuary Movement. These policies had and have a strong basis in empathy, often with the backing of churches and local aid organizations. Thus, they are designed to assist people in extremely vulnerable positions in the United States in navigating their way to a life that is as safe and healthy as possible. However, in recent years, a few high-profile incidents where undocumented immigrants have committed horrific crimes have led some political candidates—generally on the right—and other actors to make sweeping negative claims about the deleterious effects of sanctuary cities. The argument is that sanctuary cities bring crime: undocumented immigrants, who are by definition criminals, go to these cities to commit their crimes because they know their chances of deportation are much lower. Despite evidence to the contrary (e.g., Lyons et al. (2013) or Wong (2017a)), these voices argue that sanctuary policies lead to more crime and general destabilization.

We found these claims highly dubious on their face, given evidence beginning in the 1930s and continuing until today that immigrant populations tend to produce less crime because these populations are more concerned with deportation and running afoul of the law relative to the native-born population. While other research certainly indicates that relative to other cities, sanctuary policies, on average, produce less crime or no change in crime rates, we felt compelled to reexamine this question taking a different analytical approach. We did this in part because we want to evaluate the sanctuary policy definitively. Given the political saliency of the issue, we found it necessary to assess sanctuary cities using a causal inference method, in this case, matching. This approach lets us isolate the direct effect of a sanctuary policy on a variety of outcome variables while controlling for several confounding variables.

Our findings have clear normative democratic implications. Sanctuary policies in terms of leading to crime do not appear to be a problem. In fact, as we pointed out in our earlier review of the literature, almost all research that assesses links between immigration and criminality find an inverse relationship. The argument advanced by some politicians that immigration—namely "illegal" immigration—is somehow linked to crime in any sort of meaningful way is simply not true. Our findings, in addition to findings from others (e.g., Lyons et al. (2013)), suggest that sanctuary policies do not on their face lead to increase in crime.

6

Sanctuary Cities: The Way Forward

After a brief period of notoriety in the 1980s, which even then was over-shadowed by the Sanctuary Movement, sanctuary cities drifted out of the public eye. While the policies passed remained on the books, there was little conflict over them, and even the Reagan administration seemed content to ignore sanctuary cities and instead try to make an example of members of the movement. Throughout the 1990s, politicians, media, and the public paid little heed to sanctuary localities, but that would change as a result of the events of September 11, 2011.

The 9/11 attacks would lead to an immigration crackdown by the George W. Bush administration in the name of national security, with Secure Communities, Operation Return-to-Sender, and Operation Stonegarden leading to increased deportations post-9/11 by the newly formed Immigration and Customs Enforcement (ICE). In response, however, a number of cities either strengthened existing sanctuary resolutions or passed them for the very first time. These cities did this primarily for two reasons: (1) with the hope that establishing a sanctuary policy would encourage cooperation between immigrant communities and local law enforcement, and (2) to signal opposition to the administration's immigration crackdown. As stories of separated families and the demonization and dehumanization of the undocumented population increased over the 2000s, more and more cities nationwide adopted sanctuary resolutions in protest.

These new resolutions would make sanctuary policies an issue in the 2008 Republican presidential primary, when candidates including Mitt Romney and Fred Thompson attacked former New York mayor Rudy Giuliani for the city's perceived sanctuary status. While this was a nonissue in the 2008 general election it would reemerge in the Republican primaries in 2012, this time with Newt Gingrich and Rick Perry trying to use the issue to show their bona fides on immigration policy. Once again, though, sanctuary policies failed to capture the attention of either the public or media in any significant way.

All of this changed, however, on July 1, 2015, with the shooting of Kathryn Steinle in San Francisco. This incident served as perhaps the most significant focusing issue in the long history of sanctuary policies (McBeth and Lybecker, 2018). Then–Republican presidential candidate Donald Trump seized on the shooting, and San Francisco's sanctuary status, to further his narrative of immigrant criminality and threat.

While Trump's rhetoric was certainly nothing new in the United States (Gonzalez O'Brien, 2018), his willingness to embrace nativism and what some would characterize as racist attitudes toward Mexican immigrants led many analysts and political scientists to discount Trump's chances of winning the GOP nomination, let alone the presidency.

After his inauguration, one of Trump's first acts in office was to sign Executive Order 13768, titled "Enhancing Public Safety in the Interior of the United States," which would have stripped sanctuary localities of federal funds. When this act was deemed unconstitutional, there would be attempts to strip law enforcement grants from sanctuary jurisdictions, which again would be thrown out by the courts as a violation of the precepts of federalism.

What seems likely is that this fight over sanctuary policies will ultimately devolve to the state level. Increasingly, blue states like Oregon and California have passed statewide legislation that mirrors policies that had previously been passed at the city or county level. Some red states, like Texas and more recently Iowa, have banned sanctuary legislation and criminalized any behavior by local officials that tries to limit the sharing of immigration-related information with the federal government.

As this conflict has grown in prominence, media coverage of sanctuary policies has also significantly increased. The post-Steinle period has seen more media coverage of sanctuary policies than any other, and increasingly the narrative of criminality is a central feature of these stories. In addition, state legislatures have moved to introduce both anti- and prosanctuary bills that either seek to ban sanctuary cities or promote policies that protect undocumented communities.

In the 1980s, when the intended beneficiaries of sanctuary policies were a more sympathetic group in being refugees, media coverage emphasized the personal stories of the immigrants. Instead of painting Central American immigrants as threats to the nation, most print media discussed the Sanctuary Movement in terms of the conflict between law and conscience. Many articles went so far as to compare the movement to the Underground Railroad. As the intended beneficiaries of these policies shifted, so did media coverage.

By the 2000s media coverage focused more on crimes committed by undocumented immigrants, with television coverage, Fox News in particular, seizing on these crimes as examples of not only the danger of undocumented immigration but also sanctuary policies. Since 9/11, media coverage has both become more partisan, often featuring a representative of the Democratic or Republican Party, and more likely to emphasize crime over the personal stories of those protected by sanctuary legislation and sanctuary ordinances.

In the period following Steinle's death, media coverage has regularly featured sources that charged that sanctuary cities made America less safe. Often there are lurid descriptions of the alleged deaths of Americans at the hands of undocumented immigrants included in both print and television news, though the latter has leaned more heavily on this approach than the former. Trump has, somewhat unsurprisingly considering his ownership of the issue, also become a regular feature of news stories, making coverage more partisan still.

As a result, the public has increasingly become polarized regarding the issue of sanctuary, with Democrats clearly engaging in what political scientists call *negative partisanship*. In 2015, a majority of both Republicans and Democrats opposed policies barring local law enforcement from working with the federal government to enforce immigration policy. In the period following the Steinle shooting, as the issue became increasingly partisan, Republicans became even more opposed to the issue, and Democrats, taking the "correct" ideological position, shifted to the left in terms of support for sanctuary policies.

As we showed in chapter 3, ideology or partisanship is now one of the most significant predictors of support for sanctuary cities. However, despite narratives about the dangers of sanctuary policies in terms of crime, we find that anti-sanctuary attitudes are not driven by actual crime rates but instead by the size and/or growth of the local Latino population and individual-level concern about immigration and crime. In other words, support for these policies is now both partisan and driven by racial threat.

Racial threat and partisan politics also play significant roles in the introduction of pro- or anti-sanctuary legislation at the state level. We find that the likelihood of anti-sanctuary legislation being introduced is driven by factors that don't differ much from those predicting anti-sanctuary attitudes among the general public. The size or growth of the Latino population made it more likely a state would introduce anti-sanctuary legislation, suggesting they could be responding to the demographics of their state and the white panic that often results from a sizable or growing Latino population. More conservative states, as measured by public or legislator ideology, were also more likely to introduce anti-sanctuary bills. Considering the role that the American Legislative Exchange Council played in the authoring and dissemination of Arizona's SB-1070, it is unsurprising that the ALEC membership within the state legislature also was significant in predicting the introduction of anti-sanctuary legislation.

What we did not find was evidence that states introduce sanctuary legislation due to concerns about the economy or crime. Neither the state's unemployment rate or median income increased the likelihood of introducing sanctuary legislation. Similarly, actual crime rates in the state played little role in the introduction of policies. Legislators thus do not appear to be responding to actual crime threats or economic concerns when introducing legislation.

With the increasing attention to and conflict over sanctuary policies, it is important to consider the costs and benefits of these policies. Do they lead to more crime as opponents argue, or do they have tangible benefits in terms of Latino incorporation, as their proponents assert? Examining the crime rates in cities pre/post–sanctuary status adoption, we found no support for the argument that becoming a city of refuge led to an increase in crime. In some cities, crime did increase after a sanctuary policy was adopted, in others it decreased, and in some there was little tangible change.

The conclusion is that there is no relationship between crime and the passage of sanctuary legislation ordinances, and instead crime rates are driven by predictable factors like poverty. In addition, using a matching program to compare sanctuary and non-sanctuary cities with similar demographics and size, we again found no support that these policies led to a change in crime rates. Matching cities across a host of demographics allowed us to further isolate the effect of policies themselves rather than just looking at individual cities pre/post passage, but again returned a null finding.

We also looked at county-level crime data to examine whether counties that decline ICE detainers had higher crime rates. Again, we found no support for this argument. We thus find no generalizable support for the contention that sanctuary cities or counties "breed crime." Our findings are buttressed by a growing literature in this area, all of which, regardless of the methods used, similarly finds no support that sanctuary localities have higher crime rates (Lyons et al., 2013; Wong, 2017a).

While we found no support that sanctuary policies had the detrimental effects their opponents claim, we did find some evidence that they do have very real benefits. Sanctuary cities had higher levels of Latino voter turnout than did cities that did not pass legislation. In addition to increased voter turnout among Latinos, we also found that those cities that passed sanctuary bills had higher numbers of Latinos as part of their police force. Notably, we did not find a relationship between sanctuary status and police force representation for other minority group, indicating the issue is specific to the racial or ethnic group most directly targeted by the policy.

We also found that anti-sanctuary legislation tended to reduce the number of 911 calls from areas with a large number of noncitizens, though data was limited to El Paso, Texas. Anti-sanctuary legislation thus may have some very detrimental effects on cooperation between immigrant communities and the police in terms of crime reporting, something that proponents of sanctuary policies have long argued. We find it ironic, then, that a bill designed to supposedly fight crime might actually encourage it by reducing the likelihood that people call 911.

The conflict between the federal government and sanctuary localities seems poised to continue, at least for the near term. Cities, counties, and states that have declared themselves as places of refuge have refused to back down despite attempts by the Trump administration to strip them of federal funds and charges that the jurisdictions are responsible for every instance of immigrant-related crime that occurs within their borders.

As the Latino population continues to expand into new states, we can once again expect a mixed reaction from political elites and the body politic. As our results from chapter 4 show, Latino growth is negatively associated with the introduction of pro-sanctuary bills. If this is the "norm" legislative outcome, then prosanctuary interests will need to prepare and facilitate the introduction of legislation for ready legislators in order to prod a defense of such cities.

On the one hand, the GOP seems ready to drive an anti-sanctuary agenda as part of a broad anti-immigrant platform, even if it the strategy does not produce successful election outcomes (so far, the question of issue ownership is up for debate). At the moment, many GOP candidates seek to move to the right of other candidates in primary campaigns as they pursue the votes of conservative primary voters. Even in the liberal majority-minority and plurality-Latino state of California, Republican John Cox campaigned for governor on an anti-sanctuary platform.

On the other hand, Democrats, campaigning in areas of growing Latino political clout, will need to move to the left as a strategy to mobilize their increasingly diverse base. This is exemplified by Philadelphia mayor Jim Kenney, who has provided strong leadership on sanctuary cities. By moving the dial on a policy highly salient to a growing constituency, candidates and elected officials can expand their electoral coalition. All of this is likely to lead to continued polarization in the near term and potentially for the foreseeable future.

While attempts to strip sanctuary cities of funding have thus far been unsuccessful, it remains unclear whether these cases will eventually make their way to the Supreme Court and what the Court will find should the cases get a hearing. What is clear is that, like immigration, gun rights, abortion, and a host of other issues, sanctuary policies have now become part of the polarized cultural conflict in this country.

The clash over sanctuary cities is reflective of a larger problem in the United States with immigration policies that have for decades pushed some people into the shadows, making them "impossible subjects" in the words of Mae Ngai (2004). Mexican immigrants in particular have been regularly demonized and criminalized despite the long-standing reliance of the United States on the labor of these very immigrants (Gonzalez O'Brien, 2018). With the emergence of sanctuary policies as an issue of cultural conflict, these policies are now part of a larger battle in this country over who America should welcome and whether we should embrace the increasing diversity of this nation or try to fight it.

Despite broad empirical support for the fact that immigrants are no more likely to commit crime than the native-born and a growing body of literature, including this book, finding no support for sanctuary policies increasing crime, these accusations of immigrant criminality have never really been about crime or economics. They are, and always have been, about race and culture, and whether we truly are a melting pot or an Anglo-Christian country as some on the right contend. We hope our research here makes this plainly clear: hiding behind arguments of criminality is merely an attempt to masquerade protection of the racial hierarchy (Masuoka and Junn, 2013).

This book, as well as all the other research in the field of race and ethnic politics, has shown that the demonization of nonwhites, immigrants, and the undocumented has always been built on fallacies and white fear – whether we look at media, public opinion, legislation, or policy outcomes. Hopefully, with more nonwhite – especially Latino – politicians entering politics and nonwhite scholars entering academia, we can begin to have a truly balanced debate about immigration and sanctuary, one that doesn't rely on fear or misrepresented findings.

We hope this book makes a positive contribution to that debate.

Appendix A

California Data and Methodology for Hypothesis 1 and 2

For the most part, all question items in the two surveys are asked and coded in the same way. The dependent variable reads:

> Under California law, local jurisdictions like cities and counties can ignore requests from federal authorities to detain illegal immigrants who have been arrested and are about to be released. Do you believe that local authorities should be able to ignore a federal request to hold an illegal immigrant who has been detained? – Yes, local authorities should be able to ignore these federal requests (1); No, local authorities should not be able to ignore these federal requests (0).[1]

We include items on partisanship, racial identification, and a dummy variable for year of survey (1 = 2017 respondent, 0 = 2015 respondent). Party identification is a standard three-item question, which we scaled accordingly: Strong Democrat (1), Somewhat Democrat (2), Weak Democrat (3), Independent (4), Weak Republican (5), Somewhat Republican (6), Strong Republican (7). In both surveys, voters were asked to identify their race, as either Asian/Pacific Islander, black, Latino, Native American/Alaska Native, or white. We crafted dummy variables of these nominal categories, leaving white out of the model as the comparison group. To evaluate the two learning models, we interact party identification X year 2017, and also Latino X year 2017. Because the literature clearly articulates a white identity racial-learning framework, and a Latino identity racial-learning framework—when it comes to the issue of immigration—we focus our analysis among these two groups.

We include control variables available on the survey: gender, education, age, income, race, Catholic identification, as well as dummy variables for splits in each survey. All coding is included below. Finally, because our dependent variable is coded as a binary, we employ logit regression as our statistical technique.

California survey items:

- Dependent Variable 2015: [**Split A gets this plus language in split B**] An illegal immigrant who had been deported several times was recently released from jail in San Francisco and soon after shot and killed a woman walking with her parents near the Bay.

- [**2015: Split B only gets this:**] Under California law, local jurisdictions like cities and counties can ignore requests from federal authorities to detain illegal immigrants who have been arrested and are about to be released. Do you believe that local authorities should be able to ignore a federal request to hold an illegal immigrant who has been detained? 1. Yes, local authorities should be able to ignore these federal requests. 0. No, local authorities should not be able to ignore these federal requests.

- Dependent Variable 2017: [**Split A**] Under California law, local jurisdictions like cities and counties can ignore requests from federal authorities to detain illegal or undocumented immigrants who have been arrested and are about to be released. Do you believe that local authorities should be able to ignore a federal request to hold an illegal immigrant who has been detained? Yes, SHOULD be able to ignore a federal request to hold an illegal or undocumented immigrant who has been detained (1). No, SHOULD NOT be able to ignore a federal request to hold an illegal or undocumented immigrant who has been detained (0).

- **[2017 Split B]** Some communities in California have declared themselves "sanctuary cities" for undocumented immigrants living in the country illegally. This means that when local police or government employees learn that someone is here illegally, they do not automatically turn over that person to federal immigration enforcement officers for possible deportation to their home country. Generally speaking, do you favor or oppose communities in California declaring themselves as sanctuary cities for illegal or undocumented immigrants? Favor strongly (1), Favor somewhat (1), Oppose somewhat (0), Oppose strongly (0).

- Party Identification (1–7, Dem–Rep): Generally speaking, do you usually think of yourself as a Democrat, a Republican, an independent, or what?

- Do you consider yourself closer to the Republican Party or the Democratic Party?

- Would you call yourself a strong Democrat/Republican, or a not very strong Democrat/Republican?

- Race: White is comparison group; Asian/Pacific Islander (1 = yes, 0 = no); Black (1 = yes, 0 = no); Latino (1 = yes, 0 = no); Race other (1 = yes, 0 = no)

- 2017 respondent (1), 2015 respondent (0)

- 2015 Split B version (1), Split A (0)

- 2017 Split B version (1), Split A (0)

- Gender: female (1), male (0)

- Education: Less than HS (1), HS or equivalent (2), Some college (3), Bachelor's degree (4), Advanced degree (5)

- Age: 18–29 (1); 30–39 (2); 40–49 (3); 50–65 (4); 65+ (5)

- Catholic (1 = yes, 0 = no)

Texas Data and Methodology for Hypotheses 1 and 2

Our analytical approach in Texas is similar to our approach in California in the sense that we stack two years together with a dummy indicator year 2017; thus we keep the discussion about data coding to a minimum. The dependent variable, however, is asked differently: "In so-called 'sanctuary cities,' local law enforcement officials do not actively enforce some federal immigration laws. Do you approve (1) or disapprove (0) of city governments that choose not to enforce some immigration laws?"

Again, our main independent variables are party identification (seven-point), racial identification (Latino versus white/Anglo), and survey year (2017). We include controls for gender, education, age, income, and ideology. All coding and question wording appear below. Because our dependent variable is coding as a 0–1, we estimate pooled logistic regression models.

Texas survey items:

- DV 2015: In so-called "sanctuary cities," local law enforcement officials do not actively enforce some federal immigration laws. Do you approve (1) or disapprove (0) of city governments that choose not to enforce some immigration laws?

- Generally speaking, would you say that you usually think of yourself as a Democrat, Republican, or Independent? Uses the four PID3 follow-up questions: Strong Democrat (1); Not very strong Democrat (2); Lean Democrat (3); Independent (4); Lean Republican (5); Not very strong Republican (6); Strong Republican (7).
- On a scale from 1 to 7, where 1 is extremely liberal, 7 is extremely conservative, and 4 is exactly in the middle, where would you place yourself? Extremely liberal (1); Somewhat liberal (2); Lean liberal (3); In the middle (4); Lean conservative (5); Somewhat conservative (6); Extremely conservative (7).
- Please indicate your age group: 18–29 (1); 30–44 (2); 45–64 (3); 65+ (4).
- In which category would you place your household income last year (0–6 low to high), dummy for nonincome.
- What is the highest level of education that you received? Less than high school (1), High school degree (2), Some college / Two-year college degree (3), Four-year college degree (4), Post-graduate degree (5).
- What race do you consider yourself to be? Nominal with White as comparison category (0); Black (1 = yes, 0 = no); Hispanic/Latino (1 = yes, 0 = no); Asian/Pacific Islander (1 = yes, 0 = no).

Texas Data and Methodology for Hypotheses 3 and 4

Our dependent variable is asked slightly differently in the two surveys, so we code the variable into 1 = Support, 0 = Oppose. Our estimation technique is therefore logistic regression. The Texas Lyceum Poll's question on sanctuary cities is more in-depth:

> In some cities, when local police or city government employees learn that someone is in the country illegally, they do not automatically turn that person over to federal immigration enforcement officers. Supporters of these so-called "sanctuary cities" say that this improves public safety because it encourages people in immigrant communities to work with police to help arrest dangerous criminals without fear of being deported themselves. Opponents of these so-called "sanctuary cities" say that this practice is a violation of federal law and allows some dangerous criminals who are in the country illegally to continue to commit violent crimes. Thinking about your own view, do you support (1) or oppose (0) "sanctuary cities"?

The UT Poll asked respondents: "Do you [strongly/somewhat] support or [strongly/somewhat] oppose sanctuary cities?" This variable is recoded to a binary: strongly/somewhat support = 1; strongly/somewhat oppose = 0.[2]

While four of our main independent variables of interest are contextual—which we discuss below—we do include two individual-level items to assess our individual-level hypotheses related to immigration and crime. These are dummy variables that measure the most important issue in the state (1 = immigration, 0 = not immigration; 1 = crime/drugs, 0 = not crime/drugs). We include several control variables, which have been shown to influence public opinion and voting behavior. These include party identification, ideology, race/ethnicity, education, gender, and urbanity. All coding is shown above.

We include four variables to test our contextual-based hypotheses (H3a, H3b, H4a, H4b). For racial/Latino threat (H3a), we employ Latino growth measured as the percentage change in the county-level Latino population from 2000 (census) to 2010–2014 (American Community Survey).[3] The larger the number, the greater the Latino growth. To test H3b, we include percent Latino in the county as determined by the combined 2010–2014 ACS.

These measures are calculated for all Texas counties, then appended to the individual-level survey data based on county FIPS code. Based on findings from Newman and Velez (2014), if the threat argument is true, we expect Latino growth to carry more influence on sanctuary city attitudes than will Latino population.

For our crime threat hypothesis (H4), we gathered crime statistics from the Texas Department of Public Safety (2015),[4] which tracks various crime rates in Texas, and the Federal Bureau of Investigation's (FBI) Uniform Crime Reporting program 2000 county-level dataset.[5] The most recent data available are from 2015, of which we select murder rate by county (H4a), and total crime rate by county (H4b).[6] These data are scaled to crimes per one hundred thousand people. We selected the same measures from 2000, creating a percent change measure ((2015–2000) / 2000), which we include in our models.

Additional Models

Table A.1 Predictors of public opinion on sanctuary cities in California, 2015–2017 Pooled Model (Identical DV): "Do you believe that local authorities should be able to ignore a federal request to hold an illegal immigrant who has been detained? Yes, local authorities should be able to ignore these federal requests (1). No, local authorities should not be able to ignore these federal requests (0)."

	Dependent variable:	
	Sanctuary (1)	Support (2)
Party Identification 7-point (Dem-Rep)	−0.364***	−0.126**
	(0.038)	(0.050)
Female	−0.383***	−0.400***
	(0.148)	(0.152)
Education (low-high)	0.088	0.089
	(0.081)	(0.084)
Age	−0.250***	−0.255***
	(0.054)	(0.055)
Latino	0.535***	0.795***
	(0.196)	(0.252)
Black	−0.833**	−0.984***
	(0.344)	(0.366)
Asian	−0.147	−0.132
	(0.245)	(0.251)
Race: Other	0.142	0.150
	(0.274)	(0.280)
Catholic	−0.285	−0.256
	(0.178)	(0.184)
Income: Medium	−0.251	−0.223
	(0.180)	(0.186)

(*continued*)

Table A.1 Continued

	Dependent variable:	
	Sanctuary (1)	Support (2)
Income: High	−0.147 (0.217)	−0.162 (0.224)
Income: Missing	−0.327 (0.260)	−0.313 (0.268)
2017 Dummy	1.191*** (0.149)	2.776*** (0.290)
Party ID X 2017 Dummy		−0.489*** (0.077)
Latino X 2017 Dummy		−0.623* (0.360)
Constant	0.844** (0.369)	0.099 (0.396)
Observations	1,056	1,056
Log Likelihood	−586.164	−563.034
Akaike Inf. Crit.	1,200.329	1,158.068
Pseudo R2	0.161	0.194

Note: *p<0.1; **p<0.05; ***p<0.01

Appendix B

Table B.1 Predictors of count of sanctuary city bill introduction in state legislatures, 2017. (Poisson model)

	Sanctuary Bill Count	
	Anti (1)	Pro (2)
ALEC Legislator Count	0.026**	−0.023
	(0.010)	(0.023)
Percent Trump 2016	0.080**	−0.127**
	(0.032)	(0.056)
Public Opinion: Anti-Immigration Attitudes	−7.188	17.157
	(6.878)	(11.528)
Percent Latino 2015	0.053***	−0.007
	(0.020)	(0.022)
Delta Percent Latino	0.009	−0.021**
	(0.006)	(0.009)
Delta HH Median Income (2000 $)	−0.019	−0.039
	(0.021)	(0.034)
Pct. Adult Unemployment Rate 2016	−0.313**	0.230
	(0.159)	(0.209)
Violent Crime Rate 2014	−0.001	−0.001
	(0.001)	(0.002)
Divided State Government	0.916***	1.337***
	(0.321)	(0.403)
State Legislative Competition Index	0.014	−0.002
	(0.009)	(0.012)
Legislative Professionalism	2.665***	1.230
	(1.012)	(0.846)
Constant	−1.998	−2.440
	(2.458)	(4.359)
Observations	50	50
Log Likelihood	−82.122	−49.358
Akaike Inf. Crit.	188.245	122.716

Note: *p<0.1; **p<0.05; ***p<0.01

Table B.2 Summary Statistics.

	Min	Max	Median	Mean	S.D.
Anti-Sanctuary Count	0.00	12.00	2.00	1.78	2.12
Pro Sanctuary Count	0.00	11.00	0.00	1.20	2.25
Divided State Government	0.00	1.00	0.00	0.34	0.48
State Legislative Competition Index	9.80	98.24	71.91	65.35	21.63
Legislative Professionalism	0.06	0.90	0.24	0.26	0.15
Percent Trump 2016	30.00	68.60	48.85	49.31	10.22
Number of ALEC Legislators	1.00	42.00	13.50	15.54	10.68
Percent Latino 2015	1.40	47.40	8.75	11.22	10.16
Delta Percent Latino	12.62	146.09	75.18	75.14	36.41
Violent Crime Rate 2014	99.27	635.78	325.11	346.81	128.82
Delta HH Median Income 2000–2016 (2000 $)	-18.42	22.53	-3.89	-3.34	6.97
Pct. Adult Unemployment Rate 2016	2.80	6.70	4.80	4.64	0.98
Public Opinion: Anti-Immigration Attitudes	0.41	0.58	0.47	0.48	0.04
Percent Foreign-Born 2015	1.53	27.04	6.76	8.96	6.09
Delta Foreign-Born	1.21	75.39	34.78	36.58	20.95
Percent Latino Foreign-Born Non-Citizen 2015	0.10	9.20	2.00	2.51	2.13
Delta Latino Foreign-Born Non-Citizen	-16.90	200.00	47.22	57.05	50.16

Public Opinion Anti-Immigrant Sentiment, 2016 CCES

We summed up yes/no responses to four items inquiring about immigration policy. The base question asks, "What do you think the U.S. government should do
about immigration?" Each item is dummied yes (1 = anti-immigrant position) or no
(0 = pro-immigration position), aggregated, then divided by 4 for a scale ranging from
0 to 1 (pro-immigrant to anti-immigrant). We then take the mean score for each state
as our measure of anti-immigrant sentiment. The items are below:

- Grant legal status to all illegal immigrants who have held jobs and paid
  taxes for at least 3 years, and not been convicted of any felony crimes
  (1 = no, 0 = yes)
- Increase the number of border patrols on the U.S.-Mexican border
  (0 = no, 1 = yes)
- Grant legal status to people who were brought to the U.S. illegally as children, but
  who have graduated from a U.S. high school (1 = no, 0 = yes)
- Identify and deport illegal immigrants (0 = no, 1 = yes)

Appendix C

Table C.1 List of sanctuary cities by state and year.

Number	City	State	Year
1	Anchorage	ALASKA	2003
2	Haines	ALASKA	2003
3	Sitka	ALASKA	2003
4	Chandler	ARIZONA	2006
5	Berkeley	CALIFORNIA	2007
6	East Palo Alto	CALIFORNIA	2007
7	Fresno	CALIFORNIA	2003
8	Garden Grove	CALIFORNIA	2007
9	Los Angeles	CALIFORNIA	2007
10	Oakland	CALIFORNIA	2007
11	Richmond	CALIFORNIA	2007
12	San Diego	CALIFORNIA	2008
13	San Francisco	CALIFORNIA	2002
14	San Jose	CALIFORNIA	2007
15	San Rafael	CALIFORNIA	2003
16	Santa Cruz	CALIFORNIA	2007
17	Watsonville	CALIFORNIA	2007
18	Durango	COLORADO	2004
19	Hartford	CONNECTICUT	2007
20	New Haven	CONNECTICUT	2006
21	Washington	DISTRICT OF COLUMBIA	2003
22	Portland	MAINE	2004
23	Baltimore	MARYLAND	2003
24	Takoma Park	MARYLAND	2007
25	Boston	MASSACHUSETTS	2006
26	Brewster	MASSACHUSETTS	2003
27	Brookline	MASSACHUSETTS	2006
28	Cambridge	MASSACHUSETTS	2002
29	Lexington	MASSACHUSETTS	2004
30	Orleans	MASSACHUSETTS	2003
31	Ann Arbor	MICHIGAN	2003
32	Detroit	MICHIGAN	2002
33	Hamtramck	MICHIGAN	2008
34	Lansing	MICHIGAN	2004
35	Minneapolis	MINNESOTA	2007
36	St. Paul	MINNESOTA	2004
37	St. Louis	MISSOURI	2004
38	Elko	NEVADA	2004
39	Montclair	NEW JERSEY	2004
40	Newark	NEW JERSEY	2006
41	Trenton	NEW JERSEY	2004

(*continued*)

Table C.1 Continued

Number	City	State	Year
42	Albuquerque	NEW MEXICO	2007
43	New York	NEW YORK	2003
44	Syracuse	NEW YORK	2003
45	Durham	NORTH CAROLINA	2003
46	Ashland	OREGON	2003
47	Gaston	OREGON	2002
48	Portland	OREGON	2003
49	Talent	OREGON	2003
50	Philadelphia	PENNSYLVANIA	2002
51	Pittsburgh	PENNSYLVANIA	2004
52	Seattle	WASHINGTON	2003
53	Madison	WISCONSIN	2002
54	Milwaukee	WISCONSIN	2004

Table C.2 Variables, data type, and coding.

Variable	Type	Coding
Total Population (2000)	numeric	raw count
Percent White	numeric	percent
Percent Black	numeric	percent
Percent Asian	numeric	percent
Percent Hispanic	numeric	percent
Percent Unemployed (2000)	numeric	percent
Median Income (2000)	numeric	city median
Percent Poverty (1999)	numeric	percent
BA or Greater (25+)	numeric	percent
Percent Foreign-Born	numeric	percent
Percent Latino Non-Citizen (2000)	numeric	percent
Percent Foreign Born Latin American (2000)	numeric	percent
Gore Vote	Numeric	percentage
Percentage Age Male 15–19 (2000)	numeric	percent
Percentage Age Male 20–24 (2000)	numeric	percent
Percentage Age Male 25–29 (2000)	numeric	percent
Percentage Age Male 30–34 (2000)	numeric	percent
Violent Crime	numeric	per/100,000
Property Crime	numeric	per/100,000
Rape Crime	numeric	per/100,000

Table C.3 Prematch: Example covariate balance table.

	Means Treated	Means Control	SD Control	Mean Diff	eQQ Med	eQQ Mean	eQQ Max
distance	0.43	0.02	0.07	0.40	0.35	0.39	0.94
Total_Pop_2000	539373.33	41927.99	64399.29	497445.34	157917.50	475981.46	6687233.00
Pct_White_2000	59.01	78.00	18.88	−19.00	19.70	18.66	30.40
Pct_Black_2000	20.11	6.96	12.27	13.15	9.20	12.73	33.60
Pct_Asian_2000	7.13	4.79	7.22	2.34	1.85	3.02	30.90
Pct_Hisp_2000	17.30	14.08	18.89	3.21	4.05	4.92	22.30
Pct_Unemployed_16Plus_2000	4.74	3.66	2.10	1.08	1.20	1.62	23.60
Median_Income_1999	42654.77	49719.77	20264.11	−7065.00	6167.00	9006.38	96332.00
Pct_Poverty_18Plus_1999	15.04	9.73	6.71	5.31	6.30	5.94	23.90
Pct_EDU_25Plus_BAPlus_2000	34.20	27.64	15.91	6.56	6.95	6.41	10.40
Pct_ForBorn_2000	17.87	13.02	11.57	4.85	5.10	5.35	21.00
Pct_ForBorn_NotCit_2000	11.34	7.53	7.61	3.81	4.00	3.88	8.50
Pct_ForBorn_LatinAm_2000	40.08	35.36	27.19	4.72	8.90	8.66	17.70
Pct_Latino_Not_Citizen_2000	5.36	3.98	6.61	1.38	1.18	1.58	9.91
Pct_New_City_Residents_2000	23.23	28.08	8.82	−4.84	4.78	5.00	21.86
PGORE	58.67	51.49	9.90	7.18	7.60	7.44	13.10

Table C.4 Postmatch: Example covariate balance table.

	Means Treated	Means Control	SD Control	Mean Diff	eQQ Med	eQQ Mean	eQQ Max
distance	0.43	0.23	0.22	0.20	0.23	0.20	0.47
Total_Pop_2000	539373.33	184489.17	228230.82	354884.17	87319.50	354963.46	6687233.00
Pct_White_2000	59.01	62.42	20.55	-3.42	3.20	4.31	10.50
Pct_Black_2000	20.11	17.12	19.39	2.99	2.70	3.41	13.80
Pct_Asian_2000	7.13	5.48	7.11	1.65	1.00	2.00	9.40
Pct_Hisp_2000	17.30	18.48	18.05	-1.18	1.55	2.88	23.50
Pct_Unemployed_16Plus_2000	4.74	4.45	1.81	0.28	0.30	0.32	0.90
Median_Income_1999	42654.77	42292.56	13028.64	362.21	1372.00	1989.17	8717.00
Pct_Poverty_18Plus_1999	15.04	14.04	5.81	0.99	1.45	1.36	3.90
Pct_EDU_25Plus_BAPlus_2000	34.20	32.28	17.41	1.92	2.85	2.98	8.30
Pct_ForBorn_2000	17.87	16.63	11.10	1.24	1.20	1.85	6.90
Pct_ForBorn_NotCit_2000	11.34	10.63	7.56	0.71	0.90	1.15	6.30
Pct_ForBorn_LatinAm_2000	40.08	46.46	24.30	-6.38	6.50	6.38	13.50
Pct_Latino_Not_Citizen_2000	5.36	5.28	7.05	0.08	0.29	0.58	6.05
Pct_New_City_Residents_2000	23.23	25.59	8.52	-2.36	2.41	2.58	6.17
PGORE	58.68	54.39	10.47	4.28	3.95	4.67	13.70

Table C.5 Interrupted ARIMA time series models. Outcome variable = Crime; Independent variable = Change in ICE detainer policy. Santa Clara, Los Angeles (CA) and Queens (NY) Counties.

			Dependent variable:		
	Santa Clara Part 1 (1)	Santa Clara Violent (2)	Los Angeles Part 1 (3)	Queens Part 1 (4)	Queens Violent (5)
AR 1		−0.401*** (0.118)	0.474*** (0.111)	0.510*** (0.131)	
AR 2		−0.399*** (0.123)			
SAR1	−0.346*** (0.132)	−0.527*** (0.124)	−0.334*** (0.123)		
Intercept	412.095*** (14.654)	43.668*** (3.027)	6,697.123*** (115.055)	2,112.720*** (46.169)	703.362*** (17.019)
Post Interruption	−53.390* (31.950)	−14.641*** (4.348)	−1,335.666*** (296.670)	210.416* (116.027)	−7.318 (31.693)
Time Elapsed	−4.133*** (0.627)	−0.488*** (0.089)	−18.714*** (4.631)	−6.493*** (1.966)	−2.930*** (0.581)
Interruption X Time	3.650*** (0.800)	0.547*** (0.108)	40.264*** (6.634)	−5.802* (3.105)	0.632 (0.841)
February	−38.322** (15.234)	−10.216** (4.256)	−920.709*** (66.165)	−244.173*** (28.404)	−103.449*** (18.937)
March	−11.782 (15.157)	−3.624 (4.293)	−519.649*** (80.548)	−103.726*** (34.744)	−34.099* (18.952)

(continued)

Table C.5 Continued

			Dependent variable:		
	Santa Clara Part 1 (1)	Santa Clara Violent (2)	Los Angeles Part 1 (3)	Queens Part 1 (4)	Queens Violent (5)
April	−1.637 (15.188)	−6.739** (3.301)	−494.257*** (86.589)	−84.690** (36.811)	−32.862* (18.194)
May	23.241 (15.253)	−5.058 (3.752)	−190.072** (89.297)	112.884*** (38.046)	59.585*** (18.202)
June	−5.997 (15.293)	−3.466 (3.908)	−415.954*** (90.067)	76.108** (38.691)	49.032*** (18.220)
July	13.593 (15.398)	−0.093 (3.665)	−195.384** (87.974)	216.387*** (39.866)	106.172*** (18.996)
August	7.789 (16.263)	−1.753 (4.060)	−380.387*** (90.642)	237.917*** (40.048)	102.049*** (19.003)
September	−9.453 (16.291)	−13.032*** (3.976)	−569.425*** (89.600)	149.997*** (39.551)	52.926*** (19.020)
October	9.211 (16.072)	1.452 (3.520)	−281.141*** (86.673)	296.230*** (38.344)	54.603*** (19.046)
November	4.112 (16.058)	−11.992*** (4.416)	−579.932*** (80.480)	96.563*** (35.733)	8.080 (19.082)
December	−38.534** (16.021)	−7.366* (4.425)	−118.217* (66.126)	182.980*** (28.436)	16.849 (18.937)

Note: *p<0.1; **p<0.05; ***p<0.01

Table C.6 Interrupted ARIMA time series models. Outcome variable
= Crime; Independent variable = Change in ICE detainer policy.
Alameda and San Diego Counties.

| | *Dependent variable:* | | | |
	Alameda Part 1 (1)	Alameda Violent (2)	San Diego Part 1 (3)	San Diego Violent (4)
MA1	0.462*** (0.132)			
SAR1		−0.413*** (0.123)		
AR1			0.299*** (0.116)	
AR2			0.229* (0.121)	
AR3			0.232** (0.117)	
Intercept	300.518*** (15.002)	53.137*** (3.021)	6,694.479*** (328.307)	933.387*** (25.974)
Post Interruption	−44.559 (32.119)	−35.548*** (6.221)	−286.680 (840.537)	−188.522*** (48.166)
Time Elapsed	−1.395*** (0.507)	−0.315*** (0.104)	−4.102 (12.522)	−0.384 (0.772)
Interruption X Time	1.157 (0.737)	0.679*** (0.134)	−1.441 (20.754)	2.579** (1.095)
February	−40.014*** (11.443)	−0.401 (2.941)	−727.443*** (150.045)	−79.239*** (28.359)
March	−14.202 (14.555)	7.060** (2.954)	−442.776*** (153.180)	13.188 (28.377)
April	−20.717 (14.468)	−1.160 (2.946)	−419.010*** (152.022)	13.949 (28.405)
May	−2.648 (14.054)	4.206 (2.826)	−227.348 (162.747)	53.894** (27.375)
June	18.389 (14.665)	7.991*** (2.992)	−341.291** (171.646)	40.508 (28.635)
July	10.942 (14.703)	9.250*** (2.977)	−50.858 (169.026)	92.935*** (28.560)
August	−4.748 (14.652)	8.271*** (2.966)	−43.848 (168.910)	94.196*** (28.497)
September	−15.935 (14.611)	7.584** (2.957)	−357.563** (166.713)	41.957 (28.446)
October	−15.111 (14.578)	7.069** (2.952)	−111.278 (151.826)	42.051 (28.405)
November	−14.628 (14.555)	2.741 (2.945)	−545.331*** (153.165)	−43.355 (28.377)
December	1.179 (11.443)	2.095 (2.941)	120.723 (150.228)	24.073 (28.359)

Note: *p<0.1; **p<0.05; ***p<0.01

Table C.7 Difference in difference regression estimating causal relationship between sanctuary status (treatment) and Latino voter registration. (Robust clustered standard errors).

	Coef	SE	T-stat	P-value
Intercept	0.37	0.00	241.38	0.00
Treat	−0.06	0.02	−3.16	2.00
Time	0.07	0.00	55.34	0.00
Treatment X Time	0.03	0.02	1.61	0.10
Sanctuary	0.00	0.01	0.07	0.90

Table C.8 Difference in difference regression estimating causal relationship between sanctuary status (treatment) and Latino police force representation. (Robust clustered standard errors).

	Coef	SE	T-stat	P-value
Intercept	−11.41	1.39	−8.21	2.00
Treatment (sanctuary)	4.56	2.14	2.13	0.00
Time	−0.53	0.95	−0.56	1.40
Treatment X Time	2.54	1.58	1.60	0.10

Notes

Introduction

1. We define *immigration-related tweets* as tweets that include the at least one of the following terms: steinle, sanctuary, illegals, immigration, border.
2. This has been found unconstitutional thus far and little has come of it.
3. D'Angelo Gore (2017), "Ed Gillespie's 'sanctuary cities' attacks", Factcheck.org, September 26. https://www.factcheck.org/2017/09/ed-gillespies-sanctuary-cities-attacks/
4. Dixon, Matt (2018), "Sanctuary city debate erupts in Florida governor's race", *Politico.com,* February 1. https://www.politico.com/story/2018/02/01/florida-sanctuary-city-governor-race-381318
5. Golshan, Tara (2018), "Rick Saccone's Pennsylvania blunder was very expensive for Republicans," *Vox.com,* March 14. https://www.vox.com/policy-and-politics/2018/3/14/17117950/rick-saccone-pennsylvania-expensive-republicans
6. Ulloa, Jazmine (2017), "California becomes 'sanctuary state' in rebuke of Trump immigration policy", *Los Angeles Times,* October 5. http://www.latimes.com/politics/la-pol-ca-brown-california-sanctuary-state-bill-20171005-story.html
7. See the Ohio Jobs & Justice PAC website for a list of some of the actions that can lead to a city being classified as a sanctuary even if no formal policy exists: http://www.ojjpac.org/sanctuary.asp
8. http://www.ci.berkeley.ca.us/citycouncil/2007citycouncil/packet/052207/2007-05-22%20Item%2034b%20City%20Refuge%20Ordinance%20to%20Prevent%20Co-operation%20with%20Immigration%20Raids.pdf
9. Wootson, Jr., Cleve R. (2018), "Widespread panic as Oakland mayor warns sanctuary city of an ICE sweep", *Washington Post,* February 26. https://www.washingtonpost.com/news/post-nation/wp/2018/02/25/oaklands-mayor-just-warned-the-sanctuary-city-about-a-potential-ice-raid
10. This law enforcement by local officials, which had been authorized in 1996 but the first agreement did not come until after 9/11.
11. https://www.law.cornell.edu/supremecourt/text/505/144
12. https://www.law.cornell.edu/supct/html/95-1478.ZO.html
13. https://www.law.cornell.edu/uscode/text/8/1373
14. Greenberg, Jon (2015), "Tom Tancredo muffs illegal immigrant murder stats", *Politifact.com,* August 17. http://www.politifact.com/punditfact/statements/2015/aug/17/tom-tancredo/tancredo-muffs-illegal-immigrant-murder-stats/
15. Farley, Robert (2010), "Sharron Angle says Sen. Harry Reid twice voted against making English the national language", *Politifact.com,* October 29. http://www.politifact.com/truth-o-meter/statements/2010/oct/29/sharron-angle/sharron-angle-says-se-harry-reid-twice-voted-again/

16. Finnegan, Michael (2015), "On immigration, Donald Trump takes a page from Pete Wilson's 1994 playbook", *Los Angeles Times,* July 11. http://www.latimes.com/local/california/la-me-0712-trump-california-20150712-story.html

Chapter 1

1. Based on a list maintained by the National Immigration Law Center.
2. http://time.com/3923128/donald-trump-announcement-speech/
3. Los Angeles would declare itself a sanctuary city again in 2019.
4. See chapter 5 for a map of current sanctuary city locations.
5. http://archiveswest.orbiscascade.org/ark:/80444/xv93375/pdf
6. In the 2000s, faith-based organizations would start the New Sanctuary Movement, which was inspired by the Sanctuary Movement. This never gained the recognition or amount of support of the original movement, nor did it have the same amount of influence on the broader debate around immigration policy. The New Sanctuary Movement, instead of sheltering refugees, offered refuge to families in danger of separation because of the Bush administration's immigration crackdown (Freeland, 2010).
7. Ryan, Andrew (2006), "Agency nabs illegal immigrants across U.S.", *Washington Post*, June 14. http://www.washingtonpost.com/wp-dyn/content/article/2006/06/14/AR2006061401245.html
8. https://www.ice.gov/secure-communities
9. McGreevy, Patrick (2013), "Signing Trust Act is another illegal-immigration milestone for Brown, *Los Angeles Times*, October 5. http://www.latimes.com/local/la-me-brown-immigration-20131006-story.html
10. https://leginfo.legislature.ca.gov/faces/billNavClient.xhtml?bill_id=201320140AB4
11. https://www.alecexposed.org/wiki/No_Sanctuary_Cities_for_Illegal_Immigrants_Act_Exposed
12. https://www.presidency.ucsb.edu/documents/republican-presidential-candidates-debate-manchester-new-hampshire; https://www.presidency.ucsb.edu/documents/republican-presidential-candidates-debate-the-progress-energy-center-for-the-arts-st
13. https://www.presidency.ucsb.edu/documents/republican-candidates-debate-sioux-city-iowa
14. https://www.whitehouse.gov/presidential-actions/executive-order-enhancing-public-safety-interior-united-states/
15. Bomboy, Scott (2017), "Federal judge's order sets up sanctuary city showdown", *Constitutioncenter.org,* November 21. https://constitutioncenter.org/blog/federal-judges-order-sets-up-sanctuary-city-showdown
16. See *City of Philadelphia v. Sessions*; *City of Chicago v. Sessions*.
17. https://www.ice.gov/voice
18. https://leginfo.legislature.ca.gov/faces/billNavClient.xhtml?bill_id=201720180SB54
19. https://leginfo.legislature.ca.gov/faces/billNavClient.xhtml?bill_id=201720180AB450
20. https://legiscan.com/TX/text/SB4/id/1608435
21. Astor, Maggie (2018), "Texas' ban on 'Sanctuary Cities' can begin, appeals court rules", *New York Times*, March 13. https://www.nytimes.com/2018/03/13/us/texas-immigration-law-sb4.html

22. Hanks, Douglas (2017). "Miami-Dade complied with Trump to change its 'sanctuary' status. It worked", *Miami Herald*, August 7. https://www.miamiherald.com/news/local/community/miami-dade/article165837497.html

Chapter 2

1. Allan, Nicole (2010), "Whitman to Latinos: Hola", *The Atlantic,* August 5. https://www.theatlantic.com/politics/archive/2010/08/whitman-to-latinos-hola/60940/; Crowley, Michael (2010), "What does Meg Whitman's $120 million really buy?", *Time*, September 30. http://content.time.com/time/magazine/article/0,9171,2022710,00.html
2. http://www.cnn.com/ELECTION/2010/results/polls/#val=CAG00p1
3. https://www.c-span.org/video/?407380-1/1980-republican-presidential-candidates-debate
4. We also included a search for Lou Dobbs, a fervent anti-immigrant CNN anchor in the mid-2000s.

Chapter 3

1. Luhby, Tami (2016), "Trump condemns sanctuary cities, but what are they?", *Cnn.com,* September 1. http://www.cnn.com/2016/09/01/politics/sanctuary-cities-donald-trump/index.html
2. Valverde, Miriam (2016), "Compare the candidates: Clinton vs. Trump on immigration", *Politifact.com,* July 15. http://www.politifact.com/truth-o-meter/article/2016/jul/15/compare-candidates-clinton-vs-trump-immigration/
3. Gonzalez, Richard (2016), "Mayor Rahm Emanuel: 'Chicago always will be a sanctuary city' ", *NPR,* November 15. http://www.npr.org/sections/thetwo-way/2016/11/14/502066703/mayor-rahm-emanuel-chicago-always-will-be-a-sanctuary-city; https://www.nytimes.com/2017/06/28/nyregion/bill-de-blasio-defends-new-york-policies-on-immigration.html?mcubz=1&_r=0
4. Griffiths, Brent D. (2017), "California governor endorses potential 'sanctuary cities' lawsuit", *Politico.com,* August 5. http://www.politico.com/story/2017/08/05/california-trump-sanctuary-cities-lawsuit-jerry-brown-241358
5. Aguilera, Elizabeth (2017), "Gov. Jerry Brown once opposed sanctuary cities, but have time – and Trump – changed his mind?", *The Mercury News,* May 6. http://www.mercurynews.com/2017/05/06/californias-governor-once-opposed-sanctuary-status-have-time-and-trump-changed-his-mind/
6. Mendoza, Jessica (2017), "California poised to become 'sanctuary' state. But do such policies work?", *Christian Science Monitor,* September 13. https://www.csmonitor.com/USA/2017/0913/California-poised-to-become-sanctuary-state.-But-do-such-policies-work
7. Ulloa, Jazmine (2017), "California lawmakers approve landmark 'sanctuary state' bill to expand protections for immigrants", Los *Angeles Times,* September 16. http://www.latimes.com/politics/la-pol-ca-california-sanctuary-state-bill-20170916-story.html
8. Ulloa, Jazmine (2017), "How California's Trust Act shaped the debate on the new 'sanctuary state' proposal", *Los Angeles Times,* September 10. https://www.latimes.com/politics/la-pol-ca-trust-act-sanctuary-state-immigration-20170910-htmlstory.html

9. Arkin, Daniel (2017), "Kathryn Steinle killing: San Francisco defends 'sanctuary city' status amid criticism", *NBC News*, December 2. https://www.nbcnews.com/news/us-news/kathryn-steinle-killing-san-francisco-defends-sanctuary-city-status-amid-n825836

10. Associated Press (2017), "Is ICE planning California raids to retaliate against sanctuary state?", *sacramento.cbslocal.com*, January 17. https://sacramento.cbslocal.com/2018/01/17/california-ice-raids-sanctuary-state/

11. Held, Amy (2018), "Oakland mayor stands by 'fair warning' of impending ICE operation", *NPR*, March 1. https://www.npr.org/sections/thetwo-way/2018/03/01/589948064/oakland-mayor-stands-by-fair-warning-of-impending-ice-operation

12. Olsen, Kristin (2018), "GOP is dead in California. A new way must rise", *San Francisco Chronicle*, November 14. https://www.sfchronicle.com/opinion/openforum/article/GOP-is-dead-in-California-A-new-way-must-rise-13393401.php

13. Aguilar, Julián (2017), "After emotional debate, Texas House tentatively passes "sanctuary" legislation", *Texas Tribune*, April 27. https://www.texastribune.org/2017/04/27/tensions-flaring-house-members-will-debate-anti-sanctuary-city-bill/

14. Hing, Julianne (2017), "Texas's SB 4 is the most dramatic state crackdown yet on sanctuary cities", *The Nation*, June 1. https://www.thenation.com/article/texass-sb-4-dramatic-state-crackdown-yet-sanctuary-cities/

15. Aguilar, Julián (2017), "After emotional debate, Texas House tentatively passes "sanctuary" legislation", *Texas Tribune,* April 27. https://www.texastribune.org/2017/04/27/tensions-flaring-house-members-will-debate-anti-sanctuary-city-bill/

16. Selby, W. Gardner (2017), "Torching Greg Abbott's claim Travis County sheriff declared she wouldn't hold violent criminals", *Politifact.com,* May 18. https://www.politifact.com/texas/statements/2017/may/18/greg-abbott/torching-greg-abbotts-claim-travis-county-sheriff-/

17. https://www.gregabbott.com/petition-poll/sanctuary-cities/

18. Krogstad, Jens M; Flores, Antonio; and Lopez, Mark H. (2018), "Key takeaways about Latino voters in the 2018 midterm elections", *Pew Research Center*, November 9. http://www.pewresearch.org/fact-tank/2018/11/09/how-latinos-voted-in-2018-midterms/

19. E.g., people from Puerto Rican and Mexican heritage, respectively, both considering themselves as sharing common experiences as Latinos in the United States.

20. We examine these two groups because the racial learning expectations are fairly straightforward, whereas racial learning for blacks or Asians, for instance, is not so straightforward. That said, future research should apply different learning models to other racial groups within this policy domain.

21. We also investigate "current" crime rates instead of change in crime rates as a possible explanatory factor. The results are effectively the same.

22. Very few publicly available public opinion surveys inquiring about sanctuary cities exist, but we managed to acquire data from these two states. See Casellas and Wallace (2018) for a more recent national analysis. To the extent possible we conduct the same analyses in both states, to provide consistent tests of our hypotheses. However, the surveys do have some differences, which we control for and address in our analytic approach.

23. Field dates: August 11–26, 2015.
24. Blacks do change opinion from 2015 to 2017, however. We do not investigate this here because theoretical expectations for this group are not clear.
25. Aguilar, Julián (2017), "Trump administration doesn't view Austin as "sanctuary" city, mayor says", *Texas Tribune,* April 25. https://www.texastribune.org/2017/04/25/adler-told-austin-travis-co-are-not-considered-sanctuary-jurisdictions/
26. This is the same poll employed in the earlier analysis.
27. The University of Texas (UT) poll contains zip codes attached to each respondent, whereas the Lyceum poll has county FIPS codes. We matched the zip codes for the UT poll to county, then pooled the two datasets.
28. Given that the surveys were separated by a few months, the univariate sanctuary distributions do vary from poll to poll. In the February UT poll, just 37 percent of respondents supported sanctuary cities, whereas 63 percent opposed. In April, the Lyceum poll recorded 48 percent support and 52 percent opposition. These differences may be due to calling house/mode effects, wording effects, and attitude change across time related to a rapidly changing media and political environment (Schuman and Presser, 1996; Tesler, 2015).
29. We subsetted the data among whites only and found the relationship between Latino growth and sanctuary attitudes to hold, whereas with other racial groups, the relationship between Latino growth and sanctuary attitudes disappeared.

Chapter 4

1. Bolten, Kathy A. (2016), "Trump uses Iowan's death as reason to strengthen immigration laws", *Des Moines Register,* April 16. https://www.desmoinesregister.com/story/news/crime-and-courts/2016/04/16/sarah-root-eswin-mejia/82902280/
2. Peters, Jeremy W. (2018), "How Politics took over the killing of Mollie Tibbetts", *New York Times,* August 23. https://www.nytimes.com/2018/08/23/us/politics/mollie-tibbetts-republicans-immigration-trump.html
3. As of this writing, all of these attempts by the Trump administration to penalize sanctuary cities have been turned back by the courts.
4. Chokshi, Niraj (2017), "States have already passed almost twice as many immigration laws as last year", *New York Times,* August 7. https://www.nytimes.com/2017/08/07/us/sanctuary-city-immigration.html?_r=0
5. Adler, Ben (2017), "California Governor signs 'Sanctuary State' bill", *NPR,* October 5. http://www.npr.org/sections/thetwo-way/2017/10/05/555920658/california-governor-signs-sanctuary-state-bill
6. Pfannenstiel, Brianne (2018), "Iowa 'sanctuary' city ban signed into law", *Des Moines Register,* April 10. https://www.desmoinesregister.com/story/news/politics/2018/04/10/iowa-sanctuary-city-ban-becomes-law-sf-481-reynolds-signs/504176002/
7. Although recent work by Acharya et al. (2018) makes a strong case that racial threat in the South has less to do with the current demographic context and more to do with the historical presence of chattel slavery, and the resulting attitudes emanating from and justifying that institution.

8. We also examined the role of general state ideology as measured by Sorens et al. (2008). This variable is highly collinear with both presidential vote and our ALEC measure.
9. Valverde, Miriam, (2017), "Jeff Sessions cites study on sanctuary cities, researchers say he misrepresented it", *Politifact.com,* July 24. http://www.politifact.com/truth-o-meter/statements/2017/jul/24/jeff-sessions/jeff-sessions-mischaracterizes-study-sanctuary-cit/
10. Graves, Allison (2017), "Fact-checking Donald Trump's Super Bowl interview", *Politifact.com,* February 5. http://www.politifact.com/truth-o-meter/article/2017/feb/05/fact-checking-donald-trumps-interview-bill-oreilly/
11. https://www.justice.gov/opa/speech/attorney-general-jeff-sessions-delivers-remarks-sanctuary-jurisdictions
12. Casselman, Ben (2017), "Stop saying Trump's win had nothing to do with economics", *Fivethirtyeight.com,* January 9. https://fivethirtyeight.com/features/stop-saying-trumps-win-had-nothing-to-do-with-economics/; Thompson, Derek (2016), "Donald Trump and 'economic anxiety': What's fueling his support?", *The Atlantic,* August 18. https://www.theatlantic.com/business/archive/2016/08/donald-trump-and-economic-anxiety/496385/
13. http://www.ncsl.org/Portals/1/Documents/immig/StateSanctuaryBills_050817.pdf
14. One or more of the following words had to be included in the bill title or text of the bill: city, cities, town, towns, central america, central american, mexican, mexico, movement, police, immigrant, immigrants, immigration, illegal, enforcement, alien, aliens, refugee, refugees, campus, campuses.
15. We also include Poisson models in Table B.1 in the appendix. Our substantive findings remain unchanged.
16. https://www.alec.org/model-policy/a-public-safety-resolution-calling-on-the-insert-jurisdiction-to-define-insert-jurisdiction-as-a-rule-of-law-community/. We also gathered state policy liberalism measures, but this measure correlated so highly with our presidential voting measures that we dropped policy liberalism from the analysis.
17. See Collingwood et al. (2018) for more details.
18. In our text corpus, our count measure of plagiarism similarity correlates at $\rho = 0.99$ with our percentage similarity measure.
19. The measure is robust to a variety of search algorithm specifications.
20. In his study linking incarceration to mass opinion, Enns (2016) argues that cross-section analysis is not appropriate when linking actual crime to public opinion or policy outcomes. Rather, he provides convincing evidence and reasoning that over-time analysis is the best way to link how one variable influences another. Unfortunately, in our case, either for public opinion data or for sanctuary legislation, we have scant reliable over-time data, so we cannot appropriately analyze data across time. However, we maintain that sanctuary city opposition represents more a moral panic issue—where the public and legislators respond in a manner out of proportion to the actual threat (Hall et al., 2013).

Chapter 5

1. Since Trump's 2016 election victory, evidence exists that crime reporting by Latinos has likely dropped in several major U.S. cities: Medina, Jennifer, (2017), "Too scared to report sexual abuse. The fear: Deportation", *New York Times*, April 30. https://www.nytimes.com/2017/04/30/us/immigrants-deportation-sexual-abuse.html; Queally, James (2017), "Latinos are reporting fewer sexual assaults amid a climate of fear in immigrant communities, LAPD says", *Los Angeles Times,* March 21. http://www.latimes.com/local/lanow/la-me-ln-immigrant-crime-reporting-drops-20170321-story.html

2. In examining the inmigration of Latinos we found no difference in matched sanctuary/non-sanctuary cities, and thus we would not expect any population effect on crime rates based on sanctuary status alone.

3. See appendix for a list of the cities.

4. On total population, larger cities are substantively different than smaller localities so it is important to take these qualitative differences into account in the matching process. For instance, San Francisco, a city of nearly nine hundred thousand people could have similar percent estimates for a variety of demographic and economic indicators as a small town of ten thousand but it stretches credulity to say these cities are comparable.

5. Tables C.3 and C.4 in the appendix show the balance improvement across the match control variables. All variables show a dramatic increase in balance postmatch. But the balance is not perfect, which is why after our analysis with matched data we also complete a regression analysis to control for small imbalances across treatment and control.

6. Additionally, we visualize the data with a map in Figure 5.3.

7. https://www.ucrdatatool.gov/offenses.cfm

8. ARIMA models account for issues of temporal autocorrelation and seasonality by incorporating autoregressive, moving average, and month fixed effects model terms where necessary (Hyndman and Khandakar, 2008).

9. Passel, Jeffrey S. and Cohn, D'Vera (2018). "U.S. unauthorized immigrant total dips to lowest level in a decade", *Pew Research Center*, November 27. http://www.pewhispanic.org/2018/11/27/u-s-unauthorized-immigrant-total-dips-to-lowest-level-in-a-decade/

.

References

Abrajano, M. and Hajnal, Z. L. (2015), *White backlash: immigration, race, and American politics*, Princeton University Press.

Abrajano, M. and Singh, S. (2009), 'Examining the link between issue attitudes and news source: The case of latinos and immigration reform', *Political Behavior* **31**(1), 1–30.

Abramowitz, A. I. and Webster, S. (2016), 'The rise of negative partisanship and the nationalization of u.s. elections in the 21st century', *Electoral Studies* **41**, 12–22. **URL:** *http://www.sciencedirect.com/science/article/pii/S0261379415001857*

Acharya, A., Blackwell, M. and Sen, M. (2018), *Deep Roots: How Slavery Still Shapes Southern Politics*, Vol. 6, Princeton University Press.

Alamillo, R. and Collingwood, L. (2016), 'Chameleon politics: social identity and racial cross-over appeals', *Politics, Groups, and Identities* pp. 1–28.

ALEC (2016), 'Strategic plan 2016–2018'.

Alexander, M. (2012), *The New Jim Crow: Mass Incarceration in the Age of Colorblindness*, The New Press.

Alvarez, R. M. and Butterfield, T. L. (2000), 'The resurgence of nativism in california? the case of proposition 187 and illegal immigration', *Social Science Quarterly* pp. 167–179.

Amundsen, E. S. (1985), 'Moving costs and the microeconomics of intra-urban mobility', *Regional Science and Urban Economics* **15**(4), 573–583.

Anderson, G. L. and Donchik, L. M. (2016), 'Privatizing schooling and policy making: The american legislative exchange council and new political and discursive strategies of education governance', *Educational Policy* **30**(2), 322–364. **URL:** *https://doi.org/10.1177/0895904814528794*

Angus, C., Converse, P., Miller, W. and Stokes, D. E. (1960), *The American Voter Ann Arbor, MI: University of Michigan Press.*

Archibold, R. (2010), 'Judge blocks arizona's law on immigrants', *The New York Times*, July 29.

Barak, G. (1994), *Media, Process, and the Social Construction of Crime: Studies in Newsmaking Criminology*, Vol. 10, Taylor & Francis.

Barnes, B. (2012), 'California sheriffs oppose bill on illegal immigrants', *The New York Times*, August 29.

Barreto, M. A. and Collingwood, L. (2015), 'Group-based appeals and the latino vote in 2012: How immigration became a mobilizing issue', *Electoral Studies* **40**, 490–499.

Barreto, M. A., Collingwood, L. and Manzano, S. (2010), 'A new measure of group influence in presidential elections: assessing latino influence in 2008', *Political Research Quarterly* **63**(4), 908–921.

Barreto, M. A. and Nuño, S. A. (2011), 'The effectiveness of coethnic contact on latino political recruitment', *Political Research Quarterly* **64**(2), 448–459.

Barreto, M. and Segura, G. (2014), *Latino America: How America's Most Dynamic Population is Poised to Transform the Politics of the Nation*, Public Affairs.

Baumgartner, F. R. and Jones, B. D. (2010), *Agendas and Instability in American politics*, University of Chicago Press.

Bazar, E. (2007), 'Lawmakers seek 'sanctuary cities' crackdown; bills target havens of illegal immigrants', *USA Today*, October 25.

Beckett, K. (1999), *Making Crime Pay: Law and Order in Contemporary American Politics*, Oxford University Press.

Bencivenga, J. (1983), 'Church sanctuary – ancient tradition in a modern world', *Christian Science Monitor*, August 22.

Bennett, J. (2008), 'Operation return to sender', *Slate*, May 30. **URL:** https://slate.com/news-and-politics/2008/05/the-government-s-immigration-enforcers-run-amok.html.

Bentele, K. G. and O'brien, E. E. (2013), 'Jim crow 2.0? why states consider and adopt restrictive voter access policies', *Perspectives on Politics* **11**(4), 1088–1116.

Berkeley City Council (1971), *Resolution 44784*.

Berkeley City Council (1985), *Resolution 52596*.

Berkeley City Council (2007), *Resolution 63711*.

Birkland, T. A. (1997), *After Disaster: Agenda Setting, Public Policy, and Focusing Events*, Georgetown University Press.

Bishin, B. (2009), *Tyranny of the Minority: The Subconstituency Politics Theory of Representation*, Temple University Press.

Black, E., Black, M. and Black, E. (2009), *The Rise of Southern Republicans*, Harvard University Press.

Blalock, H. M. (1967), *Toward a Theory of Minority Group Relations*, Wiley.

Boushey, G. and Luedtke, A. (2006), 'Fiscal federalism and the politics of immigration: Centralized and decentralized immigration policies in canada and the united states', *Journal of Comparative Policy Analysis* **8**(3), 207–224.

Boushey, G. and Luedtke, A. (2011), 'Immigrants across the us federal laboratory: Explaining state-level innovation in immigration policy', *State Politics & Policy Quarterly* **11**(4), 390–414. **URL:** *https://doi.org/10.1177/1532440011419286.*

Box-Steffensmeier, J. M., Arnold, L. W. and Zorn, C. J. (1997), 'The strategic timing of position taking in congress: A study of the north american free trade agreement', *American Political Science Review* **91**(2), 324–338.

Brader, T., Valentino, N. A. and Suhay, E. (2008), 'What triggers public opposition to immigration? anxiety, group cues, and immigration threat', *American Journal of Political Science* **52**(4), 959–978.

Bratton, K. A. and Haynie, K. L. (1999), 'Agenda setting and legislative success in state legislatures: The effects of gender and race', *The Journal of Politics* **61**(3), 658–679.

Brown, J. (2016), 'The new" southern strategy:" immigration, race, and" welfare dependency" in contemporary us republican political discourse', *Geopolitics, History, and International Relations* 8(2), 22–41.

Brulliard, K. (2007), 'Tipping point for outrage;in hampton roads area, '07 deaths fuel policies on illegal immigrants', *The Washington Post*, June 5.

Burgess, M., Giraudy, E., Katz-Samuels, J., Walsh, J., Willis, D., Haynes, L. and Ghani, R. (2016), The legislative influence detector: Finding text reuse in state legislation, *in* 'Proceedings of the 22nd ACM SIGKDD International Conference on Knowledge Discovery and Data Mining', ACM, pp. 57–66.

Cable news caricatures immigration issue with ubiquitous footage of border crossers (2009). **URL:** *http://mediamatters.org/research/2009/04/16/cable-news-caricatures-immigration-issue-with-u/149255*

Calonico, S., Cattaneo, M. D. and Titiunik, R. (2015), 'rdrobust: An r package for robust nonparametric inference in regression-discontinuity designs', *R Journal* 7(1), 38–51.

Campbell, A. L., Wong, C. and Citrin, J. (2006), ' "Racial threat", partisan climate, and direct democracy: Contextual effects in three california initiatives', *Political Behavior* **28**(2), 129.

Cantor, D. and Land, K. C. (1985), 'Unemployment and crime rates in the post-world war ii united states: A theoretical and empirical analysis', *American Sociological Review* **50**(3), 317–332.

Cargile, I., Merolla, J. and Pantoja, A. (2014), 'The effects of media framing on attitudes toward undocumented immigration', *in* V. Carty, T. Woldemikael and R. Luévano, eds, *Scholars and Southern Californian Immigrants in Dialogue: New Conversations in Public Sociology*, Lexington Books, New York, NY, pp. 41–68.

Carmines, E. G. and Stimson, J. A. (1989), *Issue Evolution: Race and the Transformation of American Politics*, Princeton University Press.

Carpini, M. X. D. and Keeter, S. (1993), 'Measuring political knowledge: Putting first things first', *American Journal of Political Science* 37(4), pp. 1179–1206.

Carpini, M. X. D. and Keeter, S. (1996), *What Americans Know about Politics and Why It Matters*, Yale University Press.

Carrington, W. J., Detragiache, E. and Vishwanath, T. (1996), 'Migration with endogenous moving costs', *The American Economic Review* pp. 909–930.

Casellas, J. P. and Wallace, S. J. (2018), 'Sanctuary cities: Public attitudes toward enforcement collaboration between local police and federal immigration authorities', *Urban Affairs Review* 0(0), 1078087418776115. **URL:** *https://doi.org/10.1177/1078087418776115*

Cavuto, N. (Presenter) (2007), *Your World with Neil Cavuto*, Fox News, August 20.

Chandler, C. and Tsai, Y.-m. (2001), 'Social factors influencing immigration attitudes: An analysis of data from the general social survey', *The Social Science Journal* 38(2), 177–188.

Chavez, J. M. and Provine, D. M. (2009), 'Race and the response of state legislatures to unauthorized immigrants', *The ANNALS of the American Academy of Political and Social Science* 623(1), 78–92.

Chavez, L. (2010), *The Latino Threat: Constructing Immigrants, Citizens, and the Nation*, Stanford University Press.

Chiricos, T., Eschholz, S. and Gertz, M. (1997), 'Crime, news and fear of crime: Toward an identification of audience effects*', *Social Problems* 44(3), 342–357. **URL:** + *http://dx.doi.org/10.2307/3097181*

Chiricos, T., Padgett, K. and Gertz, M. (2000), 'Fear, tv news, and the reality of crime', *Criminology* 38(3), 755–786.

Cicero Safe Space Resolution (2008).

Cisneros, J. (2008), 'Contaminated communities: The metaphor of "immigrant as pollutant" in media representations of immigration', *Rhetoric and Public Affairs* 11(4), 569–601.

Citrin, J., Green, D. P., Muste, C. and Wong, C. (1997), 'Public opinion toward immigration reform: The role of economic motivations', *The Journal of Politics* 59(3), 858–881.

Citrin, J. and Wright, M. (2009), 'Defining the circle of we: American identity and immigration policy', *The Forum* 7(3).

Cohen, B. C. (1963), *The Press and Foreign Policy*, Princeton University Press.

Cohen, J. (1931), 'Report on crime and the foreign born: Comment', *Michigan Law Review* 30(1), 99–104.

Cole, C. D. (1983), *Christian Perspectives on the News*, June 17, University Baptist Church sanctuary movement records, University of Washington, Seattle, WA.

Collingwood, L. (2012), *The Pursuit of Victory and Incorporation: Elite Strategy, Group Pressure, and Cross-Racial Mobilization*, University of Washington.

Collingwood, L., Barreto, M. A. and Garcia-Rios, S. I. (2014), 'Revisiting latino voting: Cross-racial mobilization in the 2012 election', *Political Research Quarterly* 67(3), 632–645.

Collingwood, L., El-Khatib, S. O. and Gonzalez O'Brien, B. (2018), 'Sustained organizational influence: American legislative exchange council and the diffusion of anti-sanctuary policy', *Policy Studies Journal*.

Converse, P. E. (2006), 'The nature of belief systems in mass publics (1964)', *Critical review* 18(1-3), 1–74.

Costelloe, M., Chiricos, T. and Gertz, M. (2009), 'Punitive attitudes toward criminals: Exploring the relevance of crime salience and economic insecurity', *Punishment and Society* **11**(1), 25–49.

Cox, A. and Miles, T. (2013), 'Policing immigration', *University of Chicago Law Review* **80**(1), 87–136.

Craig, M. A. and Richeson, J. A. (2014), 'On the precipice of a majority-minority america: Perceived status threat from the racial demographic shift affects white americans' political ideology', *Psychological Science* **25**(6), 1189–1197.

Crenshaw, K. (1995), 'Mapping the margins: Intersectionality, identity politics, and violence against women of color', *Stanford Law Review* **43**(6), 1241–1299.

Crittenden, A. (1988), *SANCTUARY: A Story of American Conscience and the Law in Collision*, Grove Press.

Cruz, T. (2015), 'If i'm elected president the federal government will stop releasing violent criminal illegal aliens', [Press Release]. **URL:** *https://www.presidency.ucsb.edu/documents/press-release-cruz-if-im-elected-president-the-federal-government-will-stop-releasing.*

Davis, R. C. and Erez, E. (1998), Immigrant populations as victims: Toward a multicultural criminal justice system. research in brief, Reports - reseach, U.S. Department of Justice, Office of Justice Programs, National Institute of Justice. **URL:** *https://eric.ed.gov/?id=ED441882*

Dawson, M. C. (2003), *Black Visions: The Roots of Contemporary African-American Political Ideologies*, University of Chicago Press.

Democratic National Convention (1984), *Platform of the Democratic Party*, San Francisco, CA. **URL:** *https://www.presidency.ucsb.edu/documents/1984-democratic-party-platform*

DeMora, S. L. and Collingwood, L. (2018), *RCopyFind: A Package to Compare HTML output from WCopyFind*. R package version 1.0.

Dixon, T. (2007), 'Crime news and racialized beliefs: Understanding the relationship between local news viewing and perceptions of african americans and crime', *Journal of Communication* **58**(1), 106–125.

Domke, D., McCoy, K. and Torres, M. (1999), 'News media, racial perceptions, and political cognition', *Communication Research* **26**(5), 570–607.

Dowler, K. (2003), 'Media consumption and public attitudes toward crime and justice: The relationship betweeen fear of crime, punitive attitudes, and perceived police effectiveness', *Journal of Criminal Justice and Popular Culture* **10**(2), 109–126.

Dunn, A. (1994), 'In suffolk, less of a sanctuary for salvadorans', *The New York Times*, December 13.

Edelman, M. (1988), *Constructing the Political Spectacle*, University of Chicago Press.

Elazar, D. J. (1994), *The American Mosaic: The Impact of Space, Time, and Culture on American Politics*, Westview Press.

Enns, P. K. (2016), *Incarceration Nation*, Cambridge University Press.

Enos, R. D. (2014), 'Causal effect of intergroup contact on exclusionary attitudes', *Proceedings of the National Academy of Sciences* **111**(10), 3699–3704.

Entman, R. (1990), 'Modern racism and the images of blacks in local television news', *Critical Studies in Media Communication* **7**(4), 332–345.

Entman, R. (1992), 'Blacks in the news: Television, modern racism and cultural change', *Journalism and Mass Communication Quarterly* **69**(2), 341–361.

Erikson, R. S., McIver, J. P. and Wright, G. C. (1987), 'State political culture and public opinion', *American Political Science Review* **81**(3), 797–813.

Esbenshade, J. L. (2007), *Division and dislocation: Regulating immigration through local housing ordinances*, Immigration Policy Center, American Immigration Law Foundation.

Eschholz, S. (1997), 'The media and fear of crime: A survey of the research', *University of Florida Journal of Law and Public Policy* **9**, 37.

Fahim, K. and Jacobs, A. (2007), '3rd suspect, 15, held in newark killings as hunt continues', *The New York Times*, August 11.

Farris, E. M. and Mohamed, H. (2018), 'Picturing immigration: how the media criminalizes immigrants', *Politics, Groups, and Identities* pp. 1–11.

Fraga, L. R. and Leal, D. L. (2004), 'Playing the "latino card": Race, ethnicity, and national party politics', *Du Bois Review: Social Science Research on Race* **1**(2), 297–317.

Freeland, G. (2010), 'Negotiating place, space and borders: The new sanctuary movement', *Latino Studies* **8**(4), 485–508.

Gabel, M. and Scheve, K. (2007), 'Estimating the effect of elite communications on public opinion using instrumental variables', *American Journal of Political Science* **51**(4), 1013–1028.

Gadarian, S. K. and Albertson, B. (2014), 'Anxiety, immigration, and the search for information', *Political Psychology* **35**(2), 133–164.

General Board of American Baptist Churches (1985), *Resolution on Church Sanctuary*, University Baptist Church sanctuary movement records, University of Washington, Seattle, WA.

Gest, J. (2016), *The New Minority: White Working Class Politics in an Age of Immigration and Inequality*, Oxford University Press.

Gibson, J. (Presenter) (2007), *The Big Story with John Gibson*, Fox News, August 14.

Golden, R. and MacConnell, M. (1986), *Sanctuary: The New Underground Railroad*, Orbis Books.

Gonzalez O'Brien, B., Collingwood, L. and El-Khatib, S. O. (2017), 'The politics of refuge: Sanctuary cities, crime, and undocumented immigration', *Urban Affairs Review* 55(1), 3–40.

Gonzalez O'Brien, B. (2018), *Handcuffs and Chain Link: Undocumented Immigrants and the Politics of Criminality*, University of Virginia Press.

Green, D. P., Palmquist, B. and Schickler, E. (2004), *Partisan hearts and minds: Political parties and the social identities of voters*, Yale University Press.

Grimmer, J. (2013), 'Appropriators not position takers: The distorting effects of electoral incentives on congressional representation', *American Journal of Political Science* 57(3), 624–642.

Gulasekaram, P. and Ramakrishnan, S. K. (2015), *The New Immigration Federalism*, Cambridge University Press.

Gutfield, G. (Presenter) (2017a), *The Five*, Fox News, February 22.

Gutfield, G. (Presenter) (2017b), *The Five*, Fox News, March 17.

Hajnal, Z. L. and Lee, T. (2011), *Why Americans Don't Join the Party: Race, Immigration, and the Failure (of Political Parties) to Engage the Electorate*, Princeton University Press.

Hall, S., Critcher, C., Jefferson, T., Clarke, J. and Roberts, B. (2013), *Policing the crisis: Mugging, the state and law and order*, Macmillan International Higher Education.

Hannity, S. (Presenter) (2007), *Hannity and Colmes*, Fox News, August 13.

Haynes, C., Merolla, J. and Ramakrishnan, S. K. (2016), *Framing Immigrants: News Coverage, Public Opinion, and Policy*, Russell Sage Foundation.

Hebert Research and King 1090 News (1984), "Providing sanctuary for refugees from El Salvador", University Baptist Church sanctuary movement records, University of Washington, Seattle, WA.

Herbut, P. (1983), 'Church network shelters illegal aliens from INS', *Washington Post*, January 29.

Hertel-Fernandez, A. (2014), 'Who passes business's model bills? policy capacity and corporate influence in us state politics', *Perspectives on Politics* **12**(3), 582–602.

Highton, B. and Rocca, M. S. (2005), 'Beyond the roll-call arena: The determinants of position taking in congress', *Political Research Quarterly* **58**(2), 303–316.

Hillygus, D. S. and Shields, T. G. (2014), *The Persuadable Voter: Wedge Issues in Presidential Campaigns*, Princeton University Press.

Ho, D. E., Imai, K., King, G. and Stuart, E. A. (2007), 'Matching as nonparametric preprocessing for reducing model dependence in parametric causal inference', *Political analysis* **15**(3), 199–236.

Hogan, M., Chiricos, T. and Gertz, M. (2005), 'Economic insecurity, blame and punitive attitudes', *Justice Quarterly* **22**(3), 392–412.

Hohmann, J. (2015), 'The daily 202: Does donald trump know rick perry's cell phone number?', *Washington Post*, July 23.

Hood III, M. V. and Morris, I. L. (1997), '¿Amigo o Enemigo?: Context, attitudes, and Anglo public opinion toward immigration', *Social Science Quarterly* pp. 309–323.

Hood, M. V. and Morris, I. L. (1998), 'Give us your tired, your poor, ... but make sure they have a green card: The effects of documented and undocumented migrant context on anglo opinion toward immigration', *Political Behavior* **20**(1), 1–15. **URL:** *https://doi.org/10.1023/A:1024839032001*

Hopkins, D. J. (2010), 'Politicized places: Explaining where and when immigrants provoke local opposition', *American political science review* **104**(1), 40–60.

Huang, A. (2008), Similarity measures for text document clustering, *in* 'Proceedings of the sixth new zealand computer science research student conference (NZCSRSC2008), Christchurch, New Zealand', pp. 49–56.

Hughey, M. W. and Parks, G. S. (2014), *The Wrongs of the Right: Language, Race, and the Republican Party in the Age of Obama*, NYU Press.

Hume, B. (Presenter) (2007), *Special Report with Brit Hume*, Fox News, August 9.

Hutchings, V. L. and Valentino, N. A. (2004), 'The centrality of race in american politics', *Annual Review of Political Science* **7**, 383–408.

Hutchings, V. L., Walton, H., Mickey, R. W. and Jardina, A. E. (2011), 'The politics of race: How threat cues and group position can activate white identity', APSA2011 Annual Meeting Paper.

Hyndman, R. J. and Khandakar, Y. (2008), 'Automatic time series forecasting: the forecast package for R', *Journal of Statistical Software* **26**(3), 1–22. **URL:** *http://www.jstatsoft.org/article/view/v027i03*

Ingwerson, M. (1985), 'Religious freedom issue likely to be linchpin of sanctuary trial defense', *Christian Science Monitor*, February 7.

Iyengar, S. and Kinder, D. R. (1987), *News that Matters: Agenda-Setting and Priming in a Television Age*, University of Chicago Press.

Jackman, M. (2013), 'ALEC's Influence over Lawmaking in State Legislatures'. **URL:** *www.brookings.edu/articles/alecs-influence-over-lawmaking-in-state-legislatures/*

Jacobs, D. and Carmichael, J. T. (2002), 'The political sociology of the death penalty: A pooled time-series analysis', *American Sociological Review* pp. 109–131.

Jacoby, W. G. (1988), 'The impact of party identification on issue attitudes', *American Journal of Political Science* pp. 643–661.

Jardina, A. E. (2014), 'Demise of dominance: Group threat and the new relevance of white identity for american politics', APSA 2011 Annual Meeting Paper.

Johnson, C. A. (1976), 'Political culture in american states: Elazar's formulation examined', *American Journal of Political Science* pp. 491–509.

Jones, D. R. (2003), 'Position taking and position avoidance in the us senate', *Journal of Politics* **65**(3), 851–863.

Karol, D. (2009), *Party Position Change in American Politics: Coalition Management*, Cambridge University Press.

Key, V. O. (1949), *Southern Politics in State and Nation*, Alfred Knopf.

Kim, S., Carvalho, J., Davis, A. and Mullins, A. (2011), 'The view of the border: News framing of the definition, causes, and solutions to illegal immigration', *Mass Communication and Society* **14**(3), 292–314.

King, J. D. (2000), 'Changes in professionalism in us state legislatures', *Legislative Studies Quarterly* pp. 327–343.

Kittrie, O. F. (2006), 'Federalism, deportation and crime victims afraid to call the police', *Iowa Law Review* **91**, 1449–1508.

Koger, G. (2003), 'Position taking and cosponsorship in the us house', *Legislative Studies Quarterly* **28**(2), 225–246.

Kohn, A. (January 25, 1986), 'The return of cointelpro?', *The Nation*, January 25th.

Lau, R. R. and Redlawsk, D. P. (1997), 'Voting correctly', *American Political Science Review* **91**(3), 585–598.

Lee, M., Martinez, R. and Rosenfeld, R. (2001), 'Does immigration increase homicide? negative evidence from three border cities', *Sociological Quarterly* **42**(4), 559–580.

Lenz, G. S. (2013), *Follow the Leader?: How Voters Respond to Politicians' Policies and Performance*, University of Chicago Press.

Lewis-Beck, M. S. (2009), *The American Voter Revisited*, University of Michigan Press.

López, I. H. (2015), *Dog Whistle Politics: How Coded Racial Appeals have Reinvented Racism and Wrecked the Middle Class*, Oxford University Press.

Lowry, M. (1983), *Letter to Katherine Mock*, August 10, University Baptist Church sanctuary movement records, University of Washington, Seattle, WA.

Lowry, M. (1983), *Letter to Rev. Jamie Robbins*, March 14, University Baptist Church sanctuary movement records, University of Washington, Seattle, WA.

Luo, M. (2007), 'A closer look at the 'sanctuary city' argument', *The New York Times*, November 29.

Lyons, C. J., Vélez, M. B. and Santoro, W. A. (2013), 'Neighborhood immigration, violence, and city-level immigrant political opportunities', *American Sociological Review* p. 0003122413491964.

Maier, S. (1986), "A 'City of Refuge is Born", *Seattle Times*, January 14.

Major, B., Blodorn, A. and Major Blascovich, G. (2016), 'The threat of increasing diversity: Why many white americans support trump in the 2016 presidential election', *Group Processes & Intergroup Relations* p. 1368430216677304.

Marquez, T. and Schraufnagel, S. (2013), 'Hispanic population growth and state immigration policy: An analysis of restriction (2008–12)', *Publius: The Journal of Federalism* **43**(3), 347–367.

Martinez, R., Stowell, J. I. and Lee, M. T. (2010), 'Immigration and crime in an era of transformation: A longitudinal analysis of homicides in san diego neighborhoods, 1980–2000', *Criminology* **48**(3), 797–829.

Massey, D. and Pren, K. (2012), 'Unintended consequences of us immigration policy: Explaining the post--1965 surge from Latin America', *Population and Development Review* **38**(1)), 1–29.

Masuoka, N. and Junn, J. (2013), *The Politics of Belonging: Race, Public Opinion, and Immigration*, University of Chicago Press.

Mathews, J. (1985), 'Los angeles to be refugee 'sanctuary'', *The Washington Post*, November 28.

Mathews, J. (1986), 'Tough-talking ins official raises profile, ire in the west', *The Washington Post*, March 24.

Mathews, J. (1990), '500,000 immigrants granted legal status; a milestone for central american refugees', *The Washington Post*, December 19.

Matsubayashi, T. and Rocha, R. R. (2012), 'Racial diversity and public policy in the states', *Political Research Quarterly* **65**(3), 600–614. **URL:** *https://doi.org/10.1177/1065912911401418*

McBeth, M. and Lybecker, D. (2018), 'The narrative policy framework, agendas, and sanctuary cities: The construction of a public problem', *Policy Studies Journal* 46(4), 868–893.

McCarthy, C. (1983), 'For Salvadorans deportation or compassion', *The Washington Post*, April 17.

McClain, P. D., Johnson Carew, J. D., Walton Jr, E. and Watts, C. S. (2009), 'Group membership, group identity, and group consciousness: Measures of racial identity in american politics?', *Annual Review of Political Science* **12**, 471–485.

McDowall, D., Loftin, C. and Pate, M. (2012), 'Seasonal cycles in crime, and their variability', *Journal of Quantitative Criminology* **28**(3), 389–410.

Mendelberg, T. (2001), *The Race Card: Campaign Strategy, Implicit Messages, and the Norm of Equality*, Princeton University Press.

Menjivar, C. and Bejarano, C. L. (2004), 'Latino immigrants' perceptions of crime and police authorities in the united states: A case study from the phoenix metropolitan area', *Ethnic and Racial Studies* **27**(1), 120–148.

Menjivar, C. and Salcido, O. (2002), 'Immigrant women and domestic violence: Common experiences in different countries', *Gender & Society* **16**(6), 898–920.

Michelson, M. R. (2003), 'Getting out the latino vote: How door-to-door canvassing influences voter turnout in rural central california', *Political Behavior* **25**(3), 247–263.

Mihalcea, R., Corley, C., Strapparava, C. et al. (2006), Corpus-based and knowledge-based measures of text semantic similarity, *in* 'AAAI', Vol. 6, pp. 775–780.

Miles, T. and Cox, A. (2014), 'Does immigration enforcement reduce crime? evidence from secure communities', *The Journal of Law and Economics* **57**(4), 937–973.

Miller, G. and Schofield, N. (2008), 'The transformation of the republican and democratic party coalitions in the US', *Perspectives on Politics* **6**(3), 433–450.

Miller, S. (2004), 'When doing the right thing leads to arrest', *Christian Science Monitor*, January 7.

Monogan, J. E. (2009), Immigration policy in the fifty us states from 2005–2008, *in* 'Ninth Annual Conference on State Politics and Policy, Chapel Hill, NC'.

Mutz, D. C. (2018), 'Status threat, not economic hardship, explains the 2016 presidential vote', *Proceedings of the National Academy of Sciences* p. 201718155.

National Sanctuary Sites (1983), University Baptist Church sanctuary movement records, University of Washington, Seattle, WA.

Newman, B. J. (2013), 'Acculturating contexts and anglo opposition to immigration in the United States', *American Journal of Political Science* **57**(2), 374–390. **URL:** *http://dx.doi.org/10.1111/j.1540-5907.2012.00632.x*

Newman, B. J. and Johnson, J. (2012), 'Ethnic change, concern over immigration, and approval of state government', *State Politics & Policy Quarterly* **12**(4), 415–437.

Newman, B. J., Johnston, C. D., Strickland, A. A. and Citrin, J. (2012), 'Immigration crackdown in the american workplace', *State Politics & Policy Quarterly* **12**(2), 160–182. **URL:** *https://doi.org/10.1177/1532440012442910*

Newman, B. J., Shah, S. and Collingwood, L. (2018), 'Race, place, and building a base: Latino population growth and the nascent trump campaign for president', *Public Opinion Quarterly* **82**(1), 122–134.

Newman, B. J. and Velez, Y. (2014), 'Group size versus change? assessing americans perception of local immigration', *Political Research Quarterly* **67**(2), 293–303. **URL:** *http://dx.doi.org/10.1177/1065912913517303*

Newton, L. (2012), 'Policy innovation or vertical integration? a view of immigration federalism from the states', *Law & Policy* **34**(2), 113–137.

The New York Times Editorial Board (2015), "Lost in the Immigration Frenzy", *The New York Times*, July 13.

Ngai, M. (2004), *Impossible Subjects: Illegal Aliens and the Making of Modern America*, Princeton University Press.

Nicholson-Crotty, J. and Nicholson-Crotty, S. (2011), 'Industry strength and immigrant policy in the american states', *Political Research Quarterly* **64**(3), 612–624.

O'Donoghue, L. (2017), 'Berkeley is the original sanctuary city', *East Bay Express*. **URL:** *https://www.eastbayexpress.com/oakland/berkeley-the-original-sanctuary-city/ Content?oid=5306164*

Ono, K. and Sloop, J. (2002), *Shifting borders: Rhetoric, immigration, and California's Proposition 187*, Temple University Press, Philadelphia, PA.

O'Reilly, B. (Presenter) (2007a), *The O'Reilly Factor*, Fox News, April 5.

O'Reilly, B. (Presenter) (2007b), *The O'Reilly Factor*, Fox News, April 9.

O'Reilly, B. (Presenter) (2007c), *The O'Reilly Factor*, Fox News, April 27.

O'Reilly, B. (Presenter) (2007d), *The O'Reilly Factor*, Fox News, August 13.

Oskooii, K. A., Dreier, S. K. and Collingwood, L. (2018), 'Partisan attitudes toward sanctuary cities: The asymmetrical effects of political knowledge', *Politics & Policy* **46**(6), 951–984.

Ostfeld, M. C. (2018), 'The new white flight?: The effects of political appeals to latinos on white democrats', *Political Behavior* pp. 1–22.

Ousey, G. and Kubrin, C. (2009), 'Exploring the connection between immigration and violent crime rates in U.S. cities, 1980–2000', *Social Problems* **56**(3), 447–473.

Parker, C. S. and Barreto, M. A. (2014), *Change They Can't Believe In: The Tea Party and Reactionary Politics in America*, Princeton University Press.

Pedraza, F. I. (2014), 'The two-way street of acculturation, discrimination, and latino immigration restrictionism', *Political Research Quarterly* **67**(4), 889–904.

Pedraza, F., Nichols, V. and LeBron, A. (2017), 'Cautious citizenship: The deterring effect of immigration issue salience on health care use and bureaucratic interactions among latino u.s. citizens', *Journal of Health Politics* **42**(5).

Perry, R. (2012), 'Debunking false attacks regarding Texas jobs', [Press Release]. **URL:** *https://www.presidency.ucsb.edu/documents/press-release-debunking-false-attacks-regarding-texas-jobs*

Perry, R. (2015), 'Being president of the United States is serious business, not a reality tv show', [Press Release]. **URL:** *https://www.presidency.ucsb.edu/documents/press-release-icymi-governor-perry-being-president-the-united-states-serious-business-not*

Petrocik, J. (1996), 'Issue ownership in presidential elections, with a 1980 case study', *American Journal of Political Science* **40**, 825–850.

Phillip, A. (2015), 'Is san francisco's 'sanctuary city' policy to blame for a woman's death?; the man charged with the killing of a woman in downtown san francisco had been deported five times', *The Washington Post*, July 6.

Provine, D. M. and Doty, R. L. (2011), 'The criminalization of immigrants as racial project', *Journal of Contemporary Criminal Justice* **27**(3), 261–277.

Rabbinical Assembly (1984), *Resolution on Central American Refugees*.

Quillian, L. (1995), 'Prejudice as a response to perceived group threat: Population composition and anti-immigrant and racial prejudice in europe', *American Sociological Review* pp. 586–611.

Quillian, L. and Pager, D. (2010), 'Estimating risk: Stereotype amplification and the perceived risk of criminal victimization', *Social Psychology Quarterly* **73**(1), 79–104.

Ramakrishnan, S. K. and Gulasekaram, P. (2012), 'The importance of the political in immigration federalism', *Arizona State Law Journal* **44**, 1431.

Ramírez, R. (2013), *Mobilizing Opportunities: The Evolving Latino Electorate and the Future of American Politics*, University of Virginia Press.

Ramsey, R. (2011a), 'Perry puts immigration atop session's agenda', *The New York Times*, January 16.

Ramsey, R. (2011b), 'Republicans must walk fine line on immigration', *The New York Times*, February 27.

Reid, L. W., Weiss, H. E., Adelman, R. M. and Jaret, C. (2005), 'The immigration–crime relationship: Evidence across us metropolitan areas', *Social Science Research* **34**(4), 757–780.

Rennison, C. M. (2007), 'Reporting to the police by hispanic victims of violence', *Violence and victims* **22**(6), 754–772.

Reny, T. (2017), 'Demographic change, latino countermobilization, and the politics of immigration in us senate campaigns', *Political Research Quarterly* **70**(4), 735–748.

Reny, T. T., Collingwood, L. and Valenzuela, A. (2019), 'Vote switching in the 2016 election: How racial and immigration attitudes, not economics, explain shifts in white voting', *Public Opinion Quarterly* **83**(1), 91–113.

Republican National Convention (1984), *Platform of the Republican Party*, Dallas, TX. **URL:** *https://www.presidency.ucsb.edu/documents/republican-party-platform-1984*

Ridgley, J. (2008), 'Cities of refuge: Immigration enforcement, police, and the insurgent genealogies of citizenship in us sanctuary cities', *Urban Geography* **29**(1), 53–77.

Romney, M. (2007), ' "the most successful" sanctuary city', [Press Release]. **URL:** *https://www.presidency.ucsb.edu/documents/press-release-the-most-successful-sanctuary-city*

Sanchez, G. R. (2006), 'The role of group consciousness in latino public opinion', *Political Research Quarterly* **59**(3), 435–446.

Sanchez, G. R. and Masuoka, N. (2010), 'Brown-utility heuristic? the presence and contributing factors of latino linked fate', *Hispanic Journal of Behavioral Sciences* **32**(4), 519–531.

San Francisco Municipal Code, Chapter 12H, Immigration Status (2009). **URL:** *https://sfgov.org/oceia/sites/default/files/Documents/SF Admin Code 2012H-12I.pdf*

Santa Ana, O. (2002), *Brown Tide Rising: Metaphors of Latinos in Contemporary American Public Discourse*, University of Texas Press.

Santa Ana, O. (2013), *Juan in a Hundred: The Representation of Latinos on Network News*, University of Texas Press.

Schaffner, B. F. and Streb, M. J. (2002), 'The partisan heuristic in low-information elections', *Public Opinion Quarterly* **66**(4), 559–581.

Schaffner, B. F., MacWilliams, M. and Nteta, T. (2018)'Understanding white polarization in the 2016 vote for president: The sobering role of racism and sexism,' *Political Science Quarterly* **133**(1), 9–34.

Schemer, C. (2012), 'The influence of news media on stereotypic attitudes toward immigrants in a political campaign', *Journal of Communication* **62**(5), 739–757.

Scherer, J. (2016), 'Despite Trump's threat to cut federal funding, mayors pledge to protect undocumented immigrants; mayors across the united states have vowed not to help Donald Trump and federal law enforcement officials deport undocumented immigrants', *The Washington Post*, November 15.

Scheufele, D. (2000), 'Agenda-setting, priming, and framing revisited: Another look at cognitive effects of political communication', *Mass Communication and Society* **3**(2–3), 297–316.

Scheufele, D. A. and Tewksbury, D. (2007), 'Framing, agenda setting, and priming: The evolution of three media effects models', *Journal of communication* **57**(1),
9–20.

Schickler, E. (2016), *Racial Realignment: The Transformation of American Liberalism,
1932–1965*, Princeton University Press.

Schildkraut, D. (2009), 'Amnesty, guest workers, fences! oh my! public opinion about'
comprehensive immigration reform", in G. P. Freeman, R. Hansen, & D. L. Leal (eds.),
Immigration and Public Opinion in Liberal Democracies, 207–231.

Schildkraut, D. J. (2017), 'White attitudes about descriptive representation in the us: the
roles of identity, discrimination, and linked fate', *Politics, Groups, and Identities* **5**(1),
84–106.

Schuck, A. R., Vliegenthart, R. and De Vreese, C. H. (2016), 'Who's afraid of conflict? the
mobilizing effect of conflict framing in campaign news', *British Journal of Political Science*
46(1), 177–194.

Schuman, H. and Presser, S. (1996), *Questions and Answers in Attitude Surveys: Experiments
on Question Form, Wording, and Context*, Sage.

Seattle City Council (1986). *Resolution for council action declaring Seattle a sanctuary for
Salvadoran and Guatemalan refugees*, University Baptist Church sanctuary movement
records, University of Washington, Seattle, WA.

Seattle City Council (2002), *Ordinance 121063*.

Seattle City Council (2017), *Resolution 31730*.

Sides, J., Tesler, M. and Vavreck, L. (2016), 'The electoral landscape of 2016', *The ANNALS
of the American Academy of Political and Social Science* **667**(1), 50–71.

Sides, J., Tesler, M. and Vavreck, L. (2017), 'How trump lost and won', *Journal of Democracy*
28(2), 34–44.

Simon, J. (2006), *Governing Through Crime: How the War on Crime Transformed American
Democracy and Created a Culture of Fear*, Oxford University Press.

Sorens, J., Muedini, F. and Ruger, W. P. (2008), 'Us state and local public policies in 2006:
A new database', *State Politics & Policy Quarterly* **8**(3), 309–326.

Stinchcombe, A., Adams, R., Heimer, C., Scheppele, K. L., Smith, T. and Taylor, D. G. (1980),
Crime and Punishment: Changing Attitudes in America, Jossey Bass.

Sullivan, L. (2010), 'Prison economics help drive ariz. immigration law'. **URL:** *http://www.
npr.org/2010/10/28/130833741/prison-economics-help-drive-ariz-immigration-law*.

Tajfel, H. (2010), *Social Identity and Intergroup Relations*, Cambridge University Press.

Taub, R. P., Taylor, D. G. and Dunham, J. D. (1984), *Paths of Neighborhood Change: Race
and Crime in Urban America*, University of Chicago Press.

Tesler, M. (2015), 'Priming predispositions and changing policy positions: An account
of when mass opinion is primed or changed', *American Journal of Political Science*
59(4), 806–824.

The Illegal Immigration Reform and Immigrant Responsibility Act (1996). **URL:** *https://www.
uscis.gov/sites/default/files/ocomm/ilink/0-0-0-10948.html*

Thompson, F. (2007), 'Thompson proposal would enforce immigration laws', [Press
Release]. **URL:** *https://www.presidency.ucsb.edu/people/other/fred-thompson*

Tichenor, D. (2002), *Dividing Lines: The Politics of Immigration Control in America*,
Princeton University Press.

Tolbert, C. J. and Grummel, J. A. (2003), 'Revisiting the racial threat hypothesis:
White voter support for California's Proposition 209', *State Politics & Policy Quarterly*
3(2) pp. 183–202.

True, J. L., Jones, B. D. and Baumgartner, F. R. (1999), 'Punctuated-equilibrium theory:
Explaining stability and change in american policymaking', *Theories of the policy process*
pp. 97–115.

Trump, D. (2015), 'O'Reilly: Obama admin 'complicit' in murder of CA woman by illegal immigrant', [Press Release]. **URL:** *https://www.presidency.ucsb.edu/documents/press-release-oreilly-obama-admin-complicit-murder-ca-woman-illegal-immigrant*

Trump, D. (2016), 'Remarks on immigration at the Phoenix Convention Center in Phoenix Arizona', August 31. **URL:** *https://www.presidency.ucsb.edu/documents/remarks-immigration-the-phoenix-convention-center-phoenix-arizona*

Valentino, N. A., Hutchings, V. L. and White, I. K. (2002), 'Cues that matter: How political ads prime racial attitudes during campaigns', *American Political Science Review* **96**(1), 75–90.

Vavreck, L. and Rivers, D. (2008), 'The 2006 cooperative congressional election study', *Journal of Elections, Public Opinion and Parties* **18**(4), 355–366.

Villazor, R. C. (2007), 'What is a sanctuary?', *SMU Law Review* **61**, 133–156.

Volsky, G. (n.d.), 'U.S. churches offer sanctuary to aliens facing deportation', *The New York Times*, April 8.

Wadsworth, T. (2010), 'Is immigration responsible for the crime drop? an assessment of the influence of immigration on changes in violent crime between 1990 and 2000', *Social Science Quarterly* **91**(2), 531–553.

Waldman, P. (2015), 'The new Willie Horton?', *The Washington Post*, July 8.

Walker, K. E. and Leitner, H. (2011), 'The variegated landscape of local immigration policies in the united states', *Urban Geography* **32**(2), 156–178.

Wallace, S. J. (2014), 'Papers please: State-level anti-immigrant legislation in the wake of Arizona's SB 1070', *Political Science Quarterly* **129**(2), 261–291.

Wasem, R. (2012), 'Unauthorized aliens residing in the united states: Estimates since 1986'.

Weaver, D. H. (2007), 'Thoughts on agenda setting, framing, and priming', *Journal of Communication* **57**(1), 142–147.

Wells, M. J. (2004), 'The grassroots reconfiguration of us immigration policy', *International Migration Review* **38**(4), 1308–1347.

Wilkerson, J., Smith, D. and Stramp, N. (2015), 'Tracing the flow of policy ideas in legislatures: A text reuse approach', *American Journal of Political Science* **59**(4), 943–956.

Wong, T. (2017*a*), The effect of sanctuary policies on crime and the economy, Report, Center for American Progress. **URL:** *https://www.americanprogress.org/issues/immigration/reports/2017/01/26/297366/the-effects-of-sanctuary-policies-on-crime-and-the-economy/*

Wong, T. (2017*b*), *The Politics of Immigration: Partisanship, Demographic Change, and American National Identity*, Oxford University Press.

Wood, D. (2006), 'Two towns, two stands on immigration reform', *Christian Science Monitor*, April 5.

Ybarra, V. D., Sanchez, L. M. and Sanchez, G. R. (2016), 'Anti-immigrant anxieties in state policy: the great recession and punitive immigration policy in the american states, 2005–2012', *State Politics & Policy Quarterly* **16**(3), 313–339.

Zaller, J. (1992), *The Nature and Origins of Mass Opinion*, Cambridge University Press.

Zingher, J. N. (2014), 'The ideological and electoral determinants of laws targeting undocumented migrants in the us states', *State Politics & Policy Quarterly* **14**(1), 90–117.

Index